"Chris Bruni-Lowe is one of those rare political strategists who understand both polling and messaging. This new book, the first of its kind, is a timely and fascinating look at which political slogans work and why they work. Anyone wanting to understand the appeal of Donald Trump should read this book."
TIM SHIPMAN, *SUNDAY TIMES* CHIEF POLITICAL COMMENTATOR

"A compelling read. Words, so often, are the currency of politics. This book tells you the exchange rates of the words with real value: those with the power to enthuse, provoke, motivate and persuade. If you're interested in politics, campaigning and communication, this is the book for you."
CHRIS MASON, BBC NEWS POLITICAL EDITOR

"It was an idea just waiting to be turned into a book. Chris Bruni-Lowe has undertaken a deep dive into the specific words that help political parties win an election. Don't be surprised to see a copy of *Eight Words That Changed the World* in offices in and around Westminster in the coming weeks – and much further afield. There are some illuminating observations in this insightful book, not least the extent to which 'Make X Great Again' is, far from being a fresh Trump invention, one of the most clichéd phrases in the electioneering handbook."
JIM PICKARD, *FINANCIAL TIMES* DEPUTY POLITICAL EDITOR

"Few dispute that we live in the age of political sloganeering, albeit one that is badly misunderstood. This fascinating book explores the potency of political language in a brilliant new way. Chris Bruni-Lowe grasps the power and importance of these words – and you should too."
SEBASTIAN PAYNE, *THE TIMES* COLUMNIST

"Shakespeare drew on 20,000 words. The world's democracies, it seems, run on just eight! Here, Chris Bruni-Lowe explains which words work with voters and why. A surprising gap in the political library has been filled."
GARY GIBBON, *CHANNEL 4 NEWS* POLITICAL EDITOR

"Slogans are so powerful in politics; they are long overdue for a forensic analysis. For anyone who cares about communication, I don't need eight words, I can do it in three: read this book."
ADAM BOULTON, BROADCASTER AND POLITICAL JOURNALIST

"At last, a book exploring the power of political language like never before. Anyone wanting to take back control of their knowledge of sloganeering should read this insightful and entertaining march through more than a century of persuasive messaging."
CAMILLA TOMINEY, *DAILY TELEGRAPH* ASSOCIATE EDITOR

"Political slogans are both ubiquitous and under-examined. This book offers an invaluable guide to show how their usage can make or break an election campaign. Bruni-Lowe blends anecdote with data to create an engaging analysis of the eight key words that define our times. From Mandela and Clinton to Netanyahu and Trump, this is an original and stimulating study that will stand the test of time."
JAMES HEALE, *THE SPECTATOR* DEPUTY POLITICAL EDITOR

"Global in its scope, impressive in its historical sweep and written by someone who's been there and done that. This fascinating book – part in-depth exploration, part how-to guide – aptly demonstrates that just the right words, used in just the right order, have always had, and continue to have, the power to move people and their political choices in profound and often era-defining ways. Highly recommended."
TIM BALE, PROFESSOR OF POLITICS, QUEEN MARY UNIVERSITY OF LONDON

"An insightful and compelling read about the power of language – its ability to persuade and its impact on the political scene. Chris Bruni-Lowe's analysis is a must-read for anyone interested in politics and the art of framing political debate."
SIR ROBBIE GIBB, FORMER DIRECTOR OF COMMUNICATIONS AT 10 DOWNING STREET

"Chris Bruni-Lowe's *Eight Words That Changed the World* is essential, enjoyable reading for anyone wanting to craft election-winning slogans. This seasoned consultant, known for running regime-changing campaigns against the odds, shares his battle-tested wisdom. This is a book full of practical international insights from someone who gets how the right words shape political realities around the world. Don't observe history; learn how to shape it. Grab your copy now!"
PAUL BAINES, PROFESSOR OF POLITICAL MARKETING, UNIVERSITY OF LEICESTER

EIGHT WORDS THAT CHANGED THE WORLD

EIGHT WORDS THAT CHANGED THE WORLD

A MODERN HISTORY OF THE ELECTION SLOGAN

CHRIS BRUNI-LOWE

\Bb\
Biteback Publishing

First published in Great Britain in 2025 by
Biteback Publishing Ltd, London
Copyright © Chris Bruni-Lowe 2025

ISBN 978-1-78590-904-7

10 9 8 7 6 5 4 3 2 1

A CIP catalogue record for this book is available from the British Library.

Set in Trade Gothic and Minion Pro

Printed and bound in Great Britain by
CPI Group (UK) Ltd, Croydon CR0 4YY

CONTENTS

PREFACE

What's in a word? Quite a lot, it turns out, if the word in question is 'people', 'change', 'democracy', 'strong', 'together', 'new', 'time' or 'better'.

Election campaigns are remembered for the big events – the debates, the scandals, the victories and the losses. And above all, they're remembered for the big personalities: the ones who successfully cast themselves as the storytellers of their age. We scrutinise their image, their strategy, their successes and failures, yet we rarely stop to examine the language they use to tell their stories. The words. The phrases and, crucially, the slogans. These are not just throwaway lines or marketing tricks – they are the anchors of an entire campaign. If the candidate is the author, then the slogan is the title – the few words that signal everything they want their vision of the future to be.

This book reveals the remarkable fact that these eight words have changed the modern world. They are the 'hit' words that, deployed in election slogans, have shaped democratic politics. They have won elections, brought down governments, taken countries to war, ended bitter conflicts and given political life to movements of the right, left and centre.

This claim is based on data. Throughout my long career as a pollster and political strategist, I have compiled a database of more than 20,000 slogans that have been used in major elections worldwide over the past century. I have scrutinised the results of these elections and evaluated how effective a particular slogan has been. These eight words have been used in more than 9,000 slogans in the past century – many of them in the same slogan.

This database is a unique resource, allowing me to show political clients when their favoured slogans have been used before, by whom and what the result was. As I will go on to explain, being able to point to past triumphs – and disasters – when it comes to slogans has proved invaluable. Throughout this book, with a chapter devoted to each of the eight hit words, I share for the first time some of those insights with a wider audience.

Of course, these same eight words have also made up unsuccessful political slogans and have been used in campaigns that ended in defeat. Simply combining them randomly to produce a phrase – for example, 'New Time for Strong People', 'Better Together' or 'Change Democracy' – will get you nowhere. In fact, this is the other part of the story. Deploying these words alone has never been enough to guarantee victory, even with the right marketing and promotional techniques. They create a framework for tapping into public sentiment, but other factors – like economic conditions, the credibility of the candidate, and timing – are equally vital. Just as important is who uses them – charismatic leader or clumsy loser – and how that individual connects with the public. With that said, my research does show that in most countries, a majority of people are predisposed to endorse slogans that contain one or more of these eight words. Voters are more likely to respond positively to campaigns that use them. However, predisposition alone does not secure electoral success: these words must also align with the candidate's authenticity and the electorate's mood.

In my work as a professional pollster and strategist, I have surveyed the views of more than 2 million people in more than forty countries and advised numerous heads of government of the left and right on campaign messaging and strategy. This work has given me a unique understanding of what people care about and what they perceive when they see a politician and hear their words. The proliferation of messages that the public is exposed to in the digital age means it has never been more important to use the right slogan to capture people's attention.

That is why this book is about more than just eight words. It is about how democratic politics works, or doesn't work, and how politicians shape the society in which we live.

Compiling and using my database – which is effectively a catalogue of global political history right up to the present day – made me realise that no in-depth study of election slogans exists in this form. Thousands of books about politics and marketing are published every year. So are books about particular election campaigns. None, however, have looked at the bigger picture by analysing this specific aspect of political marketing on a global, historical scale. And yet the correct slogan, used to the best effect by a winning party, can have profound consequences on people's lives, whether it's a government taking a country to war or one determined to end racial apartheid. Similarly, using the wrong slogan can have disastrous consequences for a party and the people it claims to represent.

The challenge for me as a strategist lies in knowing when to deploy the right slogan and being able to explain why, so that I can craft a campaign around it. The lessons I learned through my practical involvement in electoral contests have contributed to my understanding of the power of political slogans.

The potency of these eight hit words, and the importance of using them in the right way at the right time, is illustrated by two very different campaigns in which I played a part. The first was Nigel Farage's anti-EU Brexit Party, which won the most seats in the 2019 European Parliament elections in the UK. The second was the successful 2023 general election campaign by Montenegro's Europe Now! Party, which aimed to win public support for Montenegro's bid to join the European Union. These two campaigns aimed to achieve diametrically opposed outcomes – the first to leave the EU, the second to join it. Yet the same principles were applied in both, with considerable success. Here's a brief story of how.

One morning in November 2018, I took a telephone call from Nigel Farage, the British politician whom Donald Trump calls 'Mr Brexit'. He told me he was setting up a new political party, the Brexit Party, and he wanted me to work on a message and a slogan to help promote it. By then, I had spent almost a decade advising organisations and candidates of all political persuasions, as well as national and international companies, on what it takes to run a successful campaign, be it political or commercial. These experiences had given me a clear understanding of what language moves people to action and which words could help campaigns to win.

I understood that setting up a new political party in Britain would present unique challenges, because its national electoral system had been dominated for more than a century by just two forces, the Conservative Party and the Labour Party. However, I was intrigued by Farage's proposition. When he contacted me, the UK was stuck in a political quagmire. Two and a half years previously, a clear majority of its voters had chosen to leave the European Union in the Brexit referendum. Since then, its Parliament had been paralysed by arguments and indecision over how and whether to carry out the will of the people and over the nation's future relationship with the EU. One Tory Prime Minister, David Cameron, who had campaigned to remain in the EU, had resigned in June 2016 over the referendum result. His successor, Theresa May, who had also campaigned for the UK to remain in the EU, was finding it impossible to break the stalemate and looked close to being toppled. There was a strong feeling among Brexiteers that democracy itself was under threat because of the growing movement, headed by leading Remainers, that demanded a second referendum. But this time, they hoped to get the result they wanted.

Prime Minister Theresa May had repeatedly assured the public that the UK would cease to be a member of the EU on 29 March 2019. No ifs, no buts. But Farage told me over the phone that he didn't believe this deadline would be met. The European Parliament elections, in which 400 million citizens from every member state are entitled to vote for members of the European Parliament in Brussels, were scheduled by law to take place six months later, at the end of May 2019, and Farage predicted that Britain would have to participate in them. To that end, he had conceived the idea of the Brexit Party, which would stand in those EU elections and safeguard the referendum result.

Having been the prime mover in forcing the Brexit referendum, and having played a central part in winning it, Farage had become arguably the one of the most consequential political figures in Europe. Yet my brief as a political strategist now amounted to helping him to build a new political brand, in order to fight a national election which nobody could be sure would even be held. If a poll did take place, it would probably come to be seen as a second Brexit referendum.

The stakes were high. It was an unusual political situation that posed some distinct marketing challenges. Perhaps the toughest of these was how to reintroduce Farage to the public. He was already well known in the UK, having spent the previous twenty years campaigning for Britain to leave the EU, but for this election he needed to appear fresh and credible.

By early 2019, it was obvious that most Britons were desperate for the political chaos to end, whether they were among the 17.4 million members of the electorate who had voted for Brexit or not. Farage had begun giving interviews and addressing rallies, proclaiming that the only way to overcome the deadlock was to have a 'political revolution'. He told me that he thought any logo or slogan that the Brexit Party used should contain the word 'revolution' and that the campaign should be based around root-and-branch reform of British politics once Brexit had been properly achieved. I knew he didn't advocate the violent overthrow of the government, but I pointed out to him that the potentially explosive connotations of that term made it a risky choice. It was open to attack from the media and was likely to alienate some voters. It might also attract an irresponsible element to his cause or be wilfully misunderstood and used against him and the Brexit Party by political opponents.

I also knew that 'revolution' was a poor option from a marketing perspective. Just because a word or a message is intended a certain way, it does not follow that people will perceive it in the way it is intended. I suggested that a less radical, more nuanced slogan would be preferable. To locate the best form of words, I had to take a step back and listen carefully to voters' concerns at the time. It was critical for me to understand the language that they used to express their frustrations, as well as taking into account Farage's views and the aims of the Brexit Party.

As the Brexit Party rapidly grew, I could see that what others might perceive as its weaknesses were in fact its strengths. It was unknown; it had no staff or infrastructure and it had no representation in any Parliament. This lack of baggage meant that it could focus solely on its principal ambition: to bring about Brexit.

Furthermore, I endorsed Farage's view that it must select candidates from every walk of life and that this should be one of its chief selling points. Every political party tries to claim that it represents 'ordinary people' because its candidates are themselves 'ordinary'. By virtue of being new, however, the Brexit Party had a perfect opportunity to select people who would mirror the diverse backgrounds of Britain's Brexit voters. In the most positive sense, this would set it even further apart from the UK's established political parties, none of which, the Brexit Party argued, had seemed to want to carry out the will of the majority and most of whose MPs were at that time failing to represent the interests of many of their electors.

The Brexit Party had to be different. It had to show that it was listening to the electorate and projecting its exasperation. As for Farage himself, he had led another party, UKIP, in the UK general election of 2015, securing 3.9 million votes and coming third place in terms of the popular vote. By any standards, this made him something of a political veteran. The Brexit Party's slogan would have to reflect the fact that running this new organisation in these circumstances made him the 'change' candidate. Those who understand marketing will know that this would not be a simple task. It needed to be less of a line extension of an existing product and more an entirely new brand.

By February 2019, Farage had started to assemble a body of

potential candidates comprising businesspeople, doctors, journalists and others who had not been formally involved in politics before but represented the cross-section of society who had voted for Brexit in 2016. Of course, some existing politicians were also willing to stand under the Brexit Party banner, including the former Conservative minister Ann Widdecombe, the Revolutionary Communist Party member-turned-libertarian activist Claire Fox and Farage himself. But they were sufficiently different in outlook for the *New York Times* to note in its coverage of the 2019 European elections that the Brexit Party was 'running candidates from all over the political spectrum'.

In keeping with the party's standing as an outsider whose goal was to revamp British politics by the means of Brexit, I told Farage that all of the available data suggested using the word 'change' in its slogan was far likelier to strike a chord with the public than 'revolution'. This mirrored the feedback I received from my focus group and polling work. In pure marketing terms, I knew the Brexit Party had to stake a claim to that word first in voters' minds. So I devised the slogan 'Change Politics for Good'. The double meaning of this phrase (to change politics for the better and to change it for ever) would add to its effectiveness. It was a tactic I had used successfully in other campaigns.

If adopted, this slogan would also confirm Farage as the 'change' candidate in the election, which, as this book will show, is not without risk. Succeeding with a 'change' slogan is rare for an established figure like Farage and for a party not considered to be part of the mainstream. But these messages would strengthen the idea that large numbers of fed-up voters were willing to embark on a collective exercise to alter the status quo and were open to voting for a new party. I showed some persistence, Farage concurred and the new slogan was pressed into service on placards and on official literature ahead of the party's formal launch in Coventry in April 2019.

As Farage had envisaged months earlier, it was confirmed by the government just two weeks before polling day that the UK would be participating in the 2019 European Parliament elections. This late call was advantageous to the Brexit Party, only adding to the sense of disorder engulfing British politics at the time. Even more useful for them, it helped fuel the idea that change was not just desirable but also necessary, because the established parties could not be trusted to do anything properly – including deciding whether the electorate would have a vote in a national ballot.

When the results came through, the Brexit Party was the clear winner. It had secured twenty-nine out of a possible seventy-three seats and 30.5 per cent of the available vote, crushing the mainstream parties. The governing Conservative Party lost fifteen of its eighteen seats and was reduced to 8.8 per cent of the vote, its lowest national vote share since its formation in 1834. The day after the election was held, Theresa May resigned as Prime Minister after only three years in the job. For the first time in British political history, a new party had won a national election in its maiden campaign. Despite having only existed officially for eight weeks, it had become the most powerful campaigning force in the land at that moment. How had this happened?

I am certain that one of the decisive factors in that extraordinary performance was the 'Change Politics for Good' slogan. It had acted as a magnet both to 'outsider' Brexit Party candidates and to the disgruntled voters whose anger it voiced. A winning slogan will always need to be matched by what people can see in front of them. 'Change Politics for Good' comfortably delivered on that score thanks to the mix of ages, backgrounds, occupations and sexes across its representatives. True, Farage was himself technically a professional politician, having already served as an MEP in Brussels for two decades, but the overall message worked because it was visibly verifiable and because he and the other candidates believed in it so strongly.

This idea of changing politics for good took on the status of a mission. Indeed, it was in those circumstances that Farage became seen as the overall 'change' candidate in British politics, using the word 'change' frequently in conversation, in speeches and in interviews. We had succeeded in choosing the right word for the right candidate at the right time.

A 'change' slogan has been used eleven times in British national elections in the past century. This was one of the rare occasions since the Conservative Party under Winston Churchill in 1951 used 'It's Time for a Change. Vote Conservative' that it had been successful. In the case of Farage and the Brexit Party, I knew that the circumstances at the time were so unusual that the electorate would be likely to set aside any preconceived ideas of him and of his political history. For that reason, I was aware that in this new reality, the 'change' narrative would work for Farage in a way that it never would have done for him before.

Of all the projects I have been involved with since 2018, the one that comes closest to replicating my experiences of advising the Brexit Party presented itself in January 2023 – but from a very different, pro-EU political perspective. It provides a lesson in how the use of those eight key words in political slogans can cross over all political divides in different situations.

I helped Milojko Spajić, the former Finance Minister, in Montenegro, part of the former communist state of Yugoslavia that was now a European democracy of just 600,000 citizens. He had resigned from the government six months earlier to found a new political party called Europe Now! and he wanted my help to win the presidential election in March 2023.

The parallels with the work I had conducted for the Brexit Party were striking. Like Farage, Spajić had gone against the grain by setting up a new party in a heavily contested political marketplace, in this case thanks to the sheer quantity of parties in Montenegrin politics. He too wanted to prise his country from the grip of the past and shift it onto new political terrain. And, as had also been the case in Britain in 2019, Montenegro had reached a political impasse. This was in no small part due to the Democratic Party of Socialists of Montenegro having been in power since 1991, with one man, Milo Đukanović, serving variously as Prime Minister and President throughout that 32-year period. Yet there was a key difference between Farage and Spajić: Farage wanted to pull Britain out of the EU, whereas Spajić wanted to use Europe Now! to get his country to join the EU.

Spajić's aspiration might have been the direct opposite of Farage's, but from my point of view, the initial objective was the same. Spajić needed to overturn some deeply entrenched attitudes in order to win two democratic elections.

Spajić wanted a slogan that he believed would reflect the metaphorical crossroads at which Montenegro found itself. He wanted to convey that under other parties, the country would drift politically either to the left or the right but that he would take it forward. My polling showed that the 'crossroads' analogy would not work. My focus groups showed voters believed that change was being forced upon them, something which makes electorates all over the world uncomfortable.

In this case, unlike in the UK with the Brexit Party, the campaign and language of change had to be implicit, not explicit. My research also identified in the crossroads analogy a fourth possibility – standing still. This was something that Spajić had not even considered. A sizeable chunk of those I consulted felt that, even after more than thirty years of the same party being in charge, the 'devil you know' option would be preferable to voting for a new, untested party. This again proves that a political message counts for little if the electorate's perception of it is, for whatever reason, different to the politician's own.

Based on my analysis of what approach and what language would work best, I suggested a clearer slogan, which was then trialled with focus groups: 'It's Time'. These words would be used to suggest people's lives would be improved economically, rather than merely presenting Spajić as the 'change' candidate for the sake of it.

The idea worked. This slogan chimed with Spajić's general thesis. It also invited voters to believe that change would occur naturally if they supported him over settling for the status quo. A campaign plan was based around how the economy would be improved for everyday Montenegrins so that they could finally enjoy European standards of living, which was particularly effective because Spajić's personal standing and reputation as former Finance Minister were so solid. Telling people that the moment had arrived for a better economy and that Spajić was the person to deliver it justified the use of the 'It's Time' slogan. It played to his strengths and it was the message that the electorate wanted to hear. For the people of Montenegro, it was time.

The route to success was not straightforward, however. For one thing, Spajić had initially intended to stand for the presidency of Montenegro. Weeks before the ballot, it was announced by Montenegro's official election body that he was ineligible for the post owing to the fact he had dual citizenship – despite the fact that he had renounced it. This was a politically motivated tactic used by his opponents to wrongfoot him. Nonetheless, it required a response. His Europe Now! co-founder, Jakov Milatović, stood instead and subsequently defeated the incumbent, Milo Đukanović. The momentum gained through that victory helped Europe Now!, headed by Spajić, to win the subsequent parliamentary election. In October 2023, after weeks of negotiations, a party that had only been created the previous year formed the government, with Spajić becoming Prime Minister. Aged thirty-six, he became the world's youngest head of government.

The different campaigns run by the Brexit Party and by Europe Now! stand as two useful case studies because of their reliance on good messaging. These examples show how two sets of contradictory objectives (leaving the EU and joining the EU) can lean heavily on the same rhetorical strategies. Even though Farage and Spajić knew who they needed to appeal to, they weren't always sure what language would work best. In both instances, I was able to steer them onto the most fertile political ground by finding the right hit word for the situation.

Both examples also show that politicians often have deeply held views and fixed ideas about how they want to express them, but what they want to say, what they end up saying and what voters hear do not always align. Judging the mood of the electorate is vital. The same applies to timing. Knowing when to say something is just as important as saying it. Indeed, an election slogan with the word 'time' in it had been used by opposition parties in Montenegro on several occasions prior to 2023, to no effect whatsoever. The fact that it was used by Milojko Spajić so successfully in 2023, despite its unsuccessful use in prior elections, proves the point.

The lessons I have learned through my involvement in dozens of electoral contests gave me the idea to write this book, as did my decision to compile an election slogan database. Having a catalogue of global political history at my fingertips made me realise that no in-depth study of election slogans has ever been published before. I've asked myself why not. After all, as already noted, the choice of political slogan can have profound consequences for entire nations, for better or worse.

On the one hand, it seems surprising that more attention has not been paid to the strengths of slogans. On the other hand, I can think of some obvious possible reasons that such an analysis has so far been overlooked.

Even though a slogan's words are often striking enough to remain in people's memories for years, the creative and strategic agencies behind some of them are often reluctant to acknowledge the important role that a pithy phrase can play. Perhaps the executives think to do so would diminish what they do in the eyes of others. For some, Walter Bagehot's maxim 'We must not let in daylight upon magic' is surely applicable across political life, not just in relation to the monarchy. This unwillingness to be categorised as just another part of a slogan-generating machine or a linguistic sausage factory runs counter to the fact that slogans are fundamental to the business of politics.

At another level, those who are actively involved in a political campaign will rarely concede the importance of a slogan either. They may feel that any admission that they are linked to what is essentially another form of marketing goes against the way they like to see themselves – and be seen by others. No politician would wish to undermine their own role in this way. They certainly wouldn't be keen to admit publicly to spending large sums of money on focus groups in order to find the best slogan or most popular policy, even though most of them do. Many politicians all over the world like to present themselves as being in touch with everyday people. They would hate to be shown as dependent upon marketing surveys to understand the concerns of their constituency of voters.

The electorate, the last link in the chain, is the most important, as both the target audience and the group which has the ability to hire and fire governments and politicians. Again, there is a simple reason why voters often overlook the significance of a slogan. Who would openly confess to having been seduced by a few words in order to get them to vote for one party over another, no matter how clever some of the wordplay used undoubtedly is?

As this book will show, complex calculations take place in people's minds when they are invited to vote in an election. Although the words in a slogan may seem straightforward, their use tends to encourage voters to weigh up the options and choices in front of them, whether consciously or unconsciously. Traditionally, it has been assumed that voters are less open-minded than they realise, with political habits and opinions acquired in their youth being difficult to shift – though recent election results suggest that voters' allegiances are now becoming increasingly more fluid.

I believe there is a further reason why a book like this has never been published before: too many people who are involved in politics, whether as frontline politicians or as advisers, take a tribal view of their work. Some even refuse to consort with those whom they assume are their opponents. The idea of sharing or exchanging information is anathema to them, as I found when researching this project.

Those who operate at the commercial end of politics will likely have spent their entire career representing one party or another and so the scope of their experience is limited only to that side of the political divide. The net result is that almost everybody who works in and around the political arena, including those who work as consultants, is unable or unwilling to offer a balanced view of an adversary's campaign or its principal slogan. This stands in contrast to the advertising industry, for example, in which almost every executive would at the very least be willing to express an objective opinion on the merits or otherwise of a rival firm's marketing campaign for a given product. The advertising industry even holds numerous awards ceremonies, which are dedicated to rewarding competitor firms' campaigns. Such even-handedness barely exists in politics. Who, for example, can imagine one of Donald Trump's opponents acknowledging publicly that they envied effective aspects of the successful election campaigns he ran in 2016 and 2024?

One of the dangers of our current era is that too few people are able to free themselves from their default setting, politically speaking. This intransigence has a knock-on effect in a professional sense. The fact that so many people would refuse to put aside their personal political preferences by working on a campaign whose message they might not necessarily endorse narrows their outlook. Indeed, it is an irony that those who work in an arm of the communications business can be so blinkered themselves. Democracy is the poorer for it.

Any study of words and their effectiveness requires a balanced view. The great value of my slogan database is that it is factual. As this book will detail, it can demonstrate what has worked, when it has worked and why it has worked, bypassing any preconceptions that anybody might have in the process. This serves me well professionally. I hope that it inspires others to write on the same subject.

Other than what I have described here, this book will not detail case studies of my work as a political consultant and pollster, though it will draw upon my extensive experience operating in these fields. Instead, it looks at slogans through the widest lens possible, setting out to show their impact around the world over the past century and explaining what makes one slogan work over another. Based on information produced by the database, plus extensive interviews with more than 100 politicians, advisers, academics, marketing executives and behavioural scientists, its purpose is to identify what makes an election slogan successful in the view of those who have been involved in creating them and using them.

Each chapter focuses on one of the eight 'hit' words that has helped to win an election and which has therefore contributed to changing the world. The thinkers and strategists behind some of them will explain how they came up with their slogan, how it was marketed and offer their assessment of its effectiveness. How many times has each of these eight words been used in election slogans over the course of the past 100 years? Why has it been successful? Was it used by a right-of-centre or a left-of-centre party – or both? And which factors cemented its success in one election as opposed to another? This book seeks to answer each of these questions and, for the first time, tell the story behind the slogans that shape our world.

Whether you are a politician, a campaigner, a student of politics, a marketing professional, a voter or a general reader who is interested in looking at politics from a slightly different angle, this book aims to provide the fullest account of the history and use of political slogans in an accessible and entertaining way. It would be a mistake for anybody to assume that merely using one of the eight words that have changed the world is a guarantee of success. At the risk of stating the obvious, the words alone are not enough to win. Their potency lies in who says the words, when they say them – and understanding how best to exploit them.

GREAT

Tens of thousands of electoral slogans have been produced around the world over the past century, yet most people can only remember a handful of them. One reason for this is that since the turn of the century, the proliferation of media has increased the volume of slogans produced, meaning that, paradoxically, fewer of them resonate. In the pre-digital age, political parties were able to rely upon fewer slogans and still run a successful election campaign. As the ideological ties between politicians and voters have loosened in the twenty-first century, however, party machines are prepared to use many more slogans in what can seem like a desperate effort to connect with the public. Furthermore, so much everyday language has been truncated or dumbed down into what could be termed slogan-speak that genuine political slogans have lost some of their distinctiveness and power.

Having said that, over the past twenty-five years there have been several examples of slogans becoming inextricably linked with the politicians whose campaigns they promoted. Mention 'Yes We Can' to any voter in the US and a majority of them will surely remember that these three words helped sweep Barack Obama to the White

1

House in 2008. Similarly, anybody with knowledge of contemporary British politics will recall that Boris Johnson built the Conservative Party's 2019 general election push around a vow to 'Get Brexit Done'. It worked. The party won by an eighty-seat majority landslide and Johnson's promise partly defined his three-year premiership.

Undoubtedly the best-known slogan of recent times, however, is 'Make America Great Again' or 'MAGA' for short. Even those who are not especially politically engaged, including non-American citizens who had no stake in the outcome of the 2016 presidential election, will probably know that this phrase was deployed by Donald Trump as he defeated Hillary Clinton to become the forty-fifth President of the US. He used it again in 2020 when he lost the presidency to Joe Biden and then for a third time in 2024 when he defeated Kamala Harris to become the forty-seventh President – a feat widely considered to be the most remarkable political comeback of the modern era. Many people probably assume that Trump created the slogan. He did not. It is merely the most famous example of an old phrase.

For a host of reasons, 'Make America Great Again' has become synonymous with Trump's political brand to such a degree that by 2024 it had come to be regarded not just as a slogan but also as a kind of political philosophy. But how have these four words become so piercingly effective? The marketing principles he used to advance the phrase, beginning with his highly unusual decision to submit a trademark application for the slogan with the US Patent and Trademark Office, have certainly played a key part. Yet even though the words 'great' and 'again' – neither of which is one of the eight 'hit' words – have had a surprisingly low rate of delivering electoral success over the past century, and Trump's campaigns of 2016 and 2024 are only two of relatively few examples of these words being used by a winning candidate, it would seem perverse not to examine his use of them in a book of this nature.

Unlike any previous slogan, this one has itself become something of an ideological border within America. How voters align themselves with it – or against it – is likely to remain a talking point in US politics for at least another generation, because in some ways 'MAGA' has replaced the traditional divides of left and right. Furthermore, it is probably the most famous (or infamous, depending on your point of view) political slogan of all time and it illustrates perfectly how the history and meaning of any slogan – not just this one – are often far richer than people may appreciate. Language is always evolving, meaning that people's interpretation of it is as well. This in turn raises questions about how feasible it is to suggest that a slogan can ever be said to 'belong' to any party or politician in any accepted sense, despite slogans having become much more limited in their application and more strongly identified with individuals or causes in recent years.

In the case of 'Make America Great Again', some wonder if this form of words – or something close to it – could ever be used by another candidate or party again in future or whether it is somehow tainted by virtue of a politician as controversial as Trump having apparently monopolised it. In fact, Trump's use of the slogan shouldn't be a consideration. The words should be judged on their merit, not on the figure with whom they're most often or recently associated. They should also be judged on their ability to help convey the message in relation to a candidate, encapsulating their personality and complementing their political journey. But as Trump was not the first person to use it, such concerns are not necessarily valid anyway.

Contrary to popular assumptions, almost every slogan can be

traced to a past election, public campaign or political speech, sometimes from decades before. The 'hit' words that define those slogans
usually date back even further, but as we shall see, it can take decades for them to crystalise into the neat constructions that make up
today's election slogans. Politicians of every era may claim to have
conceived their own ideas and, in some cases, they will strenuously
deny allegations of poaching, but there are few word groups that are
so unique as to be entirely original.

Take Barack Obama's use of 'Yes We Can'. His aspiration was
that this phrase would stir within voters a sense of hope and unity
irrespective of his, or their, race, creed or skin colour. It worked,
capturing the zeitgeist of progressive America at the dawn of the
twenty-first century. Yet how many members of the US electorate at
that time knew that 'Yes We Can' had been used by the Scottish National Party (SNP) during the British general election campaign of
1997? Those who were aware of its history would have understood
that the SNP, under its then leader Alex Salmond, used 'Yes We Can'
with an aim that was diametrically opposed to Obama's. Whereas
Obama wanted to bring his nation together, Salmond and the SNP
were prepared to break up Scotland's centuries-old political union
with England and Wales in order to achieve their main goal: independence for their country. To what degree Obama or any other
politician may have been consciously aware of having adopted the
SNP's election slogan is difficult to assess. But if nothing else, 'Yes
We Can' shows that the same three-word phrase can be used in two
countries at different times for distinct purposes.

As it happens, it also resulted in different outcomes. Although
it helped Obama to become the first African American to hold the
office of US President, the SNP has still not managed to gain independence for Scotland. Indeed, 'Yes We Can' was probably the

SNP's least effective slogan of the past thirty years. This contrast shows that even a resonant slogan can fail if the party's broader appeal, timing or credibility are lacking. Would Obama still have used this political slogan if he had known of its history? Arguably, yes, for this example shows not only that two politicians can use the same slogan with opposing objectives in mind but also that other factors beyond the slogan itself go into making a particular set of words work. And, of course, he should have felt no compunction about using it if he genuinely believed it conveyed the message that he wanted to send to voters.

When their respective achievements are examined, it is plain to see that Alex Salmond and Barack Obama had different qualities. It would not be unfair to say that whatever Salmond lacked in popular appeal, Obama had in larger quantities. Similarly, the SNP and the Democratic Party are two contrasting organisations with histories that bear little relation to each other. Considering all of this, the importance of personality and marketing in making a slogan work cannot be overstated. The words can work, but only if they're used by the right person at the right time.

Just as every artwork has a provenance, so every slogan has a lineage, as my database shows, beginning when it was first used in an attempt to win an election. There is more likely to be a connection between slogans when they are brought into play by politicians who are campaigning in the same country or who have a similar political outlook. The same slogan does not always hail from the same lineage, however. Politicians are often motivated to use certain word formations for reasons that are hard to pin down, and as we have seen, it is not unusual for individuals operating thousands of miles apart to stumble upon near-identical phrases independently of each other. No matter where you are in the world, when certain conditions present themselves, politicians appear naturally driven to base a campaign around certain key words – and voters are most likely to respond to them. Getting the timing right is critical. What is important to recognise is that voters are generally receptive to acting upon similar words and ideas – even if they are presented in different languages and do not translate literally. Indeed, in 2014, a left-wing political party called Podemos – meaning 'We Can' – was launched in Spain.

Donald Trump has long maintained that the expression 'Make America Great Again' came to him as he sat at his desk on the twenty-sixth floor of Trump Tower in Manhattan in November 2012, the day after the Republican Party presidential candidate Mitt Romney lost the election to Barack Obama. Thrilled by its possibilities, which chimed with his view of the US as the most powerful nation on earth and of himself as a titan of its corporate culture, he asked his lawyers to contact the US Trademark Office. They successfully registered a claim on his behalf for the exclusive right to use it for 'political action committee services, namely, promoting public awareness of political issues and fundraising in the field of politics'. The fee was $325.

Once the trademark became effective in July 2015, Trump blocked other Republican politicians from using it, including Senator Ted Cruz and Governor Scott Walker, both of whom received cease-and-desist letters for expressing their desire in speeches that summer to 'make America great again'. The upshot for Trump was that anyone in the US who wanted to use these words assembled in this order for the purpose of furthering their own political agenda could not do so without his permission. In this way, he took ownership of what had become a vital part of his brand. He did what came naturally to him as a businessman with a long career in marketing by establishing that whenever 'Make America Great Again' was mentioned, voters would think of him. He got there first in voters' minds, even though he did not coin the slogan. Trump thought he had a legal right to act in this way, and he clearly took advantage of the fact that his rivals had little or no background in marketing in comparison to him, but it is incongruous that he was able to seize control of a form of words whose origins go back much further than the point at which his lawyers contacted the Trademark Office. His version of making a country 'great again' was merely the latest iteration of what most people would agree is a potentially timeless slogan.

It would be impossible for anybody – including Trump – to say definitively how much he knew of the history of his trademarked slogan in the years leading up to his first successful bid for the White House. There is clear evidence, however, that the principle of a country becoming 'great again' has been popular with thinkers, politicians and political parties since at least the early twentieth century, when these words were most likely first used in Britain. This is particularly true of those on the right, who tend to view the past more positively than those on the progressive left. Decades before election slogans became the short, snappy creations that are familiar to the public now, they were often derived from passages and theories contained in articles, essays or speeches. In other words, they were first presented in a more formal context before their conversion into a sound bite or catchphrase. This undercurrent can be seen as the prelude to a slogan's use in an electoral context.

By the early 1900s, Britain's global dominance had peaked and some commentators had begun to consider not just the nation's global decline but also its domestic sluggishness. On 19 March 1907, the *Daily Mirror*, a newspaper then aimed at a middle-class readership and owned by the press baron Lord Northcliffe, published an article by its editor, Henry Hamilton Fyfe, which contains an early use of the 'great again' formation. In it, Fyfe railed against the 'idle poor' and 'cadgers', whom he described as those 'who would rather live without working than support themselves'. He thought that the increasing prevalence of such people was preventing Britain from being 'great' and that his contemporaries ought to 'teach everyone to work in childhood and see that they never lose the habit' in order to 'make Britain "great" again'. When using 'great again' in this early example, perhaps the author had in mind the political union between England and his native Scotland that began in 1707, thus establishing the Kingdom of Great Britain.

The 'great again' credo was also prominent during the Second World War, with leaders of the Allied and Axis powers using it in speeches and at rallies as a way to boost people's morale and, no doubt, shore up their own position. According to *Buffalo News* and the *St Louis Star and Times*, Adolf Hitler used it in a speech he gave in Munich in February 1940 as he explained the political origins of Nazism. 'Nationalism and Socialism had to be redefined and they had to be blended into one strong, new idea to carry new strength, which would make Germany great again,' the Nazi leader was quoted as saying. Dwight Eisenhower, then the Supreme Allied Commander in Europe, uttered the same expression as he praised the Free French forces in North Africa, who were fighting the Vichy colonial administration there. He was quoted in the London *Evening Standard* in December 1942 as saying, 'All Frenchmen worthy of their country's great past have forgotten their small differences of ideas and are ready to fight hand-in-hand. Your decision and courage in the face of the Axis threats will make France great again and will eject the German invader.'

In post-war Britain, leading Conservative figures also spoke of their intention to make the country great again. Anthony Eden, who served as Foreign Secretary in Winston Churchill's war Cabinet, was foremost among them, writing in the *Manchester Guardian* in September 1947, 'Our first task must be to make our country great again.' Other MPs echoed this phrase in the lead-up to the 1950 general election campaign, which the Conservatives fought under the slogan 'Make Britain Great Again'. This marked the first time that the 'great again' form was used in a national election.

The words appeared on campaign posters featuring a photograph of a British bulldog with the plea 'Vote Unionist' underneath. A leaflet titled 'You can help to make Great Britain Great Again' was also produced, railing against socialist efforts to dismantle the British Empire. Candidates were encouraged to refer to the phrase as well. One, Margaret Roberts, who stood in Dartford, told voters in a speech in February 1950, 'We Conservatives are not afraid to face the future whatever problem it entails, because it is our earnest desire to make Great Britain great again.' As it happens, Roberts was not elected as an MP until 1959, when she stood in the constituency of Finchley under her married name, Margaret Thatcher. But that rallying call in 1950 left a mark on her politics. In the years that followed, she borrowed heavily from the Conservative Party's 'great again' campaign guide, embracing many of its policies, such as lowering taxes and boosting private enterprise, during the eleven years that she served as Prime Minister between 1979 and 1990.

The slogan 'Make Britain Great Again', however, failed to strike a chord with the electorate in 1950. The Conservative Party did not quite manage to return to government on that occasion, but it was victorious at the subsequent election in 1951, which it contested under several different slogans, including 'Now is Your Chance to Take It! Vote Conservative' and 'It's Time For a Change. Vote

Conservative.' Why wasn't 'great again' more effective in 1950? Probably because only five years had passed since the Conservatives had last been in office and voters did not look back nostalgically on the war years as a happy or successful period. The idea of recapturing a sense of greatness was essentially hollow. This, arguably, goes to the heart of why the abstract term 'great again' has rarely worked in political slogans.

Although 'great again' disappeared from Conservative campaigns after 1950, it did not vanish entirely from British politics, making a brief return in July 1962 when a neo-Nazi organisation called the National Socialist Movement (NSM) gathered in Trafalgar Square. During the ensuing rally, NSM leader Colin Jordan promised to rid Britain of Jewish influence, proclaiming, 'We have in the twelve points of policy of the National Socialist Movement the only policy which can make Britain great again and put her in the front of the world where she belongs.' The NSM had a markedly chequered history and ceased to exist by 1968.

In view of the slogan's use by the Conservative Party and by the racist NSM, it is noteworthy that David Kingsley, who was a key election adviser to the British Labour Prime Minister Harold Wilson, planned to use 'Make Britain Great Again' as Labour's slogan during the general election campaign of 1970. This came to light in his *Guardian* obituary, published in April 2014. Its author, Julia Langdon, explained that Kingsley and his colleagues anticipated running a two-part poster campaign. The first part, in which the Conservative leader Edward Heath and his shadow ministers were depicted as puppets, used the slogan 'Yesterday's Men'. This was judged by the standards of the day to be overly pessimistic. Wilson himself did not like the slogan and Labour was criticised for using it. Of the second part, Langdon wrote, 'The follow-up was intended to convey the positive message "Make Britain great again". But Wilson unexpectedly brought forward the general election to June, apparently persuaded by his political adviser Marcia Williams, and the negative nature of the "Yesterday's men" slogan rebounded to his disadvantage.' Labour was voted out of office, and as far as the voting public was concerned, Wilson was yesterday's man. Kingsley's frustration at only being able to enact half of his plan would have been understandable, as he knew that those slogans needed each other to work to their full extent.

In view of the fact that Trump's first 'Make America Great Again' campaign had not begun in earnest at the point when Kingsley's obituary was published, it is noteworthy that the Labour-supporting *Guardian*, one of Trump's most trenchant critics, referred to Kingsley's nostalgic 'great again' slogan as a 'positive message'. Would the newspaper still consider it in glowing terms today? (Following Trump's victory in 2024, its editor, Katharine Viner, offered staff counselling to cope with his 'upsetting' victory'.) Would it ever mention that in October 1995, Labour leader Tony Blair said in his speech to the party conference, 'Britain can and will be a great country again'? Would it even refer to the Labour Party's link to the slogan at all? Or would it fall victim to the curse of what has come to be known as 'recency bias'?

This is the tendency for people to focus on experiences that are freshest in their memory to the detriment of historic ones, even if the 'evidence' provided to them is not reliable. One corrosive aspect of the digital age, in which some – but not all – information is available at the touch of a button, is that the last person to use a slogan is often seen as its 'owner', to the exclusion of all others. Provenance and lineage are at risk of being forgotten.

At first glance, it may seem unlikely that Harold Wilson's Labour, as a left-wing party, would have been prepared to rely on the same words in 1970 that had been (unsuccessfully) used within living memory by the Conservative wartime leader Winston Churchill and by a far-right political group that operated on the fringes of the mainstream. One explanation for Kingsley's willingness to follow their respective leads, and for Labour to regard the 'great again' message in positive terms, is that he was unencumbered by 'recency bias'. In 1970, when information was generally only available in hard copy and took longer to access by the masses because it was more compartmentalised, such concerns may not have occurred to those running a political campaign. A second reason might be that people are, by and large, predisposed to latch on to the same words and slogans to make a point or nurture an idea, wherever they stand on the political spectrum and wherever they live in the world. This is particularly true when one party has been in government for a long period of time. Opposition parties – whatever their political leanings – almost always use a slogan that promotes the idea that change is not only desirable but also necessary, that the future can be better under them or that only they carry the torch of hope. In this sense, it could be said that we are all tuned to the same frequency, though we may choose to listen to it at different times. Had the Labour Party used the 'great again' phrase in 1970, the slogan's subsequent history might have been very different, of course.

'Make Britain Great Again' returned once more to British politics in 1975 when it was used on a leaflet by the fascist National Front urging people to vote to leave the European Economic Community (EEC) during that year's referendum. It lay dormant again until 2013, the year of Margaret Thatcher's death. By then, she was widely regarded as having been the most consequential British politician to have held power since Churchill. When David Cameron, the sitting

Conservative Prime Minister, paid tribute to her, he unwittingly – though very aptly – harked back to the slogan that Thatcher had herself uttered in Dartford more than sixty years before. 'They say that cometh the hour, cometh the man,' said Cameron in his speech to Parliament. 'Well in 1979 came the hour, and came The Lady. She made the political weather. She made history. And let this be her epitaph: that she made Britain great again.' This again reinforces the point that people often think in such similar ways that they frequently use the same words and phrases, even if they stand at different points on the ideological spectrum and, indeed, live in countries that are thousands of miles apart. It should not be forgotten that Cameron spoke these words two years before Trump's trademark became effective and more than three years before the latter won the 2016 presidential election.

Just as no individual or party can be said to be able to exercise sole rights over a slogan, no nation can be said to either. More than a decade after the Conservatives made use of the 'great again' slogan in 1950, another political party on a different continent took up the same message, albeit in a comparatively toned-down manner. On 2 August 1964, during that year's presidential campaign, those acting on behalf of the Republican nominee Barry Goldwater used an advertisement in the *Orlando Sentinel* to declare:

This great man needs you, you need this great man. Enlist in the national crusade to put Barry Goldwater in the White House in 1965. He was nominated by local people working together. He will be elected by local people who want to regain their lost freedoms and make America great again.

Did the author of these words study the Conservative Party's policy documents of the 1940s and, through them, become aware of its use of the 'great again' slogan in 1950? Indeed, who can be sure that Donald Trump, who would have been eighteen when Goldwater ran for the presidency, did not know of this advertisement before he applied for it to be trademarked? The ideas that this piece of electoral literature espouses are recognisably Trumpian in nature, after all. Undeniably, half a century before Trump's political rhetoric was unleashed upon the US, Goldwater's campaign had already used the same slogan and ideas that helped to put Trump in the White House in 2016 and in 2024. Yet in Goldwater's case it had little effect, not only because of the newspaper's limited reach but also because, in the aftermath of John F. Kennedy's assassination the year before, it might have been unclear in voters' minds which period Goldwater wanted to recall. However, this certainly shows once again that people are often drawn to the same words and ideas, whether in 1964, in 2016 or in 2024. Trump's political campaign message was not new; it had just been repackaged.

Having made an appearance in America in 1964, the 'great again' slogan crossed continents once more. It was next used in December 1965 by President Ferdinand Marcos, the Filipino dictator, during his inaugural address in Manila, so beginning its distinct Filipino lineage. As he spoke of the 'greatness' that had gone into building what he called the 'first Asian Republic', Marcos said:

This nation can be great again. This I have said over and over. It is my article of faith, and Divine Providence has willed that you and I can now translate this faith into deeds … Offering all our efforts to our Creator, we must drive ourselves to be great again. This is your dream and mine. By your choice you have committed yourselves to it. Come then, let us march together towards the dream of greatness.

Marcos went on to serve as President for the next twenty years before being ousted in the People Power Revolution of 1986. He died in exile in Hawaii in September 1989, but his widow, Imelda, and their children Imee and Bongbong, returned to the Philippines two years later and were elected to various political offices over the next thirty years, culminating in Bongbong's elevation to the presidency in June 2022. The rehabilitation of Imelda Marcos is considered to be remarkable given the charges of kleptocracy that have been levelled against her since the 1980s. Although she and her husband amassed billions of dollars before his death, much of this money has been retrieved by the Philippines government after it was found to have been stolen from the state. Marcos may have denied these charges but what cannot be disputed is that she never forgot her husband's 1965 'great again' pledge, mentioning it to anybody who would listen. When she first returned to Manila in November 1991, she addressed the thousands of supporters who had gathered outside the Philippine Plaza Hotel to greet her, telling them, 'I inherited from Marcos his love for this nation. This nation can be great again'. Five days later she visited victims of a volcano eruption in Zambales province and told a crowd of 2,000 people, 'I love you all. I will fulfil Ferdinand's dream that this nation be great again.'

The 'great again' phrase seems never to have been far from Marcos's lips, also becoming her slogan in 1992 when she stood in that year's presidential election. (She also adapted one of Ronald Reagan's best-known phrases by asking voters, 'Are you better off than you were six years ago?') 'Happy days are here again,' she said in one speech. 'If we are united, I am sure this nation will be great again.' She finished fifth out of seven candidates, but for years afterwards, she continued to repeat the magic words in the campaigns of others that she became involved in, including that of Rodrigo

Duterte, whose successful bid for the presidency of the Philippines in 2016 she is believed to have sponsored. In July 2015, the *Manila Bulletin* reported that Marcos, who at that time was a member of the Philippine House of Representatives, said of the forthcoming presidential election, 'I'm sure that after six years, people will be smarter in choosing a President who will do great things for them, so this country will be great again.'

It is worth mentioning that by then, Imelda Marcos and Donald Trump were known to each other. They met during her political exile, at the eightieth birthday party of the comedian Joey Adams, held at the Helmsley Hotel in New York in January 1991, the year before her bid for the Filipino presidency. A photograph was taken of them sitting together. Who is to say they did not discuss nations becoming 'great again' that night, planting a seed in Trump's mind that became 'Make America Great Again' more than thirty years later?

An even more tangible link between Trump and the 'great again' formula can be found in the US presidential election of 1980, when Ronald Reagan was elected off the back of the slogan 'Let's Make America Great Again'. Whether Trump remembered Reagan's use of it or not, by adapting the phrase for his own purposes in 2016 he drew from Reagan's victorious campaign more than three decades later. The nostalgic effect that this might have had on Republican voters, especially those who prospered under Reagan in the 1980s, should not be underestimated. Even if Trump had no memory of Reagan's 1980 campaign message when he trademarked the 'great again' slogan, it is conceivable that he had read an article in the *National Post*, published in June 2011, written by Conrad Black, the Canadian-born former media tycoon, which was headlined 'Can the GOP make America great again?' Six months later, on

13 December, Trump issued a statement in which he said he had not decided whether he wanted to stand for the presidency himself, concluding, 'I must leave all of my options open because, above all else, we must make America great again!'

Equally plausible is that the slogan came to Trump not, as he has claimed, in November 2012 but on 2 January 2012, when he was interviewed on Fox News by Greta Van Susteren. During that interview, he was asked if he was considering running for the presidency in light of some activists in Texas having filed the paperwork to make official their new creation, the Make America Great Again Party. Its single purpose was to encourage Trump to stand. When asked about this by Van Susteren, Trump said:

Well, I do love the name. I think the name of the party is fantastic because that really is what it's all about. America soon will not be great. A lot of people would say right now it is not great. You look at what's happening in the world, you look at what's happening with other countries, they're eating our lunch. We don't have any leadership. And it's really a very sad thing, what's going on with this country. So I think the name is a great name. I will say that.

Whatever the truth of how Donald Trump developed the 'great again' phrase, it is not difficult to accept that it has its own history, which is entirely independent of him. Having said that, it is incontrovertible that 'great again' is now generally viewed only through the prism of Trump. Questions therefore turn to why this should be so and why it matters. Most obviously, Trump designed it that way thanks to his decision to trademark the slogan and to target America with the 'MAGA' attitude via millions of stickers, T-shirts and red caps. Yet people's tendency to base their thinking on what comes most easily to mind is almost certainly to blame as well. This partial attitude possibly finds a parallel with what Trump himself would call 'fake news'. People's reliance on an internet search engine to 'verify' information, coupled with their lack of curiosity to go back beyond the first few results, tends to lead to conclusions that – in this context – the phrase is Trump's alone. Evidence of others having used it is effectively expunged. Because of this, the history of the slogan is in danger of being obscured or even forgotten.

This matters because politicians are always under a certain amount of pressure to use a fresh slogan. Generally, this makes them reluctant to adopt a slogan that has been used previously – doubly so if it has been portrayed as 'controversial'. This can lead to a timidity of thoughts and ideas. The pool of words and phrases from which slogans can be drawn has already been depleted in this century thanks to 'recency bias' and marketing efforts to find language that can unite the diverse groups of people that are now able to vote. It is being further reduced by politicians' desire to pick what is believed to be the safest or least offensive slogan. Yet election slogans ought to be regarded rather like a train that is on a continuous journey. Though the carriages come to a halt at stations from time to time, they should not be judged by the last stop they made. The catalogue of examples of people and parties who have used the 'great again' blend proves that slogans can be far more versatile than people assume.

Despite this, 'Make America Great Again' is seen to epitomise the right-wing populist language of Trump only. In September 2016, Bill Clinton, when campaigning on behalf of his wife Hillary, even appeared to accuse Trump of racism over his use of the phrase, saying at a campaign event in Orlando, 'I'm actually old enough to remember the good old days, and they weren't all that good in many ways. That message where "I'll give you America great again" is if you're a white Southerner, you know exactly what it means, don't you?'

The irony here is that when Clinton himself sought election to the White House for the first time in the early 1990s, he used the very same words, telling a rally in Arkansas in 1991, 'I believe that, together, we can make America great again.' The following year he repeated himself in at least two speeches, promising 'to secure a better future for your children and your grandchildren and to make America great again' and then saying on a separate occasion, 'I want to attack these problems and make America great again.' His fondness for the phrase did not end there. In January 2008, the first year that Hillary Clinton tried to win the Democratic Party nomination for President, her team released a sixty-second nationwide radio advert entitled 'Closer' in which Bill Clinton spoke of his confidence in his wife as a problem-solver who could fix America's economy. 'It's time for another comeback, time to make America great again. I know Hillary's the one that can do it,' he said in the advert's closing statement. Given that this was a carefully planned, pre-recorded statement, Clinton clearly believed that it was in his wife's political interests for him to use these words yet again. They had served him well in 1991 and 1992 and he assumed they would benefit her as well.

Apart from inviting accusations of hypocrisy, Bill Clinton's track record of using the 'great again' phrase again demonstrates that nobody 'owns' language and that politicians should be willing to use words that they believe to be most politically expedient and best represent their brand. It also shows not only that the meaning and interpretation of language is constantly shifting but that words which work for one politician will not necessarily work for another. Although Bill Clinton was elected to the White House in

1992 having used the 'great again' phrase in several speeches – perhaps in a calculated nod to nostalgic-minded Republicans who had voted for Reagan in 1980 – the next time he used it, during his wife's attempt to win the Democratic Party nomination for President in 2008, was unsuccessful. Hillary Clinton did not receive sufficient support and she had to make way for Barack Obama, who had achieved the nomination while using the slogan 'Change We Can Believe In'. It is worth underlining that when Bill Clinton spoke of America being 'great again' in 2008, he used the phrase when trying to appeal to members of the Democratic Party only. In this sense, 'great again' was the language of the left in America at that time, despite having been popularised in Britain, the Philippines and the US by right-of-centre parties.

When Bill Clinton talked about making America great again when running for the White House, voters accepted it. When he talked about making America great again under his wife's potential presidency more than a decade later, the idea was rejected. Both Bill Clinton and Donald Trump were believable when they said they would restore their country to glory. When the slogan was linked to Hillary Clinton it was less convincing, perhaps because of her past status as First Lady between 1993 and 2001 and, presumably, because her husband's reputation was decidedly mixed by that point owing to his personal conduct. Her ability to represent the newness and change that Democratic Party members hankered after in 2008 was therefore limited.

In this way, timing is just as important as the words used. For the 'great again' slogan to work, there needs to be a common view of when a country was previously 'great'. Reagan and Trump both picked up on a desire for change and managed to convert it into electoral success with the help of the same battle cry – the more so in the case of Trump's second victory in 2024, when he won the popular vote by a decisive margin. By comparison, the Clintons misunderstood the mood music in 2008.

Regardless, the Clintons' varied use of the phrase over the course of almost twenty years supports the idea that different people will gravitate to the same form of words whether they are of the left or of the right. The range of occasions on which Bill Clinton uttered these words further illustrates the point that people are inclined to view a slogan through the eyes of the last politician to use it – especially in the digital age and specifically if, like Trump, they have trade-marked it. Bill Clinton cannot deny having talked about making America 'great again', but most people will have little memory of his having done so. Instead, the slogan has been attributed to Trump and, perhaps deliberately, misapplied by his opponents so that its true meaning has become harder to fathom. I believe this may result in politicians of the future relying on a diminishing number of slogans in order to avoid a certain phrase having an adverse effect on their campaign.

Donald Trump is rare and perhaps unique among national pol-iticians for having used only one election slogan throughout his mainstream political career. By doing so, he has certainly guaran-teed that people remember it – and him. Stamping his project with the 'great again' seal appears closer to the way a household product is marketed rather than how a system of political ideas is advocated. In understanding this, it is crucial to reflect on how the meaning and interpretation of these four words has changed, not just since Winston Churchill used them in 1950 but also since 2012, when Trump began chanting, mantra-style, his desire to 'make America great again'. The slogan came to represent an ideology, albeit one that has not, at the time of writing, been intellectualised in the way that Reaganism or Thatcherism has been. It is certainly not as clear-ly understood as either of those political philosophies, even if it did return Trump to the White House in 2024 as the first President to serve non-consecutive terms since Grover Cleveland in the 1890s. Having said that, it is not difficult to state what Trump is against: 'woke' thinking, higher taxes, the promotion of minorities and identity politics. That he successfully persuaded a broad range of communities to support him in this is testament to the wide appeal of the MAGA slogan.

What has Trump meant by making America 'great again' in the decade since he trademarked the slogan? This is a difficult question to answer, not least because his doubters and detractors have muddied the waters by projecting onto it their interpretations of its definition. Often, these have managed to override what somebody who actually voted for Trump took the slogan to mean. Friends of Trump have told me that he has kept its meaning deliberately vague and open to interpretation. There are two reasons for this. First, if specific policies were attached to it, its emotional appeal would evaporate. Secondly, part of its power revolves round the fact that it has an indefinable quality. If pushed, his friends claim that Trump would say his personal definition of MAGA is love of his country. He also believes that the MAGA slogan will outlive him. Steve Bannon, Trump's former strategist, tells me:

MAGA is a populist nationalist slogan. That's what MAGA stands for. And it's incredibly powerful. Unlike most political slogans, MAGA only gets more powerful over time. So MAGA means that you are a populist nationalist in the Trump mould, and that means aggressive, combative, no backing down and extreme love of your country. And really MAGA is now global. Because it's really Make America, Hungary. Italy, France, Israel, Germany, the Netherlands, Poland Great Again.

In a poll conducted for this book in January 2024, some 3,000 American voters were asked for their views on the Make America Great Again slogan. In view of Trump's emphatic victory ten months later, their responses at that time showed that many mainstream commentators had completely misunderstood how the American public – regardless of race, creed, colour or sex – perceives this phrase. The slogan is not seen by voters as being a dog whistle to white nationalism in the way that some commentators (and Bill Clinton) have asserted. When the poll sample was asked which policy issues they most associate with 'Make America Great Again', more than half named the economy as their top answer. Whether respondents voted for Trump or for Joe Biden in 2020, the economy eclipsed immigration as the key policy area that they felt most aligned to the slogan. Another finding of note from the poll was the commonality among Trump and Biden voters that the three past achievements in US history of which they are most proud are the Declaration of Independence, the creation of the Bill of Rights and the abolition of slavery – showing that voters from across the political spectrum see the 'great' period of American history in much the same way.

The words contained in the world's most famous slogan have been used by politicians on both the left and the right. This shows that, when not restricted by recency bias, the best phrases have a universal quality that surpasses politics. It is about who uses them and whether they can do so at the most opportune moment.

It is also worth remembering that Trump's political positions have changed over time. He was a Republican supporter in the 1980s, he was briefly involved with the Reform Party in 1999 and he became a backer of the Democratic Party in 2001 before he switched again to the Republicans in 2009. He also considered running as an independent candidate. His own version of what 'great again' means may well have been as fluid as his political allegiances, therefore.

Taking a balanced view, in 2012, the slogan was generally accepted as expressing a centre-right desire for reform to bring about easy taxes and greater personal freedom. By 2016, when Trump fought Hillary Clinton for the White House, these sentiments had been expanded. Clinton was seen as a representative of the politically correct left-of-centre metropolitan elite whose instincts were global rather than local. Trump pitched himself to the electorate as a comparative outsider, the standard bearer of a lost America who would take the country back to less complicated times.

After he left office in January 2021, 'Make America Great Again' was in the eyes of his supporters and himself effectively reborn, so that it harked back specifically to Trump's first four-year presidential term. This was because Trump's supporters preferred his politics and policies to that of Joe Biden, and subsequently Kamala Harris, and due to the various legal actions that were taken against Trump in what he regarded as an establishment plot to prevent him from returning to power. The fact that he did so in such emphatic style in November 2024 – with the same slogan – is the best demonstration of its sheer power.

The word 'great' has proved to be a hit for Donald Trump. Certainly, Trump's deployment of that word has changed the world, but 'great' is not one of the eight hit words featured in this book. Its chequered track record across campaigns, countries and decades reveals how a slogan and its key word can become iconic without being reliably effective. The Trump effect has undeniably given the word 'great' a surge in salience, but its emotional narrative – rooted in nostalgia, pride and, for some, grievance – is difficult to summon without the kind of singular persona Trump embodies. Others have tried and most have failed. His appeal was unique and so too was the potency of 'Make America Great Again'. The reality is that 'great' cannot be depended upon to stir emotion time and time again like the other eight words featured in this book. It lacks a cross-country and ideological adaptability, which are all unique features of the eight 'hit' words that we will go on to examine in the following chapters.

1

PEOPLE

The United States of America does not have a hereditary aristocracy, but its political history since the eighteenth century has to some degree been written by a small number of dynasties. The most famous of these are the Adams, Roosevelt, Kennedy and Bush families, which have produced multiple state governors, senators and Presidents. There is a school of thought that says the Clintons could be added to this list too. President Bill Clinton served two terms in office between 1993 and 2001, after which his wife Hillary was elected as a senator and appointed US Secretary of State under Barack Obama before running unsuccessfully as the Democratic Party presidential candidate in 2016.

It is true that the Clintons are effectively outsiders as far as the established dynasties are concerned: their antecedents had no political pedigree to speak of and the couple themselves did not come from notably prosperous or prominent backgrounds. Despite their relative obscurity, however, their achievements in US politics and the influence of Bill Clinton's campaigning methods on other politicians globally are plain to see. That he reached the White House aged forty-six was a huge achievement in itself, and doubly so considering the persistent questions about his private life that dogged his political career.

Bill Clinton's victory at the 1992 election is also significant because it appeared to materialise against the odds. The Democratic Party had spent only one of the previous five terms in office. Under the Republican incumbent, President George H. W. Bush, America's global reputation had been enhanced by the successful Gulf War. And the US economy, which had been in recession between 1990 and 1991, was recovering by November 1992 when the election was held. The situation was further complicated for Clinton by a strong independent candidate, billionaire businessman Ross Perot, entering the race. The year before the election, Bush had enjoyed record-breaking approval ratings that were close to 90 per cent. Yet when the ballots were counted, Clinton secured 43 per cent of the vote to Bush's 37.45 per cent.

Bill Clinton's presidency followed the dissolution of the Soviet Union and occurred before the post-9/11 invasions of Afghanistan and Iraq. Wedged between these eventful periods, the Clinton era is often considered to have been relatively unexceptional, certainly as far as its impact on global affairs is concerned. But in terms of his legacy, this interpretation could not be further from the truth. Many of the tactics that Clinton used during the 1992 campaign – particularly moving his party from the economic centre-left to the pro-business centre ground – were later copied by Anglo-European parties, including Britain's Labour Party, led by Tony Blair, and Germany's Social Democratic Party, led by Gerhard Schröder. In what could be called economic populism, he was able to use an expanding media landscape to appeal to the masses, using his own charisma as much as a concrete ideology. Those voters who felt alienated or left behind by the establishment were carefully targeted. The slogan he used in 1992 serves as the greatest reminder of this: 'Putting People First'. At the heart of his campaign was the idea of engaging directly with the public and reflecting their views in government in a way that was considered novel at that time.

The word 'people' has an almost magical quality in the lexicon of election slogans. My own research shows that it is the catchword that has been used more often than any other, anywhere in the world. Perhaps this is unsurprising. Every language has a word for 'people'. Some countries, such as the People's Republic of China, and some political parties, like Spain's Partido Popular (People's Party), even incorporate it formally. Yet despite its widespread use, 'people' remains misunderstood when it comes to political slogans, chiefly because its meaning is so malleable. Politicians frequently invoke the word 'people' without clearly defining who the people are, often allowing voters to project their own meanings onto the word. This lack of definition can obscure deeper political intentions and lead to voter disillusionment, especially when promises framed around 'people' fail to materialise.

Clinton, however, gave the word 'people' a clear definition. He wanted it to attract everybody, within reason. In a political culture that was still dominated by traditional media and had a somewhat academic attitude towards policy, this approach was innovative. Ronald Reagan, a former Hollywood actor, relied on elements of populism during his presidency, but Clinton's technique was altogether more permeating. He was the first US President to have been born after the Second World War and his relaxed demeanour reflected his desire to be seen as socially liberal, for example by admitting to having experimented with drugs. At the same time, he targeted the middle classes, specifically disaffected Republican voters, through an economically conservative outlook. By pledging to 'put people first', he not only found a way to distinguish himself from his more staid opponent, George H. W. Bush, who was more than twenty years his senior, he was also able to bypass media hostility and communicate directly with the electorate, a tactic that has been ever present in political campaigns since. Clinton's claim to represent what the people wanted didn't just propel him to the White House. It created a blueprint, which other candidates all over the world could follow. However, one potential knock-on effect of this brand of politics has been a marked rise in the levels of public cynicism towards politicians.

William Jefferson Blythe III was born in Hope, Arkansas, in 1946. His mother was a nurse and his father was a travelling salesman who died while Clinton was *in utero*. When he was four years old, his mother married Roger Clinton and his surname was changed. His stepfather's alcoholism and abuse overshadowed his childhood, but his academic prowess earned him a place at Georgetown University before he won a Rhodes scholarship to Oxford University in 1968. He then enrolled at Yale Law School. After graduating, he embarked on a political career in Arkansas, becoming Attorney General in 1976 and serving as the elected governor between 1979 and 1981 and again from 1983 to 1992.

During his governorship, he was an active proponent of the death penalty. He also focused on improving education and healthcare and promoting business. Following the defeat of the Democratic Party's Walter Mondale in the 1984 presidential election, Clinton styled himself a 'New' Democrat, who represented the future of the party. The policies he introduced in Arkansas can be seen as a model for his ambitions nationally and were a clear attempt to move the Democrats to a centrist position. The key tenets of Clinton's modernisation programme were job creation, law and order and individual responsibility. He took on several national political posts in order to further his career, notably as chairman of the National Governors Association (NGA) in 1986 and 1987. Among the contacts he made through the NGA was Frank Greer, a communications strategist who was involved in education reform for the Bill Gates Foundation. Clinton decided against running for President in 1988 because of concerns about details of his extra-marital affairs appearing in the press. By 1991, however, he had decided to set himself on the path to the White House.

Frank Greer had always regarded Clinton as an excellent communicator and he strongly believed he had the potential to become a successful national politician. He knew about Clinton's complicated upbringing and had seen how he had won over the people of Arkansas during his tenure as governor. In Greer's eyes, Clinton could relate to voters. 'It really was sincere, and he loved people, and he really cared about making it work for people,' he recalls. In other words, by 1991, Clinton captured the spirit of the slogan which had already begun percolating in Greer's mind. 'The campaign began with me and Stan Greenberg, who was a pollster, and my wife and a few other people convincing him to run,' Greer remembers.

He didn't want to run. He thought that his daughter was too young. He was also looking at President Bush, who had just won Operation Desert Storm and had a high favourability. But there are three things about Bill Clinton that were unique. He had a real sense of how to make government work, he had been governor for eight years very successfully and he knew how to communicate and connect with people. The Democratic Party had been plagued with ineffective communicators and I just knew the ability to communicate and connect was essential. I also thought he had a vision for what he wanted to do to make the country better and he really understood that we needed some vision for the future.

Crucially, Greer sensed that after twelve years of the Republicans being in power, many Americans wanted change and the youthful Clinton had the ability to embody that change.

If slogans can be said to represent the soul of an election campaign, this was especially the case for Clinton in 1992. Whichever message he chose would have to condense the rationale of his bid for the presidency into one memorable statement. As it turned out, it would at the same time have to act as a shield against media scrutiny, thanks to persistent rumours about his private life. Putting the word 'people' at the heart of the campaign was Greer's idea. His political philosophy is geared towards what he calls the 'politics of inclusion'. He believes that to be electorally successful, citizens must be able to feel as though they are part of a candidate's campaign, which is why he wanted to emphasise notions of togetherness and cooperation. 'One of the things I say to candidates is this is not about you; it's not about me; it's about "we",' he comments.

The substance of the message 'Putting People First' was worked out quickly. Its central planks were opportunity for all, responsibility for all and a greater sense of community. Seeing Clinton's compatibility with his 'people' slogan, Greer pitched his idea of an aspirational campaign to him and his advisers and explained to them his belief that public support would come most easily through involving them in the campaign so that they could feel as though they were a part of it. 'There wasn't a lot of resistance [to this suggestion],' says Greer. He goes on: 'Bill was into the slogan. He always thought it was a pretty damn good slogan.'

Demonstrating just how quickly Clinton latched on to this message, it was ready for use in the speech he delivered in October 1991 to announce his candidacy for the primaries. 'The night before, we were still drafting and he wasn't quite satisfied with it,' Greer remembers.

> We'd arranged to have a huge rally in Little Rock, Arkansas, and he was one of the last candidates to announce. All the others had done smaller events with less inspiring messages. We thought about the final draft until 2 o'clock in the morning. And he said 'Okay, I guess we can go with it. But maybe we're going to change some things in the morning.' I took the final copy of that speech to the hotel and put it under the door of the Associated Press reporter so that by the time Clinton got to the podium the speech was out there and he couldn't change it. He's forgiven me for that!

Having announced his intention to stand, Clinton's campaign quickly gathered momentum. In January 1992, he featured on the cover of *Time* magazine and he was hailed as the frontrunner to seize the Democratic Party presidential nomination ahead of the primaries, which were due to begin in February 1992. His principal opponents came from two different wings of his party. Paul Tsongas was a former senator of Massachusetts who was popular among New England and northeastern voters. Jerry Brown had been governor of California between 1975 and 1983 and attracted support in the western states. By contrast, Clinton was a moderate, running in a party that had been increasingly abandoned by his southern compatriots, who since 1964 had been drifting towards the Republican Party following Lyndon Johnson's Civil Rights Act. His challenge was to make his case beyond his party's shrinking base in the south.

Within a week of the *Time* magazine cover story appearing, disaster struck for Clinton. Accusations of a string of Clinton's marital infidelities were splashed across the pages of most American newspapers. They included specific claims of a long-standing affair with a former television reporter and cabaret singer called Gennifer Flowers, who had given a detailed interview to a tabloid newspaper called *The Star*, apparently backed up by tapes, in which she said she and Clinton had been involved with each other for twelve years.

Clinton confronted this story by giving an interview to the CBS news programme *60 Minutes*, which was broadcast straight after the Super Bowl on Sunday 26 January 1992. It was said that 50 million Americans watched as he and Hillary fielded a series of awkward questions about Flowers. At one point, Clinton claimed that Flowers's decision to sell her story to the press might even be attributable to the economic downturn, thereby subtly moving attention away from himself and onto President Bush's economic record. In hindsight, this could be described as straightforward economic populism, but it seemed to work. 'There's a recession on, times are tough,' he told the *60 Minutes* interviewer. 'You can expect more and more of these stories as long as [journalists] are down there handing out money.' Greer's slogan arguably became useful during this toe-curling exercise, as Clinton appealed to the sympathy and judgement of 'the American people' seven times. Just as his slogan showed that he was on the people's side during a difficult economic period, so he now hoped that those same people would sensibly consider the situation that he faced going into the first caucus in Iowa on 10 February.

Clinton's campaign team had to drum up support quickly or else they would be forced to watch their candidate's chances disintegrate. Relying on the 'Putting People First' slogan would not be enough on its own. No matter how much Clinton made his campaign about people, voters would not pay attention unless he could demonstrate how he would put his mission statement into action. Several strategies were devised to strengthen the appeal of his brand. Greer advised him to counter the negative news coverage of his past by excluding hostile journalists and speaking to voters directly on his own terms. 'We built a team and we stayed committed to the message. I think it was a genuine, sincere message and it got through and it overcame a lot of baggage,' Greer says.

Nowadays, presidential candidates can rely on social media to communicate with the public, as demonstrated by Donald Trump's extensive use of Twitter in 2016. In the early 1990s, however, the only mass media platforms with the same type of immediacy and reach were television and radio. Clinton's advisers felt that TV would play to his strengths. The trouble was that the airwaves were controlled by a limited number of broadcasters whose programmes were curated by journalists, making direct communication nearly impossible. An innovative approach would be required. The plan was to maximise the expedience of paid advertising and cameo appearances on entertainment programmes and to share local events with a national audience.

Interaction was seen as the key, and Clinton's 'Putting People First' advertisement in New Hampshire, whose Democratic primary was held on 18 February 1992, was a case in point. This thirty-second film promoted his economic manifesto 'Putting People First: A National Economic Strategy for America'. Although the material was dry, Clinton made a set of short, snappy points, saying trickle-down economics did not work, most Americans were working harder but receiving less money, healthcare costs were exploding – and he had a plan to improve the situation. The advert ended with him saying, 'Putting our people first. Rebuilding this economy. Making us competitive. If we do those things, we'll compete and win and we'll bring this country back.' A line of text appeared on screen as Clinton made his pitch, inviting viewers to ring a toll-free number to order a copy of the plan. In hindsight, this language bears a close resemblance to that used by Donald Trump almost a quarter of a century later.

This advertisement was distinct in several ways. Rather than relying on audio-visual technology, it was shot in a style that would now be called a 'vlog', or video blog, in that there was no background music or any sound effects. The camera angle didn't change. And a jacketless Clinton, his tie loosened and his sleeves rolled up, spoke to the camera from behind a desk as though he was having a conversation with each viewer. When he held up the manifesto on camera, it was as if he was personally handing viewers a copy. This plain but personal approach was what Greer meant when he wanted to make Clinton's outreach interactive and involve the voters. The distribution of Clinton's economic plan was a further crucial element, which Greer believed showed voters that Clinton was 'putting people first'. Thousands of copies of the manifesto booklet and thousands of videotapes of the advert were delivered throughout New Hampshire. 'People weren't going to read the manifesto necessarily, but they thought he [Clinton] was willing to have them involved in the plan and wanted them to be a part of it,' Greer says.

Another tactic deployed at this point was the televised 'town hall' meeting. Greer explains:

I think television played a key role. Rahm Emanuel, who was most recently ambassador to Japan, was a great fundraiser from

Chicago and thanks to him we were able to stay on the air and be more competitive on the air than anything else. Clinton was much better at communicating on the air and in person and so we maximised that. We began in New Hampshire, holding town halls – which was a first in US politics – and broadcasting them, and we would invite undecided voters, not partisans for Clinton, not people for other candidates but undecided voters, and let them ask questions. They were shown live on TV. And when the press was obsessed with his personal life and the accusations of infidelity and everything else, you would go into one of these town halls in New Hampshire and people wanted to talk about education and jobs, economy and transportation, and not his personal life. And it was a great way to demonstrate to the press corps that the country really wanted the campaign to be about other things. I don't know of any other candidate in that era who could have pulled off communication on television [and] the town halls. And Clinton was just really good with people.

This helps to explain why Clinton's campaign team felt the slogan worked so well for him.

Greer credits the town hall events with boosting Clinton's support ahead of the New Hampshire primary, in which Clinton finished second, allowing him to remain in the race. Yet it was clear that a broader strategy was needed to attract voters to Clinton's campaign, and that was where consultants including Stan Greenberg, James Carville, George Stephanopoulos and Dick Morris came in. Greenberg was a pollster, who later worked with Greer during Nelson Mandela's 1994 election campaign. He helped the Clinton campaign test various messages for the election, placing great emphasis on popular opinion and the need to respond to it. He liked the slogan

'Putting People First' but felt that for it to be used to its best effect, Clinton had to show people that he aligned with their values. Greer wanted to stay true to the core 'togetherness' message of the slogan, but James Carville in particular was more open to running on specific issues and doing so aggressively if necessary. Clinton began to rely more on Carville's strategy once his tactics began reaping rewards in the primaries. By 2 June, Clinton was named as the Democratic candidate, having secured thirty-seven states and a shade under 60 per cent of the popular vote.

Winning over the Democratic Party was one thing, but appealing to millions of voters around the country was a far more demanding task. Clinton's desire to reach the masses had only just begun. In early June he appeared on the *Arsenio Hall Show*, whose audience was typically young and urban, playing his saxophone (as he had done on several other television shows) to demonstrate he was not a one-dimensional politician. That month he also appeared on MTV, the music-oriented cable channel. He used a news special it hosted, called 'Choose or Lose: Facing the Future with Bill Clinton', to try to connect with its viewers. Typically, they were less educated, less interested in politics and more likely to be young, female and liberal. This collaboration, in which he took questions from a live audience, was certainly laced with unpredictability for a prospective President. Yet the potential benefits were deemed to outweigh the risks. Clinton appeared comfortable in this setting. He was able to joke about his admission that he had tried marijuana during his student days at Oxford but had not inhaled the drug. Perhaps best of all, President Bush declined the same invitation from MTV. Clinton therefore again showed that he was keen to meet the 'people' on which his campaign slogan depended, even if they were not as likely to cast a vote as their parents were.

By the time of the election campaign, Clinton had tasked James Carville with running his operation from a so-called 'war room' in his hometown of Hope, Arkansas. President Bush could speak with experience and authority on foreign affairs, having been involved with diplomatic efforts to bring an end to the Cold War in the 1980s in his capacity as Ronald Reagan's Vice-President. He could also bask in the glory of the recent Gulf War victory. But Carville understood that the faltering US economy was very likely to be the main issue for voters as the election battle progressed, which is why it became Clinton's focus.

Having agreed that the goal of the slogan was to inspire grassroots backing for Clinton, his team knew that the identity of the 'people' it referred to would have to be broad enough to fit the country's diverse population and needs – something that numerous other politicians who have used the same word before and since have been unable or unwilling to do. Clinton was advised to show strong but compassionate leadership in the face of a slowing economy. Although America's economic prospects had begun to improve by the spring of 1992, they had not returned to the levels of prosperity that had been enjoyed in the 1980s. Unemployment rates in many key electoral states were worse than the national average, notably those in California, Florida and New York. Moreover, President Bush had broken the promise he had made in 1988 when he vowed, 'Read my lips: no new taxes.' In fact, taxes had risen after the 1990 budget, and individual taxpayers were taking the hit. Yet at the same time, the American stock market was performing well. A chasm between the general taxpaying public and those elites working in and benefiting from the financial institutions opened up. This fuelled an 'us and them' narrative, which Clinton's team knew was ripe for development, not least because George H. W. Bush was himself from an established New England family that had gained its wealth from the banking and oil industries. The conditions were perfect for a slogan such as 'Putting People First' to succeed.

James Carville decided that if Clinton was going to beat Bush, his campaign would have to contrast him as often as possible, attack Bush's economic record, shy away from proactively mentioning issues relating to integrity and trust and strike back when attacked. Many believe, erroneously, that 'It's the economy, stupid' was a slogan that Bill Clinton used during the 1992 election campaign. In fact, this phrase was dreamt up by Carville, written on a poster and pinned to a wall in Clinton's office as a way of reminding his colleagues of the main themes of the campaign. The other two points on the poster were 'Change vs. more of the same' and 'Don't forget health care'.

Clinton's campaign ultimately remained focused on its core messages of 'Putting People First' and 'For People, For a Change'. Clinton even spoke about his desire to 'put people first' during the three televised presidential debates held in October 1992, the first of which he was judged in a snap poll to have won comfortably. There is little doubt that the slogans made a profound difference to the outcome of the election. Clinton's victory was, in large part, indebted to their effectiveness. They became vehicles for his campaign's charm offensive at the expense of Bush's more reserved public persona. Stan Greenberg has even claimed that the slogans 'engineered a comeback from the dead' by rescuing Clinton from the curse of his own reputation.

Clinton's landslide victory in the electoral college – 370 votes to Bush's 168 – certainly vindicated his team's strategic planning and indicated that the notion of 'togetherness' could overcome the worst of Clinton's proclivities. With that said, Clinton's popular vote count was lower than his advisers had hoped. He received 44.9 million votes, but this was still several million short of an absolute majority. Bush managed to capture 37.4 million votes while Perot won 19.7 million votes – the largest share of the vote for an independent candidate since 1918. Perot's impressive performance was taken as proof that despite Clinton successfully capturing some Republican voters with his populist messages, many of them had gravitated towards Perot instead.

The impact of Clinton's 'people' message was profound and was amplified by the innovative campaign techniques his team used. Unconventional media strategies changed the way people interacted with presidential candidates. As we have seen, video cassettes and cable television were two new forms of communication that allowed the electorate to hear more from Clinton alongside the traditional platforms, but each major candidate also broke from the orthodoxy of political advertising. Gone were the days of solely pandering to major television networks. Rather than appearing only on traditional television news shows, candidates went on popular talk shows as well, such as *The Phil Donahue Show* and *Larry King Live*. This 'unfiltered' setting was a new form of electoral participation.

On the surface, this allowed candidates to appeal to audiences in more relaxed surroundings. They wanted every viewer to feel as though they were in their living room. Usefully, it also meant they did not have to withstand rigorous questioning. The net result was that style began to trump substance across the board. One piece of analysis showed that in 1968, mainstream evening news bulletins used clips of presidential contenders speaking that were, on average, 42.3 seconds long. By 1992, the same programmes had cut candidates' clip time to a mere 7.3 seconds. Whether this decrease was a response to viewers' shorter attention spans or whether viewers' attention spans began to slide as a result of media expecting less of them, as it were, is an open question.

Bill Clinton secured a broad range of the electorate in 1992, performing especially well in states with a high working-class and middle-class vote, both of which were adversely affected by Republican-inspired welfare cuts. He also won an overwhelming majority of the ethnic minority vote, particularly from African Americans, 83 per cent of whom voted for him, and Hispanics, 61 per cent of whom backed him, according to an exit poll by Voter Research & Surveys. He also did equally well across all age groups.

The magic of the word 'people' is that politicians frequently invoke it without clearly defining whom they represent, often allowing a myriad of different group of voters to project their own meanings onto the word. It can achieve the objective of winning over a lot of voters, as Clinton did, but within a short period of time, those voters become disenfranchised.

And there were even greater consequences to Clinton's victory. The New Democrat coalition that he represented, with its heavier focus on the Reaganite values of fiscal responsibility and individual freedom, swept away more progressive American politicians like Michael Dukakis. The New Democrat brand also evolved into what became known as 'Third Way' politics. This term, which is credited to the British sociologist Anthony Giddens, blends traditional social democracy and liberalism together as a means of social advancement. Strictly speaking, it is a way of governing neither from the left nor the right and can be seen as the logical extension of the economic policies of Ronald Reagan and Margaret Thatcher. Tony Blair's landslide election victory in 1997 is perhaps the standout example of Third Way political strategy. Indeed, in a sign of the New Democrat influence, some of Clinton's advisers, including

Stan Greenberg, worked with Blair during and after his 1997 victory, exchanging ideas on economic policy and even calling themselves Blair's 'Third-Way modernisers'. Blair's campaign also had its own 'war room' of political advisers, such as Alastair Campbell and Peter Mandelson. And Blair's campaign relied on a theme tune ('Things Can Only Get Better' by D:Ream) just as Clinton's campaign had used the Fleetwood Mac song 'Don't Stop'.

The upshot of this cross-Atlantic connection is one of Clinton's lasting legacies: globalisation. His presidency promised not only to put the American people first but also to bring the world population closer together. It was 'togetherness' on a macro scale. Clinton significantly liberalised trade during his presidency, signing deals with Mexico and Canada as part of the North Atlantic Fair Trade Agreement (NAFTA) in 1993, inviting Russia to join the G7 group of economies (making it the G8) in 1997 and eventually liberalising trade with China in 2000. However, the success of Clinton's idea of 'putting people first' also conceivably marked the beginning of the end of his team's grand vision. Despite Clinton's promises of a stronger economy and more jobs, trade liberalisation meant that many American companies moved their industrial operations to countries with cheaper labour costs, leaving thousands of working-class Americans unemployed. And Clinton's formal impeachment in December 1998 on the grounds of perjury and obstruction of justice over his extra-marital affairs caused trust in all politicians to plummet.

The legacy of Clinton's political brand influenced a new rising class of populists, up to and including the 2016 presidential election. Voters said that Clinton-era free-trade agreements, particularly NAFTA, were the reason for them voting for the left-wing candidate Bernie Sanders in the Democratic primaries and, ironically, for Donald Trump over Hillary Clinton. They felt that these trade agreements had harmed American workers by outsourcing jobs to countries with lower wages, weakening America's manufacturing industry and prioritising corporate interests. This resentment fuelled support for candidates who challenged the status quo. In this sense, the word 'people' as used by Bill Clinton perhaps sowed the seed from which sprouted the stem of twenty-first century populism in American politics. In the twenty-first century, the word 'people' has become inextricably linked with populist narratives of 'us' versus 'them'. Whether it is Sanders's support for 'working people' against the 'wealthiest people' or Trump's promise to put the 'American people' first, the definition of 'people' has arguably become narrower and more divided in its meaning. In American political discourse in particular, 'people' no longer seems to represent a diverse coalition of individuals with different backgrounds and opinions but instead a cohesive grouping with shared interests. This was not always the case and, as we have seen, it was certainly not how Clinton's 'people' slogan came about.

Over the past century in the US, the Democratic Party has been most likely to use slogans featuring the word 'people', doing so nearly a dozen times in presidential campaigns. The Republican Party has used the word only once, during George W. Bush's presidential campaign in 2000, when he ran on the slogan 'Real Plans for Real People'. (The Libertarian Party also used a 'people' slogan in 2012 and 2016.) In fact, over the same period, the Democrats have been more likely than their opponents to repeat the use of other words including 'change', 'new', 'better', 'strong' and 'future'. Some might say this suggests the party has been more likely to pursue an ideological agenda than the Republican Party. It certainly reflects a mission to tackle inequality, such as economic hardship.

The lineage of the party's 'people' slogans began with Franklin D. Roosevelt, who, during the Great Depression, ran on the slogan 'Roosevelt. Friend of the People' in 1936, arguing, 'Never in history have the interests of all the people been so united in a single economic problem.' Roosevelt tried to make the word 'people' a unifying force in politics, and almost every subsequent Democratic presidential candidate until the 1970s used it in their campaign slogans, including Harry S. Truman in 1948 ('60 Million People Working. Why Change?'); Adlai Stevenson in 1952 ('For all the People. Stevenson and Sparkman'); Hubert Humphrey in 1968 ('Some People Talk Change, Others Cause It: Humphrey. The People's Democrat'); and George McGovern in 1972 ('McGovern. Democrat. For The People.'). McGovern's campaign marked a turning point for the word 'people' with his introduction of left-wing populist themes, juxtaposing 'us' (working people) and 'them' ('wealthy individuals and large corporations') in his messaging. His opponent, the incumbent President Nixon, won by a landslide.

By 1992, Frank Greer's initial idea of the 'Putting People First' slogan was closer to Roosevelt's interpretation of the word 'people' being as inclusive as possible. Yet, as we have seen, Clinton's rhetoric became more populist as the campaign progressed. He also began to use ethnic and cultural identity as markers of division, as he sought to bring different communities together through his campaign. Indeed, according to his victory speech on 3 November 1992, this was his stated goal. He told his supporters of his plans to 'bring our people together as never before so that our diversity can be a source of strength in a world that is ever smaller'. Stan Greenberg has explained that Clinton wanted his presidency to have 'a more racially diverse inner core'. By moving the term away from its socio-economic roots and focusing on racial identity, Clinton gave the word 'people' an extra dimension in US politics, helping to establish the era of identity politics – an era that remains strong a quarter of the way through the twenty-first century.

'Putting People First' played a pivotal role in connecting Clinton and his outsider campaign to a diverse group of voters. Whereas others have failed using 'people', Clinton succeeded. That word aligned with public perception of him as a relatable leader who positioned himself on the side of ordinary Americans against elite interests. The use of the 'hit' word was made even more powerful by the contrast it painted with his opponent, George H. W. Bush, who was perceived to be out of touch.

If Clinton had decided to use a different slogan, perhaps one that emphasised his 'new' approach – which undoubtedly his campaign embodied in its style – it could have backfired and would have reinforced the experience of his opponent to the detriment of his relative inexperience. But by forcing the narrative onto his territory using the right 'hit' word, it turned a long-shot candidacy into a historic victory.

The word 'people' has been used sparingly in America since 1992. Al Gore, Clinton's Vice-President, ran on 'The People... Not the Powerful' in the 2000 presidential election against George H. W. Bush's eldest son, George W. Bush, who during the same contest used 'Real Plans for Real People'. In fact, much of Bush's campaign in 2000 resembled Clinton's rhetoric in 1992. Bush touted himself as the change candidate and his 'Real Plans for Real People' slogan echoed a line in Clinton's 1992 announcement speech when he re-ferred to 'real problems of real people'. Subsequent Republican and Democratic slogans, meanwhile, have diverged into two distinct camps.

The Democratic Party has focused on the themes of change and togetherness. Examples of Clinton's legacy include John Kerry's 'It's Time for a Change in America' (2004), Barack Obama's 'Change We Can Believe In' (2008) and Hillary Clinton's 'Stronger Together' (2016). Bill Clinton's influence on these campaigns is hardly surprising. Many of his advisers worked for Obama, quite apart from Hillary Clinton being his wife. But it is noticeable that the Democratic Party's slogans have become less ideological, more linguistically diverse and more specific to particular candidates since 1992. Hillary Clinton's slogan 'Stick It To the Man By Voting for the Woman' (2016) and Joe Biden's 'No Malarkey' (2020) are prime examples of this shift, as they both reflect personal traits of the individual candidates – Hillary being the first female presidential candidate of any major party and Biden saying 'malarkey' often.

Ironically, in recent years the Republican Party has seemingly adopted some of the Democrats' thinking by being seen as more ideological in outlook when it comes to political sloganeering. Ever since Donald Trump won over the party's base with 'Make America Great Again', every major rival Republican presidential candidate has mimicked his language and tried to fit into his mould. During the 2024 Republican primaries, Nikki Haley used 'Stand for America' and Ron DeSantis took on 'Our Great American Comeback'. Both are reminiscent of the 'America First' sentiment encapsulated in Trump's original slogan.

Globally, the word 'people' has been used in a variety of contexts, from authoritarian regimes to countries which have been in the throes of revolution, by the left and the right, by radicals and by populists. All of this confirms its adaptability and powers of political expediency. While most 'people' slogans have been found in functioning democracies, a significant number have come from authoritarian states where there are no free elections. In these instances, the word 'people' appears not only in party slogans or mottos but also in the name of the party or the country itself. The best example may be the People's Republic of China, where the ruling Communist Party has used 'Serve the People' as its motto since 1944. Another example is the Cambodian People's Party, which has governed Cambodia as a de facto one-party state since 1998. During the 2018 general election, the party used the slogan 'Officials are loyal servants of the people, not master'. The main opposition, the Cambodia National Rescue Party, was banned from running, giving the ruling party every seat in the National Assembly but no legitimacy.

Authoritarian regimes often use the word 'people' in their slogans as it lends them a claim to a popular mandate. By contrast, 'people' slogans have also been used by pseudo-authoritarian governments, which lack the apparatus needed to suppress dissenting voices and protect themselves from public scrutiny. In these instances, the popular opposition is often more successful in harnessing the power of the word 'people'. The conservative Law and Justice (PiS) party in Poland was one such pseudo-authoritarian party that attempted and ultimately failed to prolong its rule by using several 'people' slogans. After eight years in power, it ran for a second re-election in 2023 on the slogans 'Everything for the People' and 'For the People, For Poland'. Its vote share dropped by more than 8 per cent, gaining 194 seats under Poland's proportional electoral system. Meanwhile, the liberal opposition won 246 seats, securing it a majority. One interpretation is that the 'people' slogans failed to work for PiS largely because of its Catholic nationalist posturing while in government. Between 2015 and 2023, it clearly defined the 'people' as those who shared its conservative values. Yet a sizeable number of citizens objected to its policies, which included 'LGBT-free zones', the strictest abortion laws in Europe and economic protectionism. The party's shortcomings confirm the importance of proper research when deploying a 'people' slogan.

Thousands of miles away, the same problem contributed to the poor performance of the pro-military parties in Thailand's general election in 2023. The United Thai Nation Party of the then-incumbent Prime Minister Prayut Chan-o-cha made 'Dismantle laws that harass people' one of its campaign slogans, but the party finished fifth overall with only thirty-six out of 500 seats. The progressive anti-military Move Forward Party ran with 'Crowds Move Forward, Choose New People' as its slogan. Its campaign focused on the party's young membership and the cosmopolitan credentials of its leader, Pita Limjaroenrat, a young businessman with a degree from Harvard. It claimed to represent the millions of Thais frustrated with the military junta that had ruled the country intermittently during the twenty-first century.

During the campaign, Pita frequently repeated demands for the government to reflect the 'will of the people'. When his party was confirmed as the largest, with 151 seats, he said, 'The people are awake. They woke up and saw hope and change that they had been waiting a long time for ... I have a duty to protect the people.' The people reciprocated Pita's calls for change and his claim to represent them, as their interests were aligned. Pita represented the cosmopolitan prosperity to which many Thais aspired. The various legal challenges to his authority that were laid down by the military establishment only made him more popular. Pita's support rested on his ability to harness the expediency of the word 'people' by defining 'people' in relation to the concerns of the general public. That he was also willing to open his personal life up to scrutiny merely reinforced that, in the context of Thai politics, he was an authentic figure. This, in turn, helped his strong brand image.

The word 'people' becomes astonishingly effective when Pita's successes are replicated in a genuine democracy, as was the case with Hugo Chávez in Venezuela. He won his first presidential election in 1998, when the country was a working democracy, by pitting the masses against the business elite. In 2006, he successfully ran for re-election under the slogan 'With Chávez the people rule' and again in 2012 using 'The heart of the people is up. Vote for Chávez'. His landslide wins allowed him to push through constitutional amendments that led to the abolishment of term limits in 2009, among other major reforms. By the time of his death in 2013, Venezuelan politics had been remade in his image and was unrecognisable from its pre-Chavismo incarnation. His success is symbolic of the word 'people' as a slogan. When employed effectively, it can be an asset. If a leader's values do not align with the 'people' they claim to represent, political victory is likely to be elusive.

Despite 'people' being the most commonly used word in political slogans around the world, it is not without hazards. Apart from anything else, it is highly dependent on real people – voters – relating to any slogan that uses it, otherwise they may question whether it truly represents them. Who are the people to which a slogan seeks to appeal? The answer to this question is always open to interpretation. 'People' could refer to the oppressed masses rising up against the self-indulgent bourgeoisie or the *Volksgeist* ('national spirit') of an ethno-nation. To make it work in a slogan, politicians must define it clearly, they must apply it broadly, they should ensure any leader using it is representative of the 'people' he or she seeks to represent and they should encourage any candidate using it to be open about themselves with the 'people'.

'People' is the ultimate populist slogan. It has the power to emotionally appeal to the grassroots by allowing politicians to align their public profile with the worldview of their support base. The core characteristic of 'people' slogans is the concept of identity, and they are ideal for those wishing to make themselves the main theme of their campaign. The advantages of the word 'people' are its universality (every culture has a word for 'people'), inclusivity (anyone who is a human being can be part of the 'people') and expediency (people become endeared if they see the politician as one of them). The disadvantages are its ambiguity (who are the 'people'?) and exposure to scrutiny (voters will raise an eyebrow if politicians claim to be one of them).

In the world of slogans, the word 'people' appears to be similar to 'together'. Both act as rallying cries for the supporters of a certain party or candidate. Yet 'people' is the more combative and populist-sounding of the two, whereas the gentle undertone of 'together' slogans is a better reflection of establishment politics. The primary dynamic between these two groups is relatability. 'People' slogans thrive on the closeness between the politician and the voter, in contrast to the traditional view of establishment figures. The more the voter feels that a politician is on their side, the more impactful 'people' slogans become.

For 'people' slogans to make an impact in an election, politicians need to understand four key points about the word 'people' in a political context:

1. 'People' is a noun, but it acts adjectivally in politics in juxtaposition to the 'elite'.
2. The government can become more aligned with the 'people' but not politicians.
3. A politician is either with the 'people' or against them – there is no in between.

4. It is easier to fall out of favour with the 'people' than to gain their favour.

An emotive strategy is the key to harnessing the strength of 'people' slogans. A politician's ability to relate to the electorate hinges entirely on the latter's perception of them. A politician forming a strong emotional bond between themself and the voters and then projecting an open and honest image is the best way to achieve this. Politicians should maintain a good balance between appearing authentic to voters while targeting their greatest concerns.

A successful example like Clinton's 'Putting People First' slogan shows how this strategy can be applied. When Clinton was weighing up his candidacy, he already benefited from President Bush's uninspiring public image and his perceived aloofness as a wealthy oil magnate. Voters were also frustrated with the state of the economy, which had shrunk due to a recession in 1991. Other successful uses, such as PiS in Poland, may also antagonise external threats such as the European Union, although this circumstance is less common and not essential. What is essential is the placement of 'people' slogans at the beginning of a political journey, especially if the politician is a relative political outsider, as Clinton was in 1992. The novelty of a politician's identity will wear off as time goes by and so will enthusiasm for what they have to offer, as Clinton found in his second term in office. However, voters may still be receptive to a 'people' slogan only if they feel there is a constant threat against their interests, which Chávez was able to exploit in Venezuela. Chávez successfully positioned himself as the defender of the poor against a corrupt elite and foreign influence. Exploiting widespread frustration with economic inequality, corruption and neoliberal policies, he framed the elite as a constant threat to ordinary Venezuelans' interests. This resonated with impoverished voters, leading to his landslide victory with 56.2 per cent of the vote, as he promised to redirect oil wealth to social programmes for the masses.

Besides circumstance and timing, 'people' slogans will only resonate with voters if politicians address its greatest disadvantage: the ambiguity of the word 'people'. Clinton defined 'people' as the stagnant middle class, which was economically independent but vulnerable to market crises and unable to climb the social ladder. It was highly specific yet still sufficiently inclusive to allow voters to relate to Clinton's background.

A 'people' slogan can be a potent rallying cry, but it does not by itself guarantee victory. It is not a magic bullet for every campaign and will fall on deaf ears if these tactics are not deployed correctly, as voters will quickly judge whether someone is truly one of them or just another career politician who is exploiting their personal circumstances to win votes, as seen in the case of Thai Prime Minister Prayut. Voters may also feel excluded if the definition of 'people' does not allow a diverse population to relate to it, while a lack of social division could also mean that voters are seeking a more gentle, unifying message rather than an inherently decisive one like 'people'. A strategy that cleverly stirs raw emotions while balancing the timing of the slogan is a winning formula that will make the right person the ultimate populist leader.

2

CHANGE

The 2010s were a bleak time in Italy. Following the global financial crisis, the country's economy – the third largest in the Eurozone – was close to collapse. GDP shrank by a staggering 4.5 per cent cumulatively between 2008 and 2011 and the government was caught in a debt crisis that threatened widespread financial ruin. In November 2011, Silvio Berlusconi, the Prime Minister, resigned. He was replaced by Mario Monti, a former European Commissioner, who was appointed by President Giorgio Napolitano as an emergency measure to try to repair the battered economy.

On Monti's technocratic watch, EU-backed austerity measures were imposed. The overall situation eventually stabilised, but the ensuing cuts in areas such as social services were deep, leaving many people poorer or even destitute. As the decade progressed, growth was slow; the average gross annual earnings of Italian workers sank below those of Portugal and Greece and by 2017 some 5 million Italians (8.3 per cent of the population) were estimated to be living in absolute poverty. At the same time, the unemployment rate rocketed, reaching 11.2 per cent by 2017. Youth unemployment was particularly severe, hitting an average of 34.7 per cent in 2017 and in some regions, such as Sicily, exceeding 50 per cent. Although this historically prosperous nation was used to an exceptionally high turnover of governments, it now seemed to be locked in a semi-permanent crisis.

Throughout this troubled period, an increasingly agitated population began to question which politician or leader they could trust in order to carry out some long-overdue repair work. Although Berlusconi had spent a decade in office and become Italy's longest-serving Prime Minister by 2011, he was infamous for being mired in scandal, including his having hosted 'bunga bunga' sex parties. He was not alone in being distrusted. Since the 1990s, politicians from every major party had been embroiled in high-level corruption cases and some had even been found to have links to the mafia. Public faith in organised politics was plummeting and there was a need for radical change.

This was the backdrop to the extraordinary result of the 2018 general election, in which the Five Star Movement (M5S) triumphed. This anti-politics organisation pursued a populist strategy that relied on pitching voters against politicians and EU bureaucrats. However, unlike other new parties that took flight in Europe in the first quarter of the twenty-first century, it was not only electorally successful but also truly radical. Its aim was to transcend the traditional left or right political positions and stand as a social faction that could alter politics in Italy forever.

M5S hoped to do this by embracing a version of what has been called cyber-utopianism, believing that computer technology could make politics more accessible to the masses by reducing the influence and autonomy of conventional politicians and increasing the use of direct democracy. This vision was ultimately realised by using the internet to build up a following. It was further enhanced through the construction of an online voting platform called 'Rousseau', which enabled members to vote on every candidate nomination, policy proposal and internal rule within the movement. M5S's electoral slogan for the 2018 election was 'Participate. Choose. Change.', which encapsulated the desire of its founders to use computer hardware to engage its supporters in this innovative way. By any measure, they achieved their aim. History has shown that running on a 'change' slogan can be fraught with difficulties, but M5S's understanding of what the Italian population wanted, coupled with a desire for authenticity, meant that they succeeded where others have failed.

Apart from attracting attention through being modern and different, M5S quickly earned the interest, backing and respect of voters, who valued its progressive outlook and green agenda. Indeed, the five stars on the movement's logo were supposed to represent its founding principles, which were 'public water, sustainable mobility, sustainable development, connectability and the environment'. When the votes were counted following the March 2018 poll, it was the clear winner, gaining 227 out of a possible 630 seats in the Chamber of Deputies – 102 more than the nationalist-populist runner-up, Lega. It was an astonishing outcome, marking the first time in Italy that an organisation with no connections to the usual post-war left- and right-wing parties had won the most seats in any election. What made it all the more noteworthy was that M5S had not existed a decade before. The message to the political elites was clear: the people demanded change, just as its slogan promised.

Despite its emphatic electoral success and the enthusiasm it generated with its 'change' slogan, M5S soon struggled to deliver on the sweeping reforms its voters had expected. Its coalition with Lega, a party it had long criticised, alienated many supporters who had bought into the M5S anti-establishment message. Internal conflicts among the leadership, disillusionment with the party's centralised governance style and the limitations of its direct democracy platform 'Rousseau' began to surface. By 2022, M5S had lost much of its initial momentum and popular support, ultimately leading to resignations, poor election results and a return of the political status quo it had once railed against. The word 'change' had propelled M5S to power, but it was the absence of any real meaningful change that ultimately brought the M5S down.

But how did the M5S secure such a victory in the first place? And why did voters flock to it in such large numbers despite its maverick status? The answers to these questions lie in its establishment in 2009.

The M5S began not as a social grouping, nor as a political party, but as a collaborative effort between the father-and-son cyber-marketing consultants Gianroberto and Davide Casaleggio, and Beppe Grillo, an outspoken comedian who became its leader. Grillo was born in the Liguria region in 1948 and had been well known in Italy in the 1980s as a political satirist, making regular television appearances at one stage until he was effectively blacklisted from the medium after using a live TV entertainment show to accuse the Italian Socialist Party of corruption in 1986. After this, he was forced to reinvent himself, and he re-emerged as an actor, author and stand-up comic who became something of a cult figure in the 1990s. This background was crucial to the founding of the M5S because his turbulent career in many ways symbolised some of the values the movement came to represent, notably a hatred of the mainstream media.

It was business, not politics, which brought the Casaleggios and Grillo together when they first met in 2004. 'Representing

Casaleggio Associates, my father and I met Beppe Grillo after he read a book my father had written,' explains Davide Casaleggio.

> We attended one of his shows, where he was performing for an audience that remembered him from his television days. Initially, we aimed to enhance his communication, as he had been side-lined from TV and turned to theatre. We saw an opportunity to use the internet to engage with younger audiences … The meeting between us was pure sales at the time.

The idea of using the internet in this way was a leap into the unknown for all of them. Indeed, Grillo was a self-confessed techno-phobe and was so sceptical of digital communication that he even mocked it as part of his act. 'We went to one of his shows and one of his pieces was getting a computer and smashing it and saying, "We can't succeed with these computers. We need to be natural,"' remembers Casaleggio. After Grillo was shown the possibilities of social media and livestreaming technology, however, a deal was struck, giving the Casaleggios distribution rights to DVD recordings of Grillo's live performances in exchange for the provision of free digital services.

The Casaleggios helped Grillo set up an online blog, www.beppegrillo.it. Following its launch in 2005, it quickly evolved into a powerful hub for political discourse and activism. Visitors were encouraged to use its interactive section to comment and debate with each other. It also shared posts and video interviews with scientists, journalists, other bloggers and everyday citizens, covering an array of political issues and generating a high volume of traffic in the process. As well as proudly flourishing outside of the mainstream media, it was clear from Grillo's blog that there was a significant level of anger about the state of Italy's politics among the public and that Grillo had a knack for expressing it. Wanting to channel this discontent constructively, Gianroberto Casaleggio persuaded him to use various technologies to coordinate the movement, including the online meeting platform Meetup.com. Events were organised to build up support and create a sense of community.

As political engagement grew, the Casaleggios sensed the potential for the blog to move beyond its commercial function. A turning point came in September 2007, when Grillo launched the first 'Vaffanculo Day' or 'V-Day' (meaning 'Fuck Off Day'), which turned into a series of protest gatherings. It attracted an estimated 2 million people in 220 towns and cities across Italy. Grillo, who anchored the event from Bologna, won cheers for reading out the names of twenty-four convicted criminals who were serving parliamentarians either in Italy or as Italian representatives in the European Parliament, proving his point that mainstream politicians were thumbing their noses at the people they were supposed to serve. It was not hard to see why he soon had the largest social media following of any politician in Europe. More V-Days were organised, primarily using Meetup.com, and their effect undoubtedly turned the M5S from a fringe organisation into a serious political player as online activism entered the real world. In many respects, M5S was something of a test case to establish whether an online pressure group could be mobilised to become something more politically significant.

In October 2009, Grillo and the Casaleggios formally established the Movimento Cinque Stelle (Five Star Movement or M5S), converting their original business project into a nationwide social movement. The trio had different ideas of what they wanted and what they believed was possible. Grillo's interest was fundamentally linked to his personal anti-politics and anti-mass media views. In an interview with *Time* magazine in 2013, he explained his disillusionment, saying, '[Political parties are] the same thing. Left and right in Italy, they've always pretended to fight.' As for the media, he called it 'the worst' and claimed, 'They're inside the system.' Asked what he hoped M5S might achieve, he replied, 'Send them all home: close the parties, take away their money, immediately. An emergency launch of a guaranteed minimum income. Two or three operations, laws against corruption, conflicts of interest, separate the financial firms from the banks.'

A revolutionary flame also flickered in the hearts of the Casaleggios. They too believed in reshaping Italian society, though their motivation was to harness the power of technology. Davide Casaleggio says his father believed that 'digital transforms politics' and could empower citizens to directly participate in the political process. Logically, this meant bypassing the usual means of communication and legislation, a stance that aligned closely with Grillo's personal convictions. Grillo stopped short of advocating the removal of these processes, believing that replacing corrupt politicians with honest ones would be sufficient, whereas the Casaleggios believed their wholesale replacement in a system of direct democracy was preferable.

The idea of emphasising the transformative role of computer science and establishing a non-political party, despite appearing like one, was derived from a business blueprint known as 'Blue Ocean Strategy'. Based on a 2005 book of the same name written by two INSEAD business professors, Chan Kim and Renée Mauborgne, it claims that lasting success comes 'not from battling competitors but from creating "blue oceans" – untapped new market spaces ripe for growth'. The book had a profound impact on Gianroberto

Casaleggio's marketing business and led him to conceive the idea of establishing the M5S. When it was published, one man, Silvio Berlusconi, controlled directly or indirectly an estimated 90 per cent of Italy's television market via his ownership of the privately run network Mediaset and the state-owned network RAI, limiting the amount of TV coverage new political parties could gain. 'My father was a big fan of Blue Ocean Strategy,' says Davide Casaleggio. 'He realised in the way that the media was working that he had to create an entirely new style of system.' Just as Elon Musk would later disrupt mainstream car manufacturing through the production of electric vehicles, so Casaleggio's cyber-utopian vision fuelled a digital movement that could compete with Italy's existing political parties and, in the process, force them to swim in the M5S's 'blue ocean'.

Conventional political campaigns typically rely on external consultants for data analytics and marketing, but Gianroberto Casaleggio used new online applications to directly influence the M5S's strategic development. As Jacopo Iacoboni, who has written two books on M5S, explains, the structure of the organisation was unique: '[It was] a web company which creates a party, with the owner directly possessing all the data.' This allowed M5S to tailor blog posts and social media content strategically in order to shape public opinion and drive support. Some might see this as a precursor to the behaviour of large news and advertising organisations today, which render users slaves to their algorithms, as they suggest what story consumers should read or which product they might want to buy.

Another unique facet of M5S was its online voting platform 'Rousseau', named after the philosopher Jean-Jacques Rousseau, which allowed members to vote on almost every aspect of party business, from candidate shortlists to policy proposals. Decision-making was decentralised and governance devolved from the founders to the increasing number of M5S members, making them far more powerful than members of other mainstream parties – though some claim the Casaleggio company retained disproportionate control over user data and final outcomes. With Grillo as its brand ambassador, the M5S fielded candidates for the first time in the 2010 regional elections. Its best performance was in the wealthy industrial region of Emilia-Romagna, where it achieved 6 per cent of the list votes. It continued to put candidates up in local and regional elections in 2011 and 2012, to ever-greater effect. Then, in the 2013 general election, it secured 8.61 million votes – a 25.6 per cent share of the vote – and 109 of the 630 seats in the Chamber of Deputies. Grillo, who has a criminal conviction dating from 1980 when he was involved in a car accident, was prevented from standing because of strict internal M5S party rules about who can take public office, but this did not seem to impact its next performance, when it came second in the 2014 European Parliament elections in Italy, using the election slogan 'We Will Win'. They may not have reached the heights of winning on that occasion, but it would not be long before they did.

After Gianroberto Casaleggio died in 2016, Grillo stood down as party leader in 2017 and was replaced by Luigi Di Maio, but he remained actively involved in M5S as the 2018 general election approached. The theme of its campaign that year was 'change'. One major challenge of basing an electoral drive in Italy around the idea of 'change' was that two rival parties had already recently done so. On the left of centre, Matteo Renzi of the Democratic Party (PD), who served as Prime Minister from 2014 to 2016, had pledged to 'Change Italy or Change Jobs' in a constitutional referendum in 2016, which he lost. He subsequently resigned. On the right of centre, Matteo Salvini rebranded the formerly separatist Lega Nord

(Northern League) into a nationalist-populist party and renamed it 'Lega', telling journalists, 'I want to change Italy … and bring [Italians] back to where they deserve to be.'

The focus of the M5S's 'change' narrative was different, however, going beyond mere policy and rhetoric. Its idea of change was systemic rather than cosmetic, and it was because of this that Gianroberto Casaleggio had turned to the Blue Ocean Strategy. His ethos helped M5S to formulate its simple, three-word slogan for the 2018 election campaign: 'Participate. Choose. Change.' (*Partecipare. Scegliere. Cambiare.*) Marketing companies had been hired to produce campaign material, but Davide Casaleggio asserts that it was he and Grillo who devised the slogan's final wording. 'It was an easy thing to come up with, simply because it fundamentally represented what we were about,' he says.

The three words were arranged in ascending order of importance to M5S, with 'change' being the most crucial. In campaign materials, this word was always written in a font that was bigger and bolder. These words also reflected Grillo's acknowledgement that the Swiss model of direct democracy was critical to the movement's decision-making process. This marriage of principle and action made the party stand out in a crowded field, attracting more and more attention from the media, which Grillo said he hated. '[The slogan] basically was our brand,' Casaleggio explains. 'It was participate in mass rallies and attend meet-ups around the country. It was choose, which was the ability of people to choose candidates and policies via the platform. It was change, because this was the ultimate goal – to transform the way politics was done.'

It should be said that M5S was also willing to actively demonstrate its 'change' philosophy, whatever the cost. Though, based on past election performances, it had been entitled to €42 million of state funding, which could be used to contest the 2018 election, it rejected the subsidy, spending only €763,000, all of which was raised from supporters via their online platform. This anti-political party wasn't just alternative in its outlook – it was cheap to run as well.

Italy's high unemployment rate and the perception that its politics were rotten meant that people turned to the M5S and its narrative of 'change' in droves. Many members of the electorate saw a political grouping which provided such a contrast with the old ways of doing politics that they were willing to trust them, even if not everybody fully understood the changes that M5S advocated. Some clearly believed that desperate times called for desperate measures, even if the M5S advocated a radical, untested form of change to Italian society.

An explicit 'change' slogan always has the greatest chance of success when the voters have their backs against the wall and feel they have no other option. The human brain tends to gravitate towards safety and survival. Opting for change is in fact quite unusual – certainly in a stable society. Yet the original aim of the slogan was not to target the anti-establishment sentiments of Italian voters or to exploit their frustrations. In fact, it had little to do with how the party wanted to be seen from the outside and more to do with the internal conversations within the core team. 'Participate. Choose. Change.' was the way Grillo and Davide Casaleggio wanted the movement to function. It was akin to a list of ingredients on a food product rather than the motto of a company, as though McDonald's had used 'Buns. Cheese. Burgers.' as a slogan rather than 'I'm Lovin' It'. For Grillo, the three words represented a shake-up of the existing political order to upset the status quo – or, as he put it, 'to open up Parliament like a can of tuna fish'.

The Casaleggios had always envisioned a much greater ultimate change, which they hoped would drastically improve the way voters interacted with the political system. According to Davide Casaleggio, 'Rousseau' was not meant to remain solely as an online voting platform for the movement. Instead, his father felt it had the potential to become a type of virtual society in which citizens would interact, with the assistance of blockchain and AI technologies. 'We intended to cross the Rousseau platform to effectively create our own economic community, where we could provide a token where our people could spend money amongst each other to buy products and services. Almost to have their own ecosystem, that was the future,' he says.

In this way, the slogan had a dual meaning. It meant one thing to the founders, but it was interpreted differently by a sympathetic electorate. This allowed M5S to appeal to a significant number of disaffected voters while also allowing them the opportunity to promote their cause authentically. Traditional political parties develop over decades, but M5S won a national election less than nine years after it was set up. This result was attributed to the widely felt political anger in Italy, which had been festering for years. But it was also undoubtedly a product of M5S being able to present itself as an exciting alternative in a political system that had repeatedly let down the electorate. In that sense, its claim to 'change' was genuine.

M5S made history in 2018 by becoming the first self-styled 'direct democracy' party to win a national election in Europe. Most Italian parties are either part of a centre-right coalition or a centre-left coalition, so the scale of its victory was particularly impressive considering its lack of political allies. Its performance meant that Italy had a hung Parliament for one of the few times in its post-war history, with no coalition claiming a majority. With the approval of its members via the Rousseau platform, it formed a cross-aisle partnership with Lega. Lega's leader, Salvini, and M5S's leader, Di Maio, were co-Deputy Prime Ministers under Giuseppe Conte, an independent lawyer nominated by M5S.

All this was thanks in large part to M5S's slogan 'Participate. Choose. Change.' However, it wasn't just in Italy where the slogan had an impact. The same distaste for the establishment was evident elsewhere in Europe, as other self-proclaimed 'direct democracy' parties began springing up, particularly Kukiz'15 in Poland and the Freedom and Direct Democracy party in the Czech Republic. There was imitation closer to home, too, as Lega began copying some of M5S's tactics. Yet, according to David Casaleggio,

> There was a clear organisational difference, not just a communication difference … They said, 'We can use the internet too and we have the money to do it,' but they wouldn't do it [set up a platform like Rousseau]. They didn't do it because they didn't want to give out power.

The slogan 'Participate. Choose. Change.' was far more than just a memorable phrase; it embodied the revolutionary essence of M5S, articulating its foundational principles – citizen engagement, electoral empowerment and institutional reform. This slogan helped distinguish M5S from the other political parties, who were all claiming their own brand of change. The clarity and order in these three words was critical in a country where distrust in politicians was high and where the system was breaking down. A less incisive and authentic slogan would risk undermining the potency of M5S's message. Instead, 'Participate. Choose. Change.' tapped into the zeitgeist of the moment among a disaffected electorate and the slogan propelled M5S to government. The hit word 'change' was not just a promise – it was a call that resonated deeply with voters craving a definitive break with the past.

The difficulty of realising genuine change on an explicit promise of change is one explanation for why the word 'change' has not been used more frequently in Italian election slogans, with it only being used in seven slogans in the country in the past century. It requires voters to believe that a certain party or candidate's identity or their policies are different from what they have seen in the past, and this can make it hard for incumbents to use the word 'change' in a meaningful way. Given that the office of Prime Minister was occupied by the Christian Democracy party for a total of forty-one years between 1945 and 1992, the word 'change' was hardly a viable narrative on which to campaign throughout most of Italy's post-war history.

Of the seven 'change' slogans that have been deployed, only two have translated into an electoral victory (a rate of 28.5 per cent). Silvio Berlusconi was the first person to campaign successfully using the word 'change', winning a non-consecutive second term in 2001. The second time it achieved a positive outcome was in its use by M5S in 2018. It is relevant to point out, however, that although the word 'change' helped Berlusconi and the M5S into office, it also brought them down in the long run – in M5S's case by setting up unrealistic expectations that it could overhaul Italy's political system within a limited time frame, when in reality it could not. The nature of a 'change' slogan is that it suggests action or change is imminent. Yet an impatient public is invariably quick to judge whether the change they desire has been delivered, which is one of the principal dangers of using this word in an election slogan.

In politics, as in most other areas of life, there are few guarantees.

Most slogans should give politicians the time to take voters on a journey. Change slogans are often mistakenly seen as the most effective start to a political journey, but ultimately, in the minds of voters, they are in fact more of a destination. By using the word 'change' in a slogan, the journey is effectively abandoned and voters are instead taken directly to the destination. It is then up to them to decide whether that destination is desirable or not.

Looking further afield, it is clear that the word 'change' is a staple of election sloganeering. Barack Obama's decision in 2008 to use 'Change We Can Believe In' is a prime example of its influence. In one sense, the word's popularity is unsurprising. Which politician, after all, would be entirely confident of victory only by promising more of the same? And yet the reality is that 'change' slogans rarely live up to their reputation, with few exceptions. A global overview shows that the conversion rate of 'change' slogans stands at no more than 30 per cent. The patterns of success and failure reveal particular circumstances that determine where, when and how 'change' slogans are more likely to be used and whether they have a chance of prospering. These circumstances can be broadly broken down into two categories.

The first category concerns where 'change' is most often used. Most of the 'change' slogans have been used in countries with lower levels of economic development and a recent history of political instability or violent conflict. Strikingly, many of these countries are former European colonies in sub-Saharan Africa that gained independence relatively recently – in the last seventy-five years or so. Indeed, the word 'change' has been used in electoral contests in Africa more than any other place on earth, with thirty-three countries there using a 'change' slogan in the past century.

The irony, however, is that 'change' slogans tend to be used most often in countries where change is least likely to occur following a democratic election. Civil wars and military coups are common in Africa, with an overthrow of the government representing the swiftest and most common form of extra-political change in these countries. At the time of writing, there had been 220 coup attempts in the whole of Africa since 1950. Since 2020, nine of them were successful. While there is not a direct correlation between the number of violent conflicts and the use of the word 'change', it is the case that countries with a greater number of uses of 'change' election slogans have experienced higher levels of political violence. For example, since 1950, four military coups have been attempted in the Gambia, where the slogan has been used nine times (more than anywhere else on the continent). Notable practitioners include Yahya Jammeh, who ran triumphantly on 'Change with Continuity' in the 1996 presidential election with the support of those who had launched a coup in the country two years previously. The current President, Adama Barrow, also ran on 'Change for the Better' in the 2016 and 2021 elections. His government most recently survived a coup attempt in 2022.

Where coups are less common, civil war has often caused immense damage instead. Cambodia and Lebanon are two countries beyond Africa where the word 'change' frequently appears in election slogans. Both are former French colonies with no more than eighty years of independence and both are known for civil wars that started in the 1960s and 1970s. With no recent golden age to hark back to, parties operating across ethnic and political divides in these countries have embraced the word 'change' in their election slogans. There are even instances of governing and opposition parties running on the same theme of 'change', as happened in Cambodia's general election in 2013. Incumbent Prime Minister

Hun Sen's authoritarian Cambodian People's Party campaigned to 'change commune chiefs who serve the party and replace them with commune chiefs who serve the people'. At the same time, the Cambodia National Rescue Party (CNRP) ran on the simpler slogan 'Vote CNRP for Change'.

Although change is often held up as a realistic prospect in impoverished and war-torn countries, these can be the very places where it is least likely to come about through a democratic election. Promises of change are often simply unrealistic given the constraints of the political system, which may be rigged or vulnerable to extra-political action such as a military coup.

When using the word 'change' as an election slogan in a context where change is least likely to come about through the ballot box, the public's exasperation is likely to show itself. Cambodia is a good example of this. In 2013, the CNRP won 2.9 million votes (44.5 per cent) and fifty-five of the 123 seats in the National Assembly (the ruling People's Party won the remaining seats). Months before the 2018 election, the party was forcibly disbanded following a court ruling that claimed it had plotted the illegal overthrow of the government. The governing People's Party secured every seat in the subsequent uncontested election.

The word 'change' therefore makes little difference in a country like Cambodia, which is effectively a one-party state. With that said, 'change' slogans are generally less effective in two-party systems as well. The word 'change' has a greater chance of enticing voters in multi-party systems with low levels of corruption. This overall pattern defines the second category of 'change' slogans, which can be found in mature democracies around the world. One such country is Japan, where every opposition party has run at least one 'change' slogan since the advent of commercial political advertising in the

1990s. The main opposition party, currently known as the Constitutional Democratic Party of Japan, has run on the word 'change' in all but one of the four elections held in Japan since 2014 and intends to fight the next election on the theme of change (its latest slogan is 'Now is the Time to Change Politics') yet it has not been able to make a breakthrough for a decade. It can take more than the mere promise of change to succeed.

When 'change' slogans are deployed in dominant party systems, as is the case in Japan, they often struggle to appeal to voters, perhaps because the electorate has become apathetic about any meaningful change being achieved. As a result, smaller parties that have few resources and little hope of victory often employ a 'change' slogan as a calling card, seeing it as the only viable means to distinguish themselves. By lighting this flame, it is hoped that other campaigners – and the public – will keep it burning at future elections.

This is also true in more pluralistic democracies like the UK, where eleven 'change' slogans have appeared in general election campaigns over the past century. Despite this high number, the two main parties have only run on 'change' four times: the Conservative Party in 1951 and 2010, and the Labour Party in 2019 and in 2024. Minor parties have been far more likely to run on a 'change' slogan, especially regional parties such as the SNP, Plaid Cymru (a Welsh nationalist party) and Sinn Féin (the former political wing of the Irish Republican Army). These parties only field candidates in their respective countries within the UK, meaning they can never secure a governing majority because 82 per cent of all seats in the House of Commons are based in England. Demanding change from the wings is their best hope of influencing decision-making. It may appear to show that power is within their grasp, but it can just as easily have the effect of diminishing their political lifespan thanks to public hopes not being met. By contrast, the larger nationwide parties are likely to be tested on the consequences of their actions: voters will judge whether they have delivered any 'change' they might have promised.

In two-party systems such as the US's, voters who are fed up of the incumbent will often choose the alternative, regardless of the slogan. In US elections, the Democratic Party has run on the word 'change' in five elections since 1972. On each occasion, the Democrats were out of office, and considering that there have been eight elections where this was the case since 1972, it is clear that 'change' has become the word of choice for the Democrats in these circumstances. In these five elections, Jimmy Carter (who ran on 'A Leader, For a Change'), Bill Clinton ('For People For a Change') and Barack Obama ('Change We Can Believe In') prevailed against their Republican opponent, while George McGovern ('McGovern for President If You REALLY Want Change') and John Kerry ('It's Time for a Change in America') both lost.

Although Democratic candidates have been more successful in being elected on 'change' slogans, it's worth taking into consideration that Clinton and Obama won when unpopular incumbents were in office. The net approval for George H. W. Bush on the eve of the 1992 election was -22, while at the end of George W. Bush's second term in 2008, his rating was -35. Meanwhile, McGovern lost against Richard Nixon, whose net approval stood at +23 in June 1972. There is a high likelihood that Clinton and Obama could have won with a different slogan, given they were the only viable alternatives at a time when the Republicans' popularity with voters was falling.

There is also an argument to be made for running on a slogan that omits the word 'change.' Consider Obama's 'Change We Can Believe In', which has become one of the best-known political slogans of the twenty-first century. Complementing his youthful image, it helped him to win a landslide over 72-year-old John McCain in the 2008 presidential election, with 365 of 538 electoral votes. Voters were inspired by Obama's aspirational outlook and promises of social progress. Yet while Obama undoubtedly implemented change in certain areas, such as legalising same-sex marriage, some people were disappointed by the perceived lack of real change to their daily lives – the rising cost of healthcare despite the Obamacare reforms being a prime example. This sense of being let down morphed into resentment in some quarters, indirectly leading to the election of Donald Trump in 2016, who vowed to undo much of Obama's promised change with his vow to 'Make America Great Again'. The fallout from Obama's presidency is a lesson that applies to all 'change' slogans and narratives in electoral politics: it is crucial to manage voters' expectations. While Obama may have seen his own election as a young black candidate as change itself, many assumed he would make a significant difference in their lives. But change is always slow to show itself in electoral democracies, as all politicians know.

Ironically, those running on slogans without the word 'change' often find more success in implementing changes on an existential level. The President of Russia, Vladimir Putin, the President of Belarus, Aleksandar Lukashenko, and the President of Turkey, Recep Tayyip Erdoğan, all used slogans featuring the word 'new' when they were initially elected under a democratic system, while the Prime Minister of Hungary, Viktor Orbán, used 'It's Time' when he was first elected. While these leaders are widely condemned as autocrats today, they did not reveal their true colours to voters to 'change' the system during their initial election campaigns. It is not difficult to imagine the initial challenges they might have encountered had they run truthfully on the word 'change'.

In Japan's general election of 2021, the Social Democratic Party ran on the slogan 'Change is Fun!' It won a single seat in the House of Representatives. In a sense, this slogan embodies everything that politicians, parties and political campaigners misunderstand about the word 'change'. There is an automatic assumption that voters crave something radical and different, especially during hard times. Even if some voters express a desire for change in opinion polls and focus groups, however, it is a safe bet that just as many others have an aversion to it. To suggest otherwise is to go against our natural inclinations towards familiarity, safety and survival.

The first step in mastering the use of the word 'change' in political slogans is to remember that even the prospect of it tends to instil in people's minds uncertainty and possibly even danger. Change is associated with unpredictability – a characteristic that is rarely popular. To promise a voter change is not dissimilar to asking them to take a train to an unknown destination. Once they understand that they could just as easily end up in a warzone as a safe haven of beauty, they may well decide that the current situation is preferable. In short, many people will conclude that it is a question of better the devil you know than the devil you don't. This is why so many 'change' slogans are countered in elections by messages that are in effect offering something far less revolutionary or that even ask, 'Are you sure that you want that change?' This can make voters feel uncomfortable about the prospect of change.

For this reason, there are four lessons to be learned before using the word 'change' in a slogan:

1. Anyone thinking of running on the word 'change' should think again. It is deceptive.
2. A politician wanting to effect fundamental change should

implicitly show it in their actions, rather than campaigning on those explicit words.

3. For those who are interested in a long and stable political career, never forget that 'change' slogans are anti-journey slogans and only work in the short-term. Heightened assumptions mean 'change' slogans become 'destination' slogans in voters' minds. Of the eight words that have been used most often in political slogans, 'change' will increase pressure on the campaign to deliver more than any other.

4. If somebody has to run on a 'change' slogan, remember that desperate measures should only be reserved for desperate times. Italy in 2018 is a good example of this.

'Change' is the ultimate default slogan word, having the ability to challenge the status quo by evoking arguably the most common sentiment in politics – the desire for something different. The advantages of using it are its ubiquity (the request for change is among the most commonly heard responses in focus groups) and its ambiguity (it is open to interpretation). Its disadvantages are its promise of immediacy (it implies it is possible to make a difference in the short term) and its ability to scare (people are instinctively wary of unfamiliarity).

'Change' slogans such as that used by the M5S often inject a sense of jeopardy into an election by encouraging voters to alter the existing situation. This can needlessly raise the stakes for the party using the word, giving some voters pause for thought and raising false hope in others. And because the promise of change often goes unfulfilled, it makes 'change' one of the most disingenuous and dishonest words in political sloganeering. It is understandable that some politicians think it desirable to be elected on a 'change' slogan. Indeed, for many, this word is considered to be the pinnacle of sloganeering, capable of providing a sort of political superpower. Yet while it may be perceived as giving strength, it can in fact weaken a politician's position precisely because if change does not occur quickly, criticism or unrest will surely follow.

The difficulties experienced in Italy earlier this century were not dissimilar to a flood, sweeping through every level of society and opening voters' minds to the possibility of a radical alternative. The M5S's anti-establishment rhetoric appealed to the electorate, but it took a series of corruption scandals in the 1990s and then economic collapse to get voters to the point where they hankered after serious reform. Long-term electoral success is more easily available to the party or candidate that implicitly reflects the change voters want rather than explicitly campaigning alongside a change slogan.

The more fundamental the change that is being advocated, the more time and effort it will take to achieve, which is why 'change' should only be used by the right candidate and directed at the most responsive group. The ideal expounder would have the means to implement the changes advocated. Their target audience would be voters who want to dispense with an incumbent government or regime. A resonance between the user's call for change and the target audience's answer to that call is undoubtedly important. Of course, there are always voters who seek change, but that is no guarantee that they will support just any candidate who stands on a 'change' slogan. They put their trust in politicians who have a realistic prospect of being able to enact the changes they pledge. These candidates are often members of the largest opposition party, but they may just as easily be dark horses with momentum behind them. A politician can enjoy long-term success with a 'change' slogan if they are able to keep the flame of their promise alive and keep the hopes of voters on their side.

A strategy of action is the key to capitalising on the strength of 'change' slogans. Voters are more convinced by a politician if they are given an idea of what tangible change looks like during an election campaign, either via an innovative campaign strategy or by a reminder of a party's previous record in government. Whichever is the case, a politician must conform to an overarching narrative, which is the bedrock of all good campaign strategies. In other words, actions must be part of a bigger plan or they risk being seen as stunts.

Voters were ready to back MS5 because it had a realistic chance of leading a government, either in a majority or a coalition. Its senior figures had also proven themselves to be genuine agents of change through their record of implementing innovative solutions to socio-political problems. These actions neatly fed into their aims of transforming society on the basis of their innovative approach to governance. The M5S's programme of 'change' was radical, but the movement was largely able to assuage voters' instinctive concerns by gradually introducing them to their methods over several years before 2018 and by banking on the fact that the total systematic change they wanted was not readily understood by those that voted for them.

The fact that MS5 swept to victory in 2018 proves that a 'change' slogan has the power to upend traditional politics. That MS5's support slipped later on shows that this strength can quickly become a weakness, however. Voters felt betrayed that election promises were broken and a pact was formed with established parties – the very opposite of the 'change' that had been promised, in other words. In this sense, 'change' is a double-edged sword, which is why it must always be handled with care.

3

DEMOCRACY

In the twenty-first century, any mention of Taiwan tends to conjure up two images in the minds of most people who live in the West: microchips and military action. This small island, 100 miles from the Chinese mainland, is estimated to produce more than 60 per cent of the world's semiconductors, which help to power everything from cars and smartphones to navigation systems and life-support machines. However, its global significance is overshadowed by the fact its 23 million-strong population lives under the constant threat of invasion. China's authoritarian communist government regards Taiwan as one of its provinces and ultimately seeks reunification by whatever means necessary. It routinely sends warplanes into Taiwanese airspace – some 1,727 were flown over the country in 2022 alone – and accentuates these intimidatory tactics by asserting its 'One China' principle on the international stage, under which acknowledgement of its territorial claim over Taiwan is a precondition for formal diplomatic relations.

As a result, Taiwan's independence, at the time of writing, is recognised by only thirteen countries, most of which are in Latin America and the Caribbean. Nevertheless, although Taiwan is often commended in the West for being a proud democracy that refuses to be bullied by China, surprisingly little is known about the first ever free and direct presidential elections that were held there in March 1996 or the election slogans that supported its transition to being autonomous. The legacy of the slogan 'Taiwan Needs Democracy', in particular, is far-reaching.

Like much of central and eastern Europe in the closing stages of the twentieth century, Taiwan emerged from decades of repression to establish itself as a newly minted democracy. Yet its history, and how it achieved this seismic political change, was quite different to the collapse of the governments of the Eastern Bloc.

Having been under Dutch colonial rule in the early seventeenth century, Taiwan was briefly self-governing until it became part of China in 1683. In 1895, it was colonised by Japan. After the Second World War ended in 1945, it returned to Chinese control. After the Chinese Civil War ended in 1949, the People's Republic of China (PRC) was established under Communist Party leader Mao Zedong, while the Republic of China (ROC) government, led by Chiang Kai-shek, who headed the nationalist Kuomintang (KMT) party, retreated to Taiwan, where it continued to function as the ROC government in exile. In effect, two Chinas existed from this point: 'Red China', led by Mao Zedong and endorsed by the Soviet Union, and Chiang Kai-shek's 'Free China', based in Taiwan and supported by America until 1979, when Washington finally recognised the communist government in Beijing and cut formal diplomatic ties with Taiwan.

Chiang's government in Taiwan also represented China at the United Nations until 1971, when UN General Assembly Resolution 2758 recognised the PRC as the legitimate representative of China, leading to the ROC's expulsion. Although American aid had by then paved the way for Taiwan's bright economic prospects to become a reality, it remained a police state whose people were unhappy at being presided over by Chinese mainlanders. When Chiang died in 1975, his son Chiang Ching-kuo became President. During the 1980s, he responded to public pressure by bringing an end to martial law and recognising opposition political parties. However, the system of the President and Vice-President being picked by a ballot of the deputies of the National Assembly remained in place.

Upon Chiang's death in 1988, his successor Lee Teng-hui became the first native Taiwanese to govern modern Taiwan. Lee introduced further constitutional changes, ultimately creating the conditions under which he would become the first democratically elected President of Taiwan in 1996 and earning himself the nickname 'Mr Democracy' among the West's media in the process. Whereas popular opposition was mostly responsible for bringing down communist regimes across Europe in the 1980s and 1990s, Taiwan's authoritarian ruling party enacted the necessary reforms itself to usher in the radical overhaul of the nation via the ballot box.

As the leader of a party that, decades before, had presided over the disappearance and deaths of thousands of dissidents in Taiwan, Lee had to gain the electorate's trust in order to become a champion of representative government. (The 'February 28 incident' of 1947, in which 28,000 Taiwanese were slaughtered by Chiang Kai-shek's troops, was the most notorious of several such incidents.) His interpretation of democracy, his strategy of selling its philosophy to the Taiwanese public, his personal background – particularly his education in the US – and the brand he created for himself all played a major part in his accomplishments and, by extension, the transformation of Taiwan. He was able to convert the word 'democracy' into a slogan to link Taiwan to the worldwide democracy movement happening at the time, helping to attract support from global superpowers to his cause. He achieved this political ambition in part by adopting 'democracy' as the key 'hit' word he wanted to use to spread his message.

Lee was born near Taipei, the capital of Taiwan, in 1923, the son of a policeman. At that time, Taiwan was still under Japanese rule and Lee, who is said to have spoken Japanese more proficiently than he did Mandarin, would often remark that he was 'Japanese until I was twenty-two years old'. He studied agriculture at Kyoto Imperial University and served during the Second World War as a second lieutenant in the Imperial Japanese Army. He married his wife in the late 1940s, converted to Christianity, and in the early 1950s moved to the US to study agrarian economics at Iowa State University. He remained in Taiwanese academia until 1965, when he enrolled at Cornell University in New York, receiving a PhD in agricultural economics in 1968. Returning to Taiwan, he worked as an agricultural expert, became a government minister in 1972, was mayor of Taipei between 1978 and 1981 and served as governor of Taiwan province from 1981 to 1984, when he was appointed Vice-President of Taiwan.

The rate of Lee's progress was remarkable given that he was viewed as an outsider by the mainland Chinese politicians who ran Taiwan's government. He also had a relatively unusual background, having spent several years living in the US, and would have been among a small minority of Taiwanese who were practising Christians. There were pragmatic reasons for his elevation, however – 85 per cent of Taiwan's population was made up of native Taiwanese, yet they had no political power and no senior political figure to represent their interests. The second President Chiang knew there was no prospect of his being able to reconquer mainland China and he wanted instead to cement the KMT party's future in Taiwan. Promoting an indigenous Taiwanese to the top of his government was in his interests. As an experienced party insider, Lee fitted the bill.

Not only did Lee's 'outsider' status help his political career but it also seems highly plausible that it spurred him on to realise his political ambitions. Although he had belonged to the Communist Party of China as a young man, his aim was to secure Taiwan's national identity and to establish Taiwan as a sovereign country. He believed that democracy would be the best means of achieving these objectives. Lee needed democracy and he made it his watchword.

When Chiang died unexpectedly in January 1988, the constitution decreed that Lee, as his deputy, should succeed him automatically. In fact, various factions were competing for power, including one backed by Chiang's widow, Song Mei-ling, who wished to influence policy behind the scenes. It was widely speculated internationally that Lee's tenure would be short-lived, but having promised to adopt his predecessor's programme, he soon built up a rapport with the party establishment. He was appointed KMT chairman in July 1988. That year he also publicly criticised the massacres of the February 28 incident, marking him out to the Taiwanese people as a leader who was willing to break with the past. In 1990, Lee was elected by the National Assembly to serve a six-year term as President. It would be the final time a Taiwanese President was elected in this anti-democratic way.

Once his position was stable, Lee made the establishment of democracy his priority. In his first speech in 1990, he spoke about 'humanity's pursuit of political democracy, economic freedom and world peace' and vowed to bring democracy to all '1.2 billion Chinese people'. He pushed through a series of constitutional amendments to secure recognition of Taiwanese national identity and declare a formal Taiwanese sovereignty that was distinct from

China's. He abolished the State of Emergency that Chiang Kai-shek had declared in 1948, reformed the legislature so that its members had to be directly elected by the people and ensured local officials also had to be elected rather than appointed by the KMT.

Mainland China's jurisdiction over Taiwan was then limited by eligible voters being declared residents of a 'Free Area', which was defined as any territory of China that was not controlled by the mainland Chinese Communist Party. This change became the foundation for Taiwan's transformation from a Chinese government in exile to the de facto government of a sovereign Taiwan. Citizens were allowed to send letters to mainland China, to visit relatives there and to demonstrate in the streets. In 1992, the *New York Times* declared, 'What had been a tight police state under Chiang Kai-shek and his son Chiang Ching-kuo is now the most democratic society in the Chinese-speaking world.'

In 1993, Lee established in law that Taiwan's President would be elected for a term of four years, beginning in 1996. The leadership of Taiwan would be contested fairly and freely for the first time in its history, with a campaign involving candidates from multiple parties. The structure was designed to be similar to the American model, whereby each party would be represented by a presidential candidate and a running mate, with their names appearing jointly on ballot papers. Yet there was no tradition of political campaigning in the country. Additionally, some wondered how Lee, like so many other politicians around the world, would be able to make the case for democracy in his capacity as the unelected leader of a former authoritarian party. Lee's attitude to these apparent stumbling blocks showed itself in June 1995 when he was invited by his alma mater, Cornell University, to give a speech on Taiwan's democratisation experience. It was to prove a turning point.

During the speech he said, 'Ever since I became President ... I have sought to ascertain just what the people of my country want and to be always guided by their wishes ... And it is obvious to me that most of all they want democracy and development.' He went on: 'Communism is dead or dying, and the peoples of many nations are anxious to try new methods of governing their societies that will better meet the basic needs that every human has.' Crucially, he then spoke of his experiences as a student at Cornell in the 1960s. 'This was a time of social turbulence in the United States, with the civil rights movement and the Vietnam War protest,' he said. 'Yet, despite that turbulence, the American democratic system prevailed.' He added that it was while studying at Cornell that 'I first recognised that full democracy could engender ultimately peaceful change ... I returned to my homeland determined to make my contribution toward achieving full democracy for our society.'

It could be said, therefore, that Taiwan's 1996 presidential election was the fulfilment of an ambition that Lee had been working towards for almost thirty years. It is worth pointing out that, officially, the Taiwanese government remained committed to eventual unification with mainland China. Lee was not seeking independence; he was only interested in establishing Taiwan as a democracy. Despite the obvious complexities of the situation, he would allow nothing to knock him off course.

Communist China was outraged by his speech. As is the case today, when it believed it had been compromised, it showed aggression. Within weeks it began firing test missiles in the waters near Taiwan, in what were the opening salvoes of the 1995–96 Taiwan Strait Crisis. After the first set of missiles was launched in July 1995, Chinese officials claimed that Lee's speech proved he was reneging on the 'One China' principle. They were already reeling from increased international speculation about the future of Hong Kong. This British colony was due to be returned to Chinese control in July 1997 after a period of 156 years, yet questions persisted about whether it would retain its common law legal system and its free press once it was in the hands of a communist state. These enquiries, which came from all corners of the globe, were difficult for the Chinese to bat away.

The missile crisis unsettled the Taiwanese electorate. In the December 1995 legislative election, Lee's KMT party performed poorly, losing seventeen seats and only scraping home with a majority of two. It could be argued that it was at this point that the public began to view Lee and the KMT as distinct from each other. With the presidential election only three months away, Lee, whose dream of winning it was beginning to look impossible based on the election results, decided that radical action was required. He realised that he had to separate himself from the failing KMT brand.

Until December 1995, all KMT election campaigns had been run internally. Yet promoting Western-style liberal democracy was an alien concept to many KMT elders, who had already begun to revolt against Lee back in 1992, albeit without consequence. Lee abandoned the KMT's propaganda department and instead hired an advertising executive called Lai Tomming to be his public relations manager. Lai was in effect Lee's campaign director. As a former deputy chairman of the United Communications Group (UCG), he was given free rein to strategise and formulate suitable election slogans. This prompted some bemusement and even mockery of Lee. No KMT politician had appointed a commercial advertiser to run a political campaign before, and this would be the first time that external advertisers had become involved in a presidential election campaign. Yet although Lee's employment of an external expert was not ultimately unique in the 1996 election – the rival Chen-Wang campaign drafted in seasoned advertiser Sun Dawei to help, while the Democratic Progressive Party (DPP), the main opposition, recruited Ye Chu-lan to work on Peng-Hsieh's campaign – Lee was privately envied by his political opponents for having secured Lai's services, such was his reputation. Lee and Lai worked well together.

A variety of slogans was devised to target voters during the 1996 election campaign, each of which relied on the theme of democracy, the key component in Lee's political project that would give Taiwan a distinct identity from authoritarian China. When China launched another set of test missiles in March 1996, its warning to the Taiwanese electorate was clear: a vote for Lee was a vote for conflict. Yet amid this military onslaught – and Lee's defiance in the face of China's intimidation – Lee's 'democracy' slogans and their message of unity took on a new significance.

An example of Lee's and Lai's successful collaboration came in the form of the campaign's principal slogan. Originally it was intended to be 'Hand in hand, we run Greater Taiwan; Hand in hand, we stride towards a new century!' Lai apparently found this too long and inappropriate for an advertisement. He suggested changing it to 'Dignity, Vitality, Grand Development'. These words, he felt, would draw attention to Lee's public image and emphasise his economic and security credentials. Lee agreed.

As it turned out, however, 'Dignity, Vitality, Grand Development' was not Lee's most important message to Taiwanese voters. The country's political development was of greater significance, especially since he would be more likely to attract the backing of the US and other international players once Taiwan had become a fully functioning democracy, a crucial achievement if the threat of China was to be countered. To win over both domestic and international support, therefore, his campaign also used the slogan 'Taiwan needs democracy, Taiwan needs stability and Taiwan needs unity all the more. Please give Lee Teng-hui one more vote.' Although not as well known as Lee's main slogan, this one arguably had a far greater impact. By linking 'democracy' with 'Taiwan', Lee responded to two of the biggest demands of the politically engaged public: political pluralism and Taiwanese independence.

The 'Taiwan Needs Democracy' message first appeared in television advertisements, which showed two hands trying unsuccessfully to break a large bundle of sticks, representing the strength and unity of a democratic Taiwan. The background showed the silhouette of a map of Taiwan while the Taiwanese national anthem played. Another key democracy slogan appeared on the side of Lee's official campaign van. It read, 'Democracy needs securing, unite and vote for No. 2.' (No. 2 was a reference to the KMT's place on the ballot paper.) Lee gave speeches from the vehicle's roof and walked alongside it while electioneering across the country. Like so many other charismatic politicians who had operated successfully in democracies around the world, he made sure he was visible to voters, mixing with them on the campaign trail in an effort to project his message still further. In China, politicians were remote figures. In Taiwan, the President could be a man of the people.

Despite having a strong track record on the economy and constitutional reform, Lee's path to power was far from assured. Four parties, including the nationalist KMT, contested the election and Lee faced competition, most notably from the centre-left DPP. He knew he had to campaign in a way that would embody the spirit of change and demonstrate to the world that Taiwanese democracy was built to last. This second point was crucial. Military threats from China were intensifying at the same time as Taiwan's isolation was growing, thanks to the West's increased engagement with China's newly opened economy. Electoral rules stated that the winning candidate could be elected President with a simple majority – in other words, the most votes of all candidates – but because this was Taiwan's first democratic presidential election, Lee wanted to make sure that he had the strongest mandate possible. He emphasised in the speeches he delivered that his goal was to secure more than 50 per cent of all votes cast. In order to achieve this, Lee and his running mate, Lien Chan, had to outmanoeuvre their opponents. They were Peng Ming-min and his running mate Frank Hsieh of the DPP, Chen Li-an and his running mate Wang Ching-feng of the Independent Party and independents Lin Yang-kang and his running mate Hau Pei-tsun.

Taiwan's people were generally supportive of the reforms that Lee had brought about since 1988, but by 1996 he had been President for eight years and there were concerns in his camp that some voters were open to the idea of a new leader taking over. Lai used three tactics as part of an overall strategy to win over the different constituencies of voters across the country. His use of election slogans would prove to be a highly significant element of that strategy.

The first tactic was targeted messaging, whereby distinct slogans were aimed at separate demographics. On the one hand, Lee pledged to serve with 'Dignity, Vitality [and] Grand Development'. This slogan was intended to reassure traditional KMT supporters that the constitutional changes that had been implemented would not alter the KMT's commitment to its core values. At the same time, Lee knew that merely offering more of the same was not a winning formula. He realised that a leap of faith was required for people to truly believe that the repression that Taiwan had endured between the 1940s and 1980s had been extinguished permanently.

He hoped that other Taiwanese voters who had historically felt marginalised by the KMT would respond positively to a slogan such as 'Taiwan Needs Democracy'. By linking 'democracy' to 'Taiwan' in this way, Lee's aim was to reassure sceptics that his reforms would pave the way for a new, home-grown elective government.

That the doubters were, ultimately, convinced was in no small part due to what they saw in Lee himself. Unlike his predecessors in Taiwan and elsewhere around the world, he had a record of tolerating opposition and of sympathising with those behind it. When more than 20,000 students took part in a six-day demonstration for democracy in Taipei in 1990 as part of what was known as the Wild Lily movement, Lee ordered his Interior Minister to hold back the police, no doubt mindful of the international condemnation that followed the previous year's Tiananmen Square massacre. Moreover, Lee actually visited the Wild Lily protests, though for security reasons he was unable to interact with the demonstrators. Nonetheless, he could claim with some legitimacy to have been on the same journey as those who called for a democratic Taiwan, albeit he had operated from a position of power.

This liberal attitude reflected well on him, fostering a sense of trust. The success of an election slogan often lives or dies according to the public's perception of its proponent's sincerity. Lee passed this test convincingly. But the message had to be implicit. If voters overtly interpreted the slogan as a dog whistle for independence, traditional KMT voters might have deserted Lee en masse. For this reason, 'Taiwan Needs Democracy' was always displayed alongside KMT imagery and iconography. The message it strove to send was that the reforms were not only safe for the country but they were also in line with its founding values, as well as being necessary for its survival.

The second tactic to be deployed was centred on branding. Lai urged Lee to exploit his personality by using methods that were familiar in the commercial advertising industry but had not been used in Taiwanese politics before. Lee's history as a reformer and a maverick within the KMT had earned him a strong public profile. In many ways, he stood apart from his party – so much so that he was happy to encourage people to vote for the KMT despite its poor performance in the December 1995 legislative elections.

Lai believed that the electorate would engage more with Lee's campaign if he ran positive messages that highlighted his brand, rather than the negative attributes of his opponents. As a result, the promotion of democracy became part of a wider nexus of television and print advertisements, all of which were thematic and represented Lee's progressive attitudes and his vision for Taiwan. One renowned advertisement was titled 'Leader – Quitting Smoking' and featured Lee explaining how the late President Chiang Ching-kuo had convinced him to give up cigarettes. In a series of six other advertisements, Lee was presented as being 'ordinary', as he spoke about routine subjects such as housework and marriage. In some advertisements, he spoke to voters in Taiwanese, as opposed to the KMT-imposed Mandarin, but most KMT television advertisements were faithful to the idea of tradition, featuring, for example, Taiwan's national anthem. Similarly, most posters and pictures of Lee and his running mate, Lien, used the national flag (which was also the KMT party flag) as a backdrop. In this way, he did enough to appeal to both sides simultaneously.

Marketing Lee on television, just as a business would sell a commercial product, required a lot of resources. According to contemporary figures supplied by the Central News Agency, Lai reported that between January and March 1996, the Lee–Lien campaign spent the equivalent of $3.3 million on just over eighty-three hours of on-air advertisements. This accounted for 27.73 per cent of the total airtime of all candidates. The rival Chen–Wang campaign paid the equivalent of $3.6 million for just over fifty-seven hours of television advertisements, accounting for 44 per cent of the total airtime of all candidates.

Based on these figures, Lee's rate of connectivity was clearly higher than his rival's. This was partially informed by Lai's third tactic: polling. Lee not only took a gamble by embracing commercial advertising, but in another first for a Taiwanese presidential election campaign, he commissioned Lai to conduct opinion polling to gauge the effectiveness of the slogans that were being used. According to one of Lai's polls from February 1996, 70.3 per cent of all television viewers could identify the slogan and campaign message as belonging to Lee when the names of the candidates were concealed via 'blind testing', putting him comfortably ahead of his rivals. These polls vindicated Lai's overall strategy.

When the results came through, the ruling candidate was shown to have won by a wide margin. Lee secured his second term in office with 5.81 million votes, or 54 per cent, comfortably meeting his self-imposed target. His closest competitor, Peng Ming-min of the DPP, trailed with 2.27 million votes, or just 21.1 per cent of the vote. Only three months before, Lee's KMT party had almost lost its majority in the legislative elections, making his success all the more impressive.

Taiwan is a rare example of a country where an authoritarian party has led a successful transition to democracy while continuing to play a dominant role in subsequent elections. This was in no small part due to Lee's skills as a politician and strategist. So wedded to the concept of democracy was Lee that he arguably even sacrificed his own political legacy in its name. Having stepped down in 2000, his successor as KMT leader, Lien Chan, lost the election that year to the DPP. That the political apparatus established by Lee allowed for such an outcome showed that he understood that democracy is as much about losing power as it is about winning it.

Unlike other freedom fighters of the 1990s such as Nelson Mandela in South Africa and Lech Wałęsa in Poland, Lee never enjoyed widespread international recognition, despite the great strides towards prosperity and democracy that Taiwan was able to make during the twelve years that he held the presidency. Yet Taiwan stands out as one of the few examples in electoral history where a slogan has proved more successful and significant in the long term than in the short term. Lee's 'democracy' slogans are unusual in that their impact has oscillated in the years since 1996, as the country's need to reassert its democratic status has ebbed and flowed. Normally, a slogan is useful for one time only, but the Lee slogan has regained importance over the years as Taiwan has felt externally threatened.

Lee Teng-hui's adoption of the slogan 'Taiwan Needs Democracy' turned his campaign into a historic mandate for change. Amid external threats and the KMT's faltering legislative performance, this democracy slogan cleverly positioned the election as a referendum on Taiwan's democratic identity, distinguishing it from authoritarian China and rallying both domestic and international support. The slogan achieved its two objectives: assuring KMT diehards of continuity and presenting progressive voters with an existential chance for self-government. Without this slogan, Lee's message might have lacked the emotional simplicity to mobilise a diverse electorate against his rivals. A less evocative phrase had the potential to muddle his vision, risking a split vote and a weakened mandate.

Instead, 'Taiwan Needs Democracy' defined Lee's reformist agenda, securing a landslide 54 per cent of the vote and imparting a seal of approval on Taiwan's democratic transition. The hit word 'democracy' was more than an abstraction – it was the rallying cry that defined Taiwan's fate and emphasised the slogan's irreplaceable role in Lee's triumph.

It is not far-fetched to suggest that the US might not be as economically and politically invested in Taiwan in the twenty-first century as it is had Lee not based his campaign around the word 'democracy' and established a democratic legacy for his successors. For example, when Antony Blinken, then US Secretary of State, congratulated Lai Ching-te, the newly elected Taiwanese President, on his victory following the 2024 Taiwanese presidential election, he was careful to praise Taiwan's 'robust democratic system and electoral process'. In doing so, Blinken acknowledged a political line that goes directly back to Lee. The US government also refers openly to defending Taiwan's democracy against authoritarian China, emphasising how this form of government has become one of the only international buffers between the free world and communist China.

Whereas many slogans are used for a specific election or campaign and forgotten soon afterwards, Lee's 'democracy' slogan transcended the 1996 Taiwanese poll and became a critical part of his overall political brand, legacy and vision for his country, much in the way that 'Make America Great Again' has for Donald Trump or 'Yes We Can' did for Barack Obama. The slogan that Lee used was deliberately unoriginal and inoffensive, in contrast to popular expectations that every political slogan must be fresh, but it continues to be as relevant as ever, domestically and further afield.

Yet despite Trump's and Obama's slogans remaining in people's memories, the same cannot be said of Lee and 'Taiwan Needs

Democracy'. In part this is because Taiwanese politics tends not to generate as much attention as American politics does. It is also because relatively few people attribute the slogan to Lee in a distinct way. Furthermore, the word 'democracy' is so well known globally that it would be almost impossible to link it solely to Lee. In this sense, he might be described as one of democracy's forgotten champions. As Lee would no doubt agree, what is more important is that voters remember the word 'democracy' itself as they acknowledge the extent to which Lee's vision of Taiwanese democracy has taken root, rather than thinking of Lee first and foremost. Through the guiding principles underlined in 'Taiwan Needs Democracy', Lee was able to achieve most of his political ambitions. The new constitutional order that Lee founded in the 1990s remains the basis for democratic governance in Taiwan. The Taiwanese people clearly take pride in democracy and have made it a core part of their identity without much direct input from Lee.

Lee died in 2020, but his legacy did not die with him and nor did the influence of his slogan. 'Taiwan Needs Democracy' became the essence of the democratic development of the island nation, so much so that successive political leaders there have sought to adapt his words for electoral and geopolitical reasons. In the three decades since Taiwan's democratisation, every major party there has used the word 'democracy' in an election slogan.

Yet despite the word 'democracy' being one of the eight most commonly used hit words in election slogans around the world, it is, perhaps surprisingly, a difficult concept to sell – perhaps because, as a political system, democracy takes many different forms. In Taiwan's case, democracy was supposed to embody another political idea: positive liberty. It was intended by Lee to convey hope, change and empowerment for a nation freeing itself from oppression.

Democracy's application in political campaigns can have a profound impact on a country's political development. Nowhere else outside Taiwan is Lee's 'democracy' slogan as relevant today as it is in Ukraine. Like Taiwan, this eastern European country finds itself right next to a hostile superpower, and at the time of writing, it is engaged in a bitter war with Russia. Ukraine has been trying to pursue closer relations with the EU ever since the so-called Revolution of Dignity of 2014 removed its former President, Viktor Yanukovych, and his pro-Russia regime. This rebellion incurred the wrath of Russia's President, Vladimir Putin, who annexed large swathes of the country and even denied the existence of Ukrainian sovereignty in his infamous 2021 essay, 'On the Historical Unity of Russians and Ukrainians', before invading and occupying Ukraine in February 2022.

Like Taiwan, Ukraine finds its very existence challenged by a more powerful neighbour threatening to 'reunite' it with the 'motherland'. Since the conflict began in 2014, 'democracy' has featured often in Ukrainian political campaigning and sloganeering, not only to gain international attention and military aid from the West but also, in common with many unstable countries, as a patriotic *cri de coeur*. In his inaugural speech of 2014, the newly elected President, Petro Poroshenko, declared, 'European democracy, for me, is the best form of government invented by mankind.' In June 2023, his successor, Volodymyr Zelenskyy, gave an impassioned speech in London about the importance of democracy, telling his audience, 'Democracy is in the nature of Ukrainians.'

There are clear parallels between Poroshenko's and Zelenskyy's speeches and the one made by Lee at Cornell in 1995, both in style and purpose. Yet although Poroshenko and Zelenskyy are two of the most recognisable standard bearers of Ukrainian democracy internationally, no Ukrainian politician has campaigned on the idea of democracy as much as Yulia Tymoshenko, the country's former Prime Minister. As a longtime pro-EU activist, Tymoshenko and her Fatherland Party have campaigned on the promise of democratising her country ever since she became involved in Ukraine's Orange Revolution of 2004–5. Most recently, Tymoshenko ran in the 2019 general election on the slogan 'For a Strong and Democratic Ukraine' as part of her 'New Deal for Ukraine' policy. Citing inspiration from US President Franklin D. Roosevelt's 'New Deal,' Tymoshenko promised a better life for all through a series of democratic anti-corruption reforms. These include constitutional amendments to transfer more power from the President to the Prime Minister and convert Ukraine's presidential system to a parliamentary one.

By 2019, the Ukrainian people did not show overwhelming interest in Tymoshenko's Fatherland Party or her message; not because they were uninterested in it but because they did not believe that she was, at that stage, a credible representative of it. She failed to proceed to the run-off after coming third with 2.53 million votes, or 13.5 per cent of the total. The winner of that election was President Zelenskyy, who received 5.71 million votes, or 30.61 per cent, in the first round and 13.54 million votes, or 74.96 per cent, in the run-off against Poroshenko, who received 4.52 million votes, or 25.04 per cent.

Zelenskyy's victory shook the political establishment, largely because he was a political novice who had previously been a comedian and actor. The slogans he used in that election were 'Change' and 'No to Corruption', which were prominently displayed alongside the logo of his Servant of the People Party. So why did the Ukrainian people react so positively to Zelenskyy's message of change rather than Tymoshenko's arguably more meaningful promise of democracy?

Brand image provides at least part of the answer. Tymoshenko's reputation at that time did not fit the mould of a democratic champion and changemaker in the public's mind, but Zelenskyy's did.

During her time in office as Prime Minister, Tymoshenko had been derided for a gas deal struck with Russia, which imposed one of the highest ever export prices on Ukraine, and her failed coalition government with the pro-Russia party of Viktor Fedorovych Yanukovych in 2010. Tymoshenko's old brand made her 'New Deal' hard to sell and her promise of 'democracy' even more unconvincing. Zelenskyy's 'Change' slogan was successful at the polls for the opposite reason. He did not carry any political baggage and he was able to exploit his career in comedy to his advantage. The fact that he had played a fictional Ukrainian President in the television series *Servant of the People* (which his party was named after) gave him the opportunity to bring to life the change he wished to bring. In this respect, he was similar to Donald Trump, whose fame was cemented before he entered mainstream politics via the television series *The Apprentice*. Zelenskyy's unorthodox, long-term campaign allowed the Ukrainian public to warm to him and his brand before he became a leader.

Democracy is the most highly prized political system in the world, despite being the haziest political concept. This explains why 'democracy' is the ultimate single-issue slogan word. It has the power to instil hope in oppressed peoples by energising them with the promise of freedom. The core characteristic of 'democracy' slogans is symbolism, and they are ideal for those wishing to make freedom the main theme of their campaign. The advantages of using the word 'democracy' are its malleability and universality. The disadvantages are its narrowness ('democracy' slogans only resonate with voters under very specific circumstances) and its complexity ('democracy' is an intangible system of government, making it one of the most complicated slogan words).

'Democracy' is similar to other single-issue slogans, which focus more on specific policies rather than brand identity or overarching visions. In this sense, 'democracy' is functionally similar to words such as 'economy' or 'immigration'. Single-issue slogans are most effective when voters are exclusively invested in one problem, which is why the Second World War dominated the 1944 US presidential election and why Britain's 2019 poll was known as the 'Brexit' election. 'Democracy' slogans thrive when voters agree with a politician's definition of democracy and are willing to work with them by voting them into power. For 'democracy' slogans to make an impact in an election, politicians need to understand four key points about the word in a political context:

1. 'Democracy' is a noun with an adjectival form ('democratic').
2. Authoritarianism/dictatorship is the political opposite of democracy.
3. 'Democracy' is a neutral word in linguistics, but it is seen positively in politics.
4. Democratic reforms can take centuries to enact and mature.

Lee became Taiwan's first democratically elected President despite his previous tenure as an unelected leader thanks to his successful campaign on a message of democracy. 'Taiwan Needs Democracy' perfectly captured the mood of the nation in the mid-1990s. The Taiwanese people had been antagonised by the authoritarian KMT for decades and frustrations among young activists who were sympathetic towards the opposition DPP party had reached boiling point. Many voters supported Lee due to his record of democratic actions, communicating with the opposition rather than persecuting them. Lee showed he understood the high stakes associated with democratic reform by slowly dismantling the KMT's plans to reclaim China and allow civil society to freely flourish.

'Democracy' was therefore less about the complex constitutional reforms themselves and more about Lee's efforts to liberate Taiwan from the grip of the KMT. Voters were also confident that Lee could withstand external threats from China's authoritarian regime given his cooperation with the US, making Lee's 'democracy' slogan highly successful and becoming an integral part of his legacy as 'Mr Democracy'. The irony of Lee's titanic reputation is that his 1996 campaign also marked the end of his political career, his democratic reforms having been completed.

'Democracy' resonates with people who feel marginalised or frustrated, but invoking it as a slogan does not automatically lead to victory. This word carries emotional weight, but it cannot carry a campaign alone. If the candidate or party lacks real democratic credentials, 'democracy' is reduced to a hollow promise.

If there is a problem with 'democracy' slogans, it is that they are so-called destination slogans, meaning that voters need a new reason to support a politician once they have reached the promised point. That destination should be built on a long-term journey kind of slogan, such as 'better' or 'new'.

Although 'democracy' slogans can mark the end of a journey, they leave behind a strong political legacy envied by many politicians. Democracy activists are forever admired by voters for their role in freeing them from oppression, which makes 'democracy' the ultimate legacy slogan, in addition to being the ultimate single-issue slogan.

There is a good chance that the word 'democracy' may become

a more prominent election slogan around the world in future. The threats faced by Taiwan and by Ukraine were both external, coming from mainland China and Russia respectively. Yet a 'democracy' slogan could just as easily be used to try to settle struggles that occur within a country, for example following a coup or civil war. The principal lesson to be learned from Ukraine is that although a 'democracy' slogan might be highly effective in this troubled country, it could easily fail unless it finds a politician who can represent it plausibly. Tymoshenko and the KMT conservatives were the wrong ambassadors for 'democracy' given their flawed track records.

Whereas in their case it was their record that failed the slogan, others who have unsuccessfully used a 'democracy' slogan were defeated by a mix of system pressures, authoritarian opponents and a voting population who prioritised immediate economic relief over uncertain democratic advancement. When the going gets tough for voters, their primary aim is survival, not democratic progress. The problem with democracy slogans is that most are naturally deployed in an election battle against an authoritarian or semi-authoritarian regime, propped up by state-controlled media and rigged elections. The authoritarian incumbents and their offer of stability appeals to voters' primal need to survive.

In most countries where a 'democracy' slogan has been used by the opposition, there is high unemployment, poverty and hardship. The four opposition campaigns in which this is most apparent are Kizza Besigye's 2011 Ugandan presidential campaign ('One Uganda, One People: Democracy Now!'), Morgan Tsvangirai's 2008 Zimbabwean presidential campaign ('Democracy for a New Zimbabwe'), Henrique Capriles's 2012 Venezuelan campaign ('Democracy for Progress') and Ben Ulenga's 2004 Namibian campaign ('Together for Democracy and Prosperity').

As mentioned, the failures of 'democracy' slogans in this context stem from state repression, voter prioritisation of economic stability over abstract ideals and messaging that lacks emotional resonance or tangible promises, revealing critical lessons about the limitations of democracy-centric slogans. One of many examples of this can be seen in the 2004 presidential election in Namibia. The incumbents were the South West Africa People's Organisation (SWAPO), a political party founded in 1960, emerging from years spent fighting as an independence movement. It has been the governing party in Namibia since the country achieved independence in 1990. This sense of legitimacy overshadowed Ben Ulenga's vague promises of democracy. Economic inequality and unemployment rates of 30 per cent fuelled opposition hopes, but Ulenga's slogan lacked specific economic solutions, failing to counter SWAPO's tangible offerings.

The campaigns in Uganda, Zimbabwe, Venezuela and Namibia reveal that 'democracy' slogans struggle in repressive systems where state control – via media, security or electoral manipulation – stifles opposition. Voters facing poverty or instability prioritise immediate relief (jobs, food, welfare) over abstract reforms. Democracy-centric slogans, when detached from voters' lived realities, risk seeming elitist or unattainable, failing to mobilise beyond idealistic or educated audiences. What this also shows is that the ideal of democracy, to which so many countries aspire and which so many in the West take for granted, is, ironically, one of the hardest political messages to persuade people to buy.

4

STRONG

The story of Israeli politics in the twenty-first century has become inseparable from Benjamin Netanyahu, who has served as Prime Minister of this complicated country three times: first from 1996 until 1999, then from 2009 until 2021 and, at the time of writing, since 2022. His ubiquity over the past thirty years has been such that many Israelis cannot recall a time when he was not in or close to power. His rise as a right-wing politician coincided with the gradual decline of the left, which, after the creation of the state of Israel in 1948, was in government for thirty-five of the subsequent forty-eight years. Since 1996, Netanyahu's conservative Likud party, and its splinter group Kadima, has been in charge for all but three years.

Netanyahu has always cultivated an image of strength and charisma, but by 2018, Israel had once again fallen into political instability. Contributory factors to this crisis included a controversial Supreme Court ruling ordering the conscription of ultra-Orthodox Jews and Netanyahu facing a corruption investigation. In April 2019, he called a snap general election in a bid to shore up his position. Given the sturdiness of the right-leaning coalition bloc that he led, his re-election was treated almost as a foregone conclusion. However, Netanyahu had underestimated the popularity of the retired army general Benny Gantz, who had formed the new centrist Blue and White party. Opinion polls predicted a close race.

Faced with the possibility of losing office and the prospect of a criminal prosecution, Netanyahu and his advisers devised the election slogan 'Right. Strong. Successful.' This was a direct challenge to Gantz, whom they labelled in a separate 'duo' slogan, 'Left. Weak. Bankrupt.' Given the perpetual state of conflict that has existed between Israel and its Arab neighbours since 1948, Netanyahu used his military experience and successful international relations record to boost his image as a 'strong' leader, contrasting his achievements with Gantz's untested credentials. The 'Right. Strong. Successful.' slogan helped Netanyahu to a narrow victory against Gantz – both secured thirty-five seats but Netanyahu's allies in smaller parties kept him in power – and ultimately extended his tenure as Prime Minister for two more years. It also damaged Gantz's public image, leading to a decline in support for his party. Only the appalling events of 7 October 2023 were able to reverse the public's perceptions of both men.

Netanyahu chose the word 'strong' in order to project his robustness on policy and to emphasise his personal durability against Israel's domestic and foreign adversaries. In common with many strongman leaders around the world, he used the April 2019 election as something of a referendum on himself as an individual politician, in which he wished to be seen as an irreplaceable king who was locked in battle with malign external forces and with his own country's judiciary and media. Such tactics have been increasingly prevalent globally since 2016. Donald Trump in the US, Narendra Modi in India, Jair Bolsonaro in Brazil and Recep Tayyip Erdoğan in Turkey are all examples of democratic leaders who have exploited their authority to undermine convention, with the word 'strong' often being used to describe them as a separate entity that is distinct from a particular party, country or cause. This type of slogan stands in contrast to countries that have used the word 'strong' to inspire fortitude at a time of national crisis. It is also distinguishable from slogans where the express aim is to take voters on a 'big-vision' journey. The choice of 'strong' as a central theme in Netanyahu's campaign resonated with Israeli voters in April 2019 because of the security concerns threatening Israel at that time. Netanyahu's message to the electorate was that in the final analysis, only he could be trusted to protect them and their interests.

Benjamin Netanyahu was born in Tel Aviv in 1949 to a secular Jewish family of Ashkenazi and Mizrahi heritage. He spent his teenage years in Philadelphia, where his father taught at Dropsie College, and returned to his homeland to enlist in the Israel Defense Forces (IDF) in 1967. Spending at least thirty-two months in the military was compulsory for Israeli men, but Netanyahu chose to serve for five years, taking part in numerous cross-border missions until he was discharged in 1972 after being shot in the shoulder. He returned to the US in 1972 to study architecture and political science at the Massachusetts Institute of Technology (MIT), completing his four-year course in less than three years, during which he took time off in 1973 to fight in the Yom Kippur War. Professor Leon B. Groisser at MIT has recalled, 'He was very bright. Organised. Strong. Powerful. He knew what he wanted to do and how to get it done.'

Netanyahu worked in both the private sector and in diplomatic circles as a young man, equipping him with a wide understanding of economics, security and the art of negotiation. After employment as a management consultant at the Boston Consulting Group, where he formed enduring connections with influential figures including the future Republican presidential candidate Mitt Romney, he returned to Israel to found the Jonathan Netanyahu Anti-Terror Institute in 1978. Named in memory of his late brother, his directorship of this organisation was a reflection of his commitment to national security. He joined the Likud (meaning 'consolidation') party in the early 1980s and quickly scaled its ranks, serving as a Deputy Minister in the office of the Prime Minister, Menachem Begin, in the aftermath of the 1982 Lebanon War and becoming Israel's permanent representative to the United Nations between 1984 and 1988. Subsequently, he was a deputy Foreign Minister until Likud lost the 1992 legislative elections. Although he was still in his early forties, the breadth of diplomatic and military experience established him as a 'strong' leader, and in March 1993, he won the party leadership election.

During his first spell as opposition leader, Netanyahu bolstered his credentials by taking a hardline stance against the Oslo Accords, which were negotiated as a long-term peace settlement between the Labor Party-led Israeli government and the Palestine Liberation Organisation (PLO) led by Yasser Arafat. Netanyahu seized on public opposition to the peace plan, which reached its peak in November 1995 when a nationalist assassinated the Labor Prime Minister Yitzhak Rabin at a rally held in support of the negotiations.

Netanyahu won the subsequent general election in May 1996 over Labor's Shimon Peres by a tiny margin, becoming the youngest Prime Minister in Israel's history and the first person to hold the office who had been born in Israel. During the campaign, he had promised 'A Secure Peace' in response to Labor's strategy of giving up land for peace, but difficulties in the Israel–Palestine peace process and complications passing the state budget led to Likud's coalition government falling apart. Another election was held in May 1999, in which Netanyahu lost power to the Labor Party, then led by Ehud Barak. Netanyahu decided to suspend his political career, opting to work in business, but after Barak's administration collapsed in 2000, he re-entered the political fray. When Likud regained power in 2003, he was asked to serve as Finance Minister. After two years, Likud was out of office and Netanyahu once again secured the party leadership in opposition. In 2009, he became Prime Minister for the second time after defeating Ehud Olmert of the Kadima party, a splinter group of Likud formed by Ariel Sharon and other economic liberals within the party.

Netanyahu had been Prime Minister for a decade when he called a snap election in April 2019. Arguably, he was at his most vulnerable, politically speaking. The allegations about his personal conduct – not the first he had faced – were deeply unhelpful, but the emergence of Benny Gantz as his main opponent presented Netanyahu with a problem he had not encountered before. As a retired army general, Gantz was able to outflank Netanyahu in certain key areas. Most obviously, he could speak of a 38-year military career as opposed to the five years Netanyahu had spent in the IDF. Furthermore, Gantz's views on national security were at least as hawkish as Likud's. By any definition, Gantz was a 'strong' figure in his own right, but his lack of political experience left him vulnerable to mischaracterisation by his opponents.

By staking his political future on an election, Netanyahu set himself the challenge of nipping Gantz's burgeoning political project in the bud. His advisers at the Likud's Tel Aviv office, nicknamed 'The Fortress', included the political strategist Srulik Einhorn. Einhorn understood the need to overcome Gantz's rising popularity as quickly as possible, and his solution, which earned Netanyahu's approval, was to contrast Netanyahu's right-wing credentials with the characterisation of Gantz as a left-wing novice. 'We were in a room with the team and Netanyahu, reviewing the polls and the public sentiment,' remembers Einhorn. 'We understood that we needed to push Gantz in the minds of the public to the left and reinforce the image of Netanyahu as being on the right.'

Einhorn's solution was to filter these sentiments into two short 'duo' slogans, which would present the men in opposite terms. Netanyahu was held up as being 'Right. Strong. Successful.' and Gantz was presented as 'Left. Weak. Bankrupt.' Each slogan was supposed to serve a twin purpose. The slogan working in favour of Netanyahu highlighted his qualities against what it was hoped the electorate would regard as Gantz's deficiencies. And the slogan belittling Gantz emphasised his weaknesses and was designed to force voters to measure these shortcomings against Netanyahu's merits. The slogans were always used separately, but their undoubted simplicity made them very effective. What also worked in his favour was that the public at large had little knowledge or understanding of who Gantz was. In marketing terms, his brand was unknown.

The rationale was to align the slogan with Netanyahu's political brand and play to its strengths while damaging Gantz's political prospects by tying him to the political left. When a candidate does not themselves have a strong brand, others can begin to form their brand – be it negative or positive – on their behalf. This is dangerous because it means they can have little or no control over how others see them. Netanyahu's long political career meant that most Israeli voters had an opinion about him. It was obviously unlikely that one slogan would change impressions that had been formed over many years. Yet it was well known that his secular-conservative brand was particularly popular in suburban areas outside of Jerusalem and

Tel Aviv. Even if voters did not like Netanyahu personally, Einhorn believed that a potent slogan could give them a sufficient reason to conclude to themselves, 'Okay, we'll hold our nose and vote for Netanyahu.'

Given these circumstances, the slogan had to reflect Netanyahu's personality and the public's perception of his political style. Voters knew Netanyahu as a divisive hardliner, particularly on security matters. This meant that devising a big-vision slogan with words like 'better' and 'new' – which are often used at the beginning of a political journey – was out of the question. However, 'strong' was considered an appropriate word to describe Netanyahu for two reasons. First, he had successfully used other slogans containing the words 'strong' and 'secure' in three of the five elections held since 1996. The first of these slogans was 'A Strong Leader for a Strong Country' in 1999, which Netanyahu reprised verbatim in 2009 when he returned to power after that year's general election. He also stood on 'A Strong Prime Minister, A Strong Israel' in 2013.

Second, the word 'strong' matched Netanyahu's personal convictions. It also chimed with his preference for concise and blunt communications, which, remarkably, even stretched to his personal involvement in working out how to present the message. Einhorn recalls receiving instructions from Netanyahu during the election campaign and he paints a picture of a highly knowledgeable leader whose media instincts are sufficiently well honed that he can edit campaign videos having seen them only once. 'Mr Netanyahu is the master and he knows exactly how to tell a story,' explains Einhorn.

Every comment was so precise; his feedback is always so precious to receive. One of the first videos I made for Likud and Netanyahu was around twenty-five to twenty-seven seconds long.

Upon showing it to him, he said, 'Seconds nine to eleven, put after second sixteen. Seconds seventeen to eighteen, delete and bring it closer.' While we often spent months refining a video with corporate clients, his input resulted in a perfect edit after just one review. Netanyahu is amazing, as he knew precisely what image he wanted to present of himself.

This anecdote demonstrates just how well Netanyahu knew his own political brand in contrast to Gantz, who was yet to find his political feet.

The confidence that Netanyahu demonstrated to his campaign team extended to his conduct in the public sphere. He made an effort to embody the 'strong' persona that he had asked his colleagues to craft, for example by being open about his personal friendships with strongmen politicians such as Vladimir Putin and Donald Trump. The shortness of the slogan – 'Right. Strong. Successful.' – also matched his preference for direct messages, according to Einhorn. 'Netanyahu says to stick to one message and repeat the message,' he comments. 'That's his thing. Don't divert and don't change attention.'

In truth, Netanyahu's reputation was so mixed at this point that it was calculated that the best way for him to avoid losing office was, in essence, to drag his opponent down with him. On that basis, the slogan would almost certainly not have worked without its negative component, as Einhorn explains. 'I think [the two slogans] came simultaneously. We were talking together and we said, "The right is strong, the left is weak. The right is successful and the left is bankrupt."'

The slogan provided Netanyahu with a 'first-mover' advantage, allowing him to damage Gantz's reputation in the process. And its negative slant was certainly damaging to Gantz. For one thing, it resurrected memories of his association with an IT company called Fifth Dimension, which went bankrupt in 2018, thereby raising questions about his financial competence in contrast to Netanyahu's 'success'. Furthermore, Einhorn claims that the words 'right' and 'left' were crucial to the slogans working to their full potential. In Israel, the left is, by default, seen as 'weak' for various historical reasons. By tying Netanyahu to the political right, and Gantz to the political left, the campaign team could portray Netanyahu as a 'strong' leader while pigeonholing Gantz as 'weak'. Indeed, Einhorn insists that the distinction between the 'right' and the 'left' was the focal point of the slogans, rather than the more concrete adjectives 'strong' and 'weak'. 'Left and right, that's the main issue,' says Einhorn. '"Weak" is just the description of the left.'

These differences were closely linked to the action that the Labor Party and Likud took over Israel's national security between the 1970s and the 1990s, culminating in the Oslo Accords. These two agreements, signed in 1993 and 1995 when Netanyahu was leader of the opposition, were supposed to bring peace between Israel and Palestine. Having taken the pulse of public sentiment, Netanyahu had campaigned against them at the time, calling them 'deeply flawed' and 'terribly wrong'. Recognising that Israeli public opinion had moved to the right on national security issues during the 1990s, he also refused to commit to implementation of the Accords, promising instead to crack down on Palestinian terrorist attacks to achieve, as per his slogan at the time, 'A Secure Peace'. By contrast, Labor's main offering was security through negotiations. Peres made this promise a key part of his slogan, proclaiming 'Vote for Peres. Vote for Peace' in the 1996 election, which Netanyahu won.

The continuation of Palestinian attacks (which Netanyahu failed to prevent) and the collapse of the Accords hardened Israeli attitudes throughout the 2000s, with the Labor Party bearing the brunt of the backlash after leaving government for the last time in 2001. A legacy of this is that many Israelis see the left as having capitulated to Palestinian demands in the 1990s, while the right took a more pragmatic stance to protect Israeli interests. This is reflected in the fact that 46 per cent of Israelis identified themselves as right-leaning in 2019, against 17 per cent who said they were left-wing. Einhorn and his associates were aware of this rightward tilt and cited the political climate as a primary reason for emphasising the words 'right' and 'left' in the two slogans that were used in April 2019. 'We chose "right", as in right-wing, because in Israel the vast majority of the population identify themselves as right-wing,' he says.

In other words, the slogans merely reinforced the political instincts of the voting public – a trait that the most successful slogans share. They were not an attempt to revitalise Netanyahu's ailing popularity or to overhaul his public image. If the slogans did create anything new, it was the perception that Gantz had a negative brand through being tied to the historically 'weak' political left. This was one of Einhorn's stated goals. 'When Gantz entered the contest, he was new in politics, so his message was "There is no more right or left, Israel first" and [this message] even rhymed in Hebrew,' he says.

This signalled to us that we needed to position Gantz and his party as leftist. Our narrative was helped by the fact that they couldn't form a coalition without the Arab parties and voters knew this. We were also helped by their leftist behaviour in public – for example, they supported a two-state solution.

Gantz found it hard to counter these suggestions. He knew that if he hardened his rhetoric, he would alienate the fragmented left-leaning voting bloc on which he would probably have to rely. At the same time, by allowing Einhorn's message to permeate, he risked walking straight into the trap Netanyahu had set for him. The dilemma became a lose–lose situation for Gantz, and it was made worse by Netanyahu's effective campaign strategy, which accentuated his political achievements and, in doing so, drew attention away from his personal shortcomings. This followed a similar pattern adopted by many up-and-coming strongmen of the time, such as Trump and Bolsonaro, when they were politically challenged. Netanyahu's campaign team pitched him as the only credible champion of the Israeli people and cast social and political institutions as obstacles to people's aspirations – which in Israel's case meant a safe and secure country. Netanyahu's team helped to implement this plan by creating a narrative that distinguished him from his opponents, leveraged his foreign policy credentials to strengthen his political position domestically and diversified his public relations away from traditional media.

One of the biggest difficulties Netanyahu faced was how to expand his support base despite the apparent growth in right-wing sentiments in Israel. Likud's vote share had first slipped below 30 per cent in 1992 and had never exceeded 29.4 per cent since then, instead relying on coalition partners to stay in power. Indeed, since returning to power in 2009, Netanyahu had never been able to match his best performance of 25.1 per cent, which he achieved in the 1996 general election.

Rather than attempting to build a new coalition in the face of a non-traditional challenger, he used the formula that he had relied on throughout his career: he demonised his opponent. He had done this in 1996 by claiming that Shimon Peres's involvement in the Oslo

Accords meant '[he] will redivide Jerusalem'. Einhorn says, 'With Netanyahu campaigns, there's always a clear distinction between us versus them. That's the whole idea. It's us versus them, black versus white, good versus bad.' Netanyahu's preference for binary narratives is the main reason that the April 2019 slogans, and the campaign in general, so forcefully depicted Gantz as a weak leftist, despite the retired general's military credentials being far stronger than Netanyahu's, having spent thirty-eight years in active service compared to Netanyahu's five.

Trump's popularity in Israel also made him particularly helpful to Netanyahu's campaign. Although Netanyahu already embodied the politics of muscular nationalism and the resentment of elites, Trump's anti-establishment election victory in 2016 gave him the confidence to pursue this further. Netanyahu could claim several diplomatic victories through his amiable relationship with Trump, the most impressive of which was Trump's decision to recognise Jerusalem as Israel's capital and his acknowledgement of Israeli sovereignty over the Golan Heights, an area which is disputed with Syria.

Such achievements were highlighted in campaign advertisements, which simultaneously sought to tie Gantz to Trump's predecessor Barack Obama, who is unpopular in Israel, and to Palestinian leader Mahmoud Abbas. One video advert posted on Netanyahu's official YouTube channel even put images of Gantz next to Obama and Abbas while a narrator claimed, 'Benny Gantz supported the establishment of a Palestinian state, together with Obama's people.' The damaging association with Obama, who displayed a willingness to negotiate with Palestine during his presidency, helped in the portrayal of Gantz as 'weak'.

Ironically, Gantz had only ever met Obama, not Abbas, prior to the April 2019 election. Netanyahu had met Obama, Abbas and, before his death in 2004, the chairman of the PLO, Yasser Arafat. Yet by selectively reminding the public of the triumphant elements of Netanyahu's foreign policy record, the campaign highlighted his strengths. Netanyahu also reminded voters how, unlike the predominant 'boots on the ground' approach of his predecessors Ehud Barak and Ariel Sharon, he favoured airstrikes against Israel's enemies in order to save soldiers' lives. Small policy details like this meant a lot to Israeli voters, who were hyperaware of the threats posed by hostile forces like Hezbollah, Iran and Hamas.

Despite standing on such strong messages, Netanyahu's campaign was sceptical of traditional means of communications. In fact, much like Donald Trump, Netanyahu and his team were convinced that social and government institutions, such as the mainstream media and the Ministry of Justice, were stacked with political opponents determined to undermine his authority. Einhorn reiterates this view, claiming that about 95 per cent of the media in Israel is left-leaning, anti-Netanyahu and anti-Likud. This perceived bias meant that Netanyahu faced an uphill battle, despite half of all Israelis being right-leaning. 'The media did everything they could to promote Gantz, and to explain that he's no more right than left,' says Einhorn. 'They were so aligned with his messaging. It's beyond any perception. You wouldn't believe how far the objective media goes against Netanyahu and supports Gantz.'

With political advertising banned in Israel, Netanyahu – in a style reminiscent of Trump – operated mostly in the online arena. Considering Israelis are heavy users of social media platforms, this played to his advantage. 'We did everything: social media, grassroots and door-to-door field operations,' says Einhorn. Incidentally, Netanyahu took 'everything' rather literally, even if his tactics challenged the law, including rallying voters at a beach using a megaphone. Despite being legally dubious, it showed his strength as well as his disregard for convention.

By April 2019, Netanyahu's online empire had about 6 million followers. It included a private Facebook page and dozens of accounts across Twitter, Instagram, YouTube and Telegram. This network had thousands of shares, likes and one of the highest user response rates for any politician, certainly in Israel but also internationally. The Likud party even had its own mobile app, through which supporters could organise and communicate. The sophistication of the campaign was shown by the technology used on Netanyahu's Facebook page. When entering the page, users were greeted with a chatbot pretending to be Netanyahu. The chatbot would ask users their voting intentions, allowing Netanyahu's team to gather data prior to the election. Such strategies allowed Netanyahu to communicate directly with his supporters and create an alternative media space where his messages could flourish. This was particularly useful in reinforcing the dichotomy between 'strong' Netanyahu and 'weak' Gantz.

When it came to polling day, Likud won 26.5 per cent of the overall vote, just 0.4 per cent more than the 26.1 per cent of the Blue and White party. However, this marginal victory was tempered by the fact that neither party got anywhere near the sixty-one seats needed to form a majority government. The support of smaller parties was therefore needed to form a ruling coalition. Although this was forthcoming, it soon fell apart, and another election had to be held in September 2019.

Despite this, the slogans 'Right. Strong. Successful.' and 'Left. Weak. Bankrupt.' were not in vain. There is little doubt that voters heeded the messages and backed Netanyahu, perhaps begrudgingly, over other secular nationalist alternatives even though he seemed to be in a precarious position. The slogans also made a longer-lasting impact in Israeli politics by defining Netanyahu and Gantz. Netanyahu reaffirmed his position as the undisputed strongman leader of the Israeli right, while Gantz was seen as a left-wing sympathiser who lacked Netanyahu's determination. The men did eventually enter into a coalition, and following the 7 October 2023 attacks on Israel by Hamas, Gantz was invited to serve in the war Cabinet formed by Netanyahu.

Netanyahu undeniably dealt a decisive blow against Gantz in April 2019, but the 2023 attacks did highlight a problem with a duo slogan that uses the word 'strong', namely the need for the description to continue to withstand public scrutiny long after the slogan was initially used. This principle makes duo slogans a double-edged sword, for the attacks undermined Netanyahu's perceived strength and invincibility. At the time of writing, public polling in Israel suggests that perceptions of the two politicians have been reversed, so that Netanyahu is seen as weak and Gantz is seen as strong. In fact, in a move that arguably damaged Netanyahu, in June 2024 Gantz resigned from Netanyahu's emergency government, claiming that Netanyahu was 'preventing real victory' over Hamas.

The success of the word 'strong' and its accompanying sentiments reflect the fact that the state of Israel has been in a precarious situation for so long that Israelis are constantly looking for a guarantor of security and sovereignty. By using a 'strong' slogan in April 2019, Netanyahu merely pushed at an open door. His success almost certainly had less to do with any personal qualities or achievements and more to do with the fact that the Likud has historically been more closely linked with muscular ethno-nationalism. By contrast, the Labor Party has largely retreated from security issues on the national stage, instead opting to stand on abstract promises of fighting for the 'truth' or some variation of this idea in every election since 2009.

The slogan 'Right. Strong. Successful.' wasn't just a slogan for one election. It featured a 'hit' word that has been the bedrock of Netanyahu's politics for decades – 'strong'. In using that word, Netanyahu and his campaign team tapped into a deep-seated concern among the Israeli population of perceived neighbouring threats. Opting for a different slogan and perhaps one with a more policy-based approach undoubtedly could have allowed Gantz, with his superior military experience, to shape the narrative of the campaign. That word proved for Netanyahu, as it has for so many others, that the right slogan featuring one of the eight hit words can transform electoral outcomes, even in the narrowest of circumstances.

Some of the slogans of Labor's left-wing allies have been equally vague, with the political party Meretz standing on 'Fighting for the Weak' in 1992 and 'We Must Not Lose Meretz. It Depends on You Alone.' in 2015. Centrist liberal parties, like Gantz's Blue and White party and Yair Lapid's Yesh Atid, have also lacked a distinct brand identity due to their wish to attract a diverse pool of voters. Most of their slogans have carried anti-corruption undertones targeted at Netanyahu's government, with 'What They Broke, We Will Fix' (Yesh Atid, April 2019) and 'Netanyahu Only Cares About Netanyahu' (Blue and White, September 2019) being prime examples.

In fact, the lack of optimism among left-leaning and liberal parties in Israel is unusual. Big-vision slogans are, typically, hallmarks of the political left around the world. The lack of them in Israeli left-wing politics is just another reminder of the constant threats facing Israel and the people's desire for strength against their adversaries. Perhaps the only party to have consistently stood on a big-vision slogan is the Ra'am party, which appeals to conservative Arab voters in Israel. Messages such as 2003's 'The Key to Change' and 2009's

'For a Better Future' are closer to those used by transformative leaders like Nelson Mandela and Lee Teng-hui in the 1990s.

Ra'am's slogans have had little sway in Israeli elections, almost certainly because the majority of Israel's electorate is Jewish. With this in mind, it is fair to say the inability of any other party to fully embody the essence of national strength has allowed Netanyahu to monopolise the word 'strong' and its associated qualities over time. The word has almost become an elixir to Netanyahu's faltering political career, extending its lifespan when it appeared to be in considerable doubt. The same problem arguably torments other strongman leaders around the world who have attempted to use the word 'strong' in their mid-journey slogans. Some have been more successful than others, but how the word is used, and under what circumstances, is what counts.

An analysis of 'strong' slogans around the world over the past 100 years shows that they have been used most frequently in Europe, where they have appeared in thirty-one countries. They are less common elsewhere. Sub-Saharan Africa comes a distant second, with eleven countries having used one, followed by Asia, the Caribbean and Central and South America, the Middle East and North Africa, and Oceania and North America.

As the concentration of 'strong' slogans in Europe suggests, they are most likely to be taken up by Anglo-European countries. Britain has used 'strong' slogans the most, followed by Australia and Israel. There has been a relatively even left–right split between the parties using 'strong' slogans, with those on the right using the word slightly more. The slight lean to the right could be a reflection of the traditional association of strength with conservative ideals and the right's interest in national defence.

Leaders who take ideas of strength to the extreme are often described as strongmen. They are over-represented in the list of 'strong' slogans surveyed. These types of slogans are often – though not always – used at about the midway point of a strongman's political journey, with the intention of extending it indefinitely by deploying tactics similar to those used by Netanyahu in April 2019. The defining characteristic of this type of 'strong' slogan is the focus on an individual rather than a party or country, as was the case with Netanyahu. A politician who goes down this path seeks to embody the idea of strength and so reinforce a narrative of uniqueness and irreplaceability. Those who have attempted this strategy include many well-known authoritarian leaders, most notably in former Soviet countries. For example, 'strong' slogans are among Russian President Vladmir Putin's favourite rhetorical tools. As of 2024, he has used them in four of the six elections in which he has stood, including his first in 2000, when one of the slogans he used was 'A Strong President, A Strong Russia'. In 2012, he opted for 'A Strong Leader for a Great Country' and in 2018 he used 'Strong President, Strong Russia'. In 2024, his slogan was 'Together We Are Strong'.

As with Netanyahu and Israel, Putin's slogans imply that Russia can only be strong if it picks a strong leader – him. By extension, it is inferred that voting the opposition into government would leave the country weaker and less prosperous. The President of Belarus, Alexander Lukashenko, a close ally of Putin, tried something similar in the 2001 presidential election, in which one of his slogans was 'Together for a Strong and Prosperous Belarus'. He then used a similar slogan in 2010, stating that he was standing 'for a prosperous and strong Belarus'. The President of Azerbaijan, Ilham Aliyev, adapted the same idea in his 2018 slogan 'A Strong Azerbaijan', while the President of Turkey, Recep Tayyip Erdoğan, stood on 'Strong President, Strong Assembly' in the same year.

While 'strong' slogans are usually effective at fostering a sense of power and security, they only tend to work if the electorate can identify a reason to put their faith in the 'strongman' leader. Voters quickly lose interest in 'strong' leaders when they are perceived to be incapable of solving big problems, as Erdoğan found to his cost during local elections held in 2024. Indeed, the public will likely vote most enthusiastically for a 'strong' candidate when faced with an existential crisis, such as a financial meltdown or war. Responses to such crises constitute the second type of 'strong' slogans, which are more commonly found in smaller and weaker countries that are trying to punch above their weight. The target of the 'strong' slogan's description is typically that of the country or the national community, which creates a sense of national unity at a desperate time.

This tendency probably explains why there have been so many 'strong' slogans in Lithuania, whose citizens live under the near-constant threat of a Russian invasion. Despite only having a three-decade-long history of democratic elections since the collapse of the Soviet Union, five different major parties in Lithuania have used the word 'strong' in their slogans, including the Labour Party ('For Justice and a Strong State') in 2014 and the Lithuanian Farmers and Greens Union ('Strong Region, Strong Lithuania') in 2019. Even the incumbent Prime Minister Ingrida Šimonytė wanted to stand on 'Strong President, Strong Lithuania' for her presidential bid in 2024. As it happens, she was forced to drop this idea because it was considered to be too close to that used by Vladimir Putin in 2000. If nothing else, however, this does show that two competing forces could, in theory, repackage the same form of words for different reasons if they were minded to do so.

While the intimidation facing Lithuania could evolve into an active conflict, the possibility of violence does not always have to be present. Scotland, where a large number of voters view England's dominance in British politics as a danger to their national identity, is a good example of the word 'strong' being used in a more benign setting. The pro-independence Scottish National Party (SNP) stood on 'Make Scotland Strong Again' at the 2003 Holyrood election, on 'Stronger for Scotland' in 2011 and 'Make Scotland Stronger at Westminster' in the 2015 general election. Yet the SNP's popularity began to decline in the early 2020s when the Scottish public's attention shifted away from worries over national identity and onto more general issues. Though 'strong' slogans have been used to address more run-of-the-mill topics too, and politicians have used the word in various big-vision slogans in the past, they are relatively weak in this context when compared with those that incorporate more optimistic words like 'better' or 'new'.

The other way in which the word 'strong' is used typically features it in conjunction with one of the other seven most commonly used slogan words examined in this book, and as a result, it consequently ends up being dull or redundant. Examples include the Liberal Prime Minister of Canada Justin Trudeau's 'Real Change for a Strong Middle Class' in 2015, the UK Liberal Democrats' 'Stronger Economy. Fairer Society. Opportunity for Everyone.' in the same year and the UK Conservative Party's 'Keep the Economy Strong' re-election slogan, also in 2015. The problem with this type of 'strong' slogan is its lack of narrative. It is hard to construct a convincing story over a long period of time about abstract issues that may be troubling voters when they are themselves the target of the 'strong' message.

None of these three parties lived in a society that faced an immediate shock or disaster; nor did the words point to a leader who could more concretely embody the word 'strong.' Two of them – Trudeau's Liberal Party and the British Conservative Party – subsequently won their respective elections. However, it is questionable whether the word 'strong' was pivotal to these victories. The Conservatives could probably have replaced 'strong' with another adjective and Trudeau could have omitted 'strong' altogether so that his slogan simply read 'Real Change for the Middle Class' and the end result would have likely been the same. On that basis, it is fair to say that the word 'strong' is most effective when there is a good reason to use it. Of the many examples of the word 'strong' being used around the world, the best reasons to do so are to extend an individual leader's political journey or for individual countries to inspire strength when facing some sort of struggle.

The question of whether the word 'strong' makes for a good slogan word depends on the toughness of the individual using it or the severity of the crisis to which a particular slogan is responding. 'Strong' slogans are the ultimate mid-journey slogans for those aspiring to be strongman leaders. They can also act as a rallying call.

'Strong' could be called the ultimate 'reality check' slogan word. It has the power to reassure voters seeking security by projecting an air of competence. The core characteristic of 'strong' slogans is power, and they are ideal for those wishing to make security the main theme of their campaign. The main advantage of the word 'strong' is the sense of empowerment it can bring. Its disadvantages are its aggressiveness (some voters may interpret the word as a boast or a taunt) and exposure to scrutiny (a campaign can unravel quickly if voters perceive the candidate to be weak).

The word 'strong' is often used in conjunction with words such as 'safe' and 'secure' to refer to an individual politician, a political party, the economy or country. Leaders will use 'strong' slogans to rally voters around themselves or a particular cause. This usage of the word 'strong' gives it equivalence to the word 'together', which is also deployed as a means to coalesce support, though 'strong' places greater emphasis on individual power as opposed to collective strength. The relationship between voters and politicians is more imbalanced in 'strong' slogans, with the implication being that voters can rely on the politicians to deliver. This means that the ideal users and target audience of 'strong' slogans also differ from those of 'together' slogans. Anybody considering using a 'strong' slogan should take note of the following points:

1. The mirroring twin: even if it is not stated explicitly, 'strong' slogans always have a mirroring negative slogan, which implies the weakness of one's opponent.
2. The double-edged sword: the public will expect political figures to demonstrate strength if they describe themselves as 'strong', raising the stakes once that person is in government.
3. Rally around the flag: 'strong' slogans are particularly powerful at times of crisis or threat, whether natural or manufactured.
4. No room for creativity: a politician is, or is not, regarded as strong by other people. A perception of strength cannot be created immediately if such a narrative does not already exist. It takes time to be established.
5. Anti-utopian: 'strong' narratives fall flat when leaders include them in a big-vision slogan, especially if there is no existential crisis threatening the public.

The most important point to remember when using the word 'strong' is the negative implication that there is something weak about your opponent. This is useful when, as with Benny Gantz in April 2019, the public has not yet formed an opinion of them. This is especially true for 'strong' slogans when the word describes an individual. The existence of a mirroring negative slogan means that a campaign is likely to turn negative and potentially become polarising through the use of the word 'strong', which may or may not work to a candidate's advantage depending on the public's acceptance of this style of campaigning. If the public has little appetite for it, a 'strong' slogan may turn them towards a political rival who is running on a more optimistic, big-vision slogan. Netanyahu prevented this in April 2019 because he was able to characterise Gantz before Gantz had managed to get his own message across.

Even if the public is receptive to a 'strong' slogan, however, they will expect strength from the person who stands on the 'strong' slogan, which is a risk in itself. People may become disillusioned if a politician fails to meet their expectations, especially if that politician is overwhelmed by a series of economic or political difficulties.

The problem for Benjamin Netanyahu was one that he could not have foreseen, but one that is inherent to 'strong' slogans. Hamas's surprise attack on 7 October 2023 proved to be a chink in his armour. No leader can be strong forever, and his chaotic initial response only further weakened his position. The case of Netanyahu shows why 'strong' slogans are like energy drinks: they can boost a politician's prospects halfway through an embattled tenure, but they can never sustain their journey in the long term after that initial rush of caffeine and sugar.

5

TOGETHER

The presidential and legislative elections held in Kenya in August 2017 were predicted by international analysts to have a straightforward outcome. Although security risks were forecast during the campaign in this tribal East African nation of 48 million people, the incumbent, President Uhuru Kenyatta of the Jubilee Party, was expected to win a second term in office and see off the National Super Alliance led by Raila Odinga. Under Kenyatta, Kenya's capitalist economy was regarded as viable, international relations with key global players including the US and Britain were stable and a brighter future was promised, thanks to several infrastructure projects in the pipeline.

Yet as the campaign entered its final stages, it was clear that the national mood had changed. Not only was the race much closer than anybody had previously reckoned, but a week before the poll, the man in charge of Kenya's computerised voting system was found dead. He had been tortured and murdered. Kenyatta and his party's election slogan 'We Are Together' looked even less appropriate when the results were declared and the 54.17 per cent of the vote his party secured was rejected by the opposition on the grounds that the ballot had been manipulated. Violent protests followed, leading to the deaths of up to fifty people. Then, in an unprecedented ruling, the Supreme Court ordered the election be rerun within sixty days because of 'irregularities'.

Kenyatta achieved a landslide victory in the subsequent election, with 98.26 per cent of the vote – but only because millions of Kenyans boycotted it, with turnout falling from 79 per cent in August to 39 per cent in October. These events stand as an abject lesson in the perils of using the word 'together' in any election slogan. In a complicated country such as Kenya, which has more than forty recognised tribes, most of which belong to two distinct ethnic groups, those divisions are obvious. But in any democracy, it is a statement of logic that divisions exist, and the weakness of the idea of everybody being 'together' can be exposed all too easily.

Uhuru Kenyatta was born into Kenyan politics. In 1963, when he was two years old, his father Jomo Kenyatta became the country's first Prime Minister after independence from Britain had been gained. The following year, Jomo was elected Kenya's first President, a position he held until his death in 1978. Jomo was a polygamist and Uhuru was the second of his eight children and his eldest son. The family belonged to the Kikuyu tribe, the largest in Kenya, making them members of the Bantu people. Uhuru was sent to a private Catholic school in Nairobi before attending Amherst College in Massachusetts. He then returned to Kenya to manage his family's multi-million-dollar business interests, which included land, hotels, transport and media assets.

It was only a matter of time until he followed in his father's footsteps, and after embarking on a political career in the 1990s, he stood for the presidency in the 2002 election. Despite his inexperience, he had the endorsement of the retiring President, Daniel arap Moi.

Like Kenyatta's father, Moi belonged to the Kenya African National Union (KANU) party, which had governed since 1964. Kenyatta fared badly in the ensuing poll, ending up with only 31 per cent of the vote and finishing second to Mwai Kibaki of the National Alliance of Rainbow Coalition. Kenyatta was once again the KANU candidate at the next presidential election in 2007, but he withdrew late on, ensuring Kibaki's second, controversial victory – controversial due to widespread allegations of vote rigging, tallying irregularities and a lack of transparency by the Electoral Commission of Kenya. The country descended into crisis as opposition to Kibaki's victory grew. In the nationwide violence that ensued in 2007 and 2008, about 1,200 people were killed and 600,000 were displaced. Kenyatta, who served in Kibaki's government, was later accused of inciting ethnic violence to help seal Kibaki's second victory and he was one of six individuals to face an indictment by the International Criminal Court (ICC) on charges of crimes against humanity. He would become the world's first serving President to sit in front of the ICC.

The ICC accusations reflected the persistent ethnic tensions that characterise Kenyan electoral politics and they cast a shadow over Kenyatta's political career. With his fortunes within the KANU party diminished, he ultimately joined forces with William Ruto's United Republican Party. The ICC's case against Kenyatta was abandoned in December 2014, by which time he had defeated Raila Odinga to win the 2013 presidential election, this time under the flag of the National Alliance party with Ruto as his deputy. Ruto was instrumental in Kenyatta's 2013 campaign, largely because of his standing among his tribe, the Kalenjin, the third largest ethnic group in Kenya. The Kenyatta-Ruto coalition was initially met with scepticism from the Kalenjin, who had been locked in bitter conflict for years with Kenyatta's tribe, the Kikuyu. This made the coming together of the two former rivals even more remarkable and the unlikely nature of their alliance was a central theme of the presidential campaign in 2017.

Kenyatta's August 2017 election campaign bore a close resemblance to the one he had run four years earlier, up to and including the use of its principal slogan, 'We Are Together'. Recycling this message word for word, it was judged by him to be just as relevant as it had been in 2013, if not more so. Not only had he deepened his political partnership with Ruto – they had by then merged their parties to form the Jubilee Party – they were able to boast of thousands of new jobs having been created and the completion of a new standard-gauge railway line between Nairobi and Mombasa. Following decades of economic and political failures, in which youth unemployment had risen dramatically and nepotism and bribery were standard practice, 'We Are Together' was considered the perfect slogan to urge Kenyans to unite under the Kenyatta-Ruto axis. Kenyatta understood that Kenyans wanted a leader who could promise them better prospects. For this reason, the language of his campaign matched the public optimism of his slogan, emphasising ideas such as 'potential', 'growth', 'modernisation' and 'prosperity'. The narrative of his second term was about 'overcoming' political turmoil, 'listen[ing] to the different points of view' and forging a 'better future'.

Kenyatta hired a British political consultancy firm called Strategic Communication Laboratories (SCL), the parent company of Cambridge Analytica, which specialised in behavioural science, to work on the August 2017 campaign. Its consultants by and large endorsed his ideas. Speaking on condition of anonymity, one former SCL employee observes that while Kenyan politics is mostly divided along ethnic lines, it was possible to define Kenyatta as a more right-leaning politician, in contrast to his rival for the presidency, Raila Odinga. 'On some level, Raila Odinga is a traditional left-wing communist type. Kenyatta was the right-winger,' says the former employee. 'The Jubilee Party was a multi-ethnic, multi-tribal party that was going to be built for longevity in Kenya.' The SCL team advised Kenyatta to stick with a positive message: 'The big issue we faced was: how do you sell an incumbent candidate as being fresh and new? It genuinely was a positive campaign to try and move Kenya to a more progressive, democratic future, with elections fought on policies and pledges, not on tribal loyalties.'

Kenyatta saw a dual meaning in 'We Are Together'. On the surface, the phrase contained the veneer of progress and positivity that was meant to have a broad appeal, especially internationally. It was also hoped that voters would see the slogan as a symbol of the coming together of the Kikuyu and the Kalenjin, transcending tribal loyalties. The slogan could symbolise ethnic unity only because Kenyatta allied himself with Ruto. It would not have made sense if his running mate was another Kikuyu. In this sense, Kenyatta pitched himself as a manifestation of 'togetherness', even though this idea might have appeared contradictory in view of his alleged role in stoking ethnic tensions and his subsequent brush with the ICC.

But whereas the forward-thinking interpretation of 'We Are Together' focused on the 'we' – that is, the people of Kenya and the country's overall development – the second meaning had more to do with Kenyatta himself – the 'me'. The word 'together' was closely related to the politics of his father, who in 1928 founded the newspaper *Mwigithania* (meaning 'he who brings together' in the Kikuyu language) in order to promote a sense of collective identity among the Kikuyu. In the context of Kenyatta's re-election campaign, 'together' was more than just a rallying call – it was also a historic reference to his family's dynastic motto. The word had such resonance in Kenya that Kenyatta had already used the slogan to help gather support against the ICC's allegations in 2011 and 2012, a tactic that ultimately paid off, as shown by his 2013 presidential victory.

In truth, however, the unity suggested by the word 'together' was somewhat disingenuous. It concealed political divisions, whether it was used by Jomo Kenyatta in 1928 or Uhuru Kenyatta in 2011. It was never meant to include everybody in Kenya. When Jomo – a campaigner for Kenyan independence in the twentieth century – used it, he intended the word 'together' to focus on the Kikuyu's interests versus those of the British colonialists. And when Uhuru used 'together' in the twenty-first century, he did so in a bid to persuade Kenyans to unite behind him in his battle against the ICC.

It should be said that although the Kenyan public perceived Kenyatta to be an outspoken and controversial but ultimately effective politician, some SCL sources who worked on the campaign were surprised to discover a man who was more laissez-faire in his approach to campaigning. Certainly, they say, he did not seem as committed to the strategy as Sebastian Kurz (see Chapter 7) or Nelson Mandela (see Chapter 8) might have been. Indeed, it was their experience that he rarely, if ever, involved himself in political discussions with his team, deferring responsibility to his brother, Muhoho, who was SCL's main point of contact throughout the 2017 campaign. 'Muhoho ran things behind the scenes,' says one former SCL source. 'We barely saw Kenyatta. He was just rattling around [his official residence] State House. The younger brother was the power behind the throne and ran everything. Every meeting we did was with him. Every bit of strategy we did was with him and everyone deferred to him.' Kenyatta would even repeat unedited entire speeches that had been written for him. 'I'd be asked to write a speech. I'd write it, send it over and then by the time I heard it spoken, it was pretty much verbatim,' adds the SCL source.

Kenyatta's strategy could be described as having been reliant on an old-fashioned, bare-bones campaign with a twist to attract support from Kenya's young population and the international press. In fact, the strategy was so straightforward that Kenyatta could almost certainly have managed without the help of SCL, but the firm did give the enterprise an air of professionalism and international recognition that it would have otherwise been lacking.

The reality of Kenyan politics was dictated by what SCL called a 'tyranny of numbers'. Quite simply, whichever candidate attracted the most support from certain blocs of ethnic voters would automatically win the election, regardless of their political positions or policy offerings. 'In Kenya, a lot of elections work on what is called the tyranny of numbers,' says a former SCL source. 'You get tribal voting blocs who come together. And what you had was the Kalenjin and the Kikuyu lumping together to become the Jubilee Party. You put the two biggest tribes together and it's a massive voting bloc.'

Kenyatta's objective was to maximise turnout among his supporters and among undecided young voters using his 'We Are Together' slogan. His engagement with them relied on traditional methods – rallies in particular, plus the distribution of posters and other printed materials. Despite being one of the more advanced economies in sub-Saharan Africa, a minority of Kenyans had access to the internet at the time and many households still did not own a television set, so television and other broadcast media, such as YouTube, played a relatively small part in the overall communications strategy.

SCL contributed to certain aspects of the campaign's rhetoric and digital output, but its consultants were otherwise sidelined throughout the election period. The contradiction between the international perception of Kenyatta's campaign and the situation on the ground reveals the two competing visions within his team. On one side was SCL, which sought to maximise Kenyatta's progressive vision and expand it into a comprehensive programme of national renewal that would form the basis of his long-term political journey. On the other side were Kenyatta's and Ruto's own interests, which were less visionary and more grounded in political expediency.

The SCL team had sought to create a bigger profile for Kenyatta based on his economic achievements, particularly the completion of the Nairobi–Mombasa railway and a record number of dams having been built across the country. In an effort to capitalise on these successes, one SCL employee pitched the idea of a 'New Kenya' brand to Kenyatta's campaign team. The envisioned slogan was similar to that used by Tony Blair in 1997, 'New Labour, New Life for Britain'. The aim was to relaunch Kenyatta using a 'new' slogan that would highlight the future opportunities under Kenyatta's second term in office. 'My idea was to present [Kenyatta's record] as a New Kenya,' says the source.

[As if to say] you're now living in the era of New Kenya. And I wanted New Kenya to be the centre point of the whole campaign. I came up with an idea of New Kenya around their young demographic. Making this a youth movement with T-shirts saying, 'New Kenya', 'I am New Kenya'. I wanted this built into the slogans. We were even going to do a guerilla campaign where we started having billboards going up around the country just saying hashtag New Kenya and have a New Kenya website but didn't say anything. And then at some point we would flip the switch and it all becomes an identity owned by the Jubilee Party.

The underlying rationale behind this idea was clear. For years, Kenya has been associated with ethnic violence, poverty and corruption. Yet at the same time, it is one of the strongest economies in sub-Saharan Africa, ranking fourth in terms of nominal GDP. Control of billions of dollars of investment from China and the West was at stake. SCL saw the potential for Kenyatta to develop the Kenyan brand internationally and believed he could inspire voters to join him on his journey towards that goal. Younger voters in particular would have been susceptible to this rhetoric, given that inter-tribal hostilities are less entrenched among their age group. 'Younger people don't identify as Kenyans as much as people would think,' says the former SCL source. 'Muhoho Kenyatta [Uhuru's brother] is the power behind the throne. He realised if Kenya is going to survive and become an advanced economy, it needs to move to advanced politics. It needs to move to a more Western model of peace and proper democracy.' The 'New Kenya' strategy mirrors attempts by other national leaders to change their country's international reputations. Indian Prime Minister Narendra Modi launched the 'Clean India Mission' to promote cleanliness and hygiene. In a similar way, Saudi Arabia has begun a process of liberalisation in order to help attract more foreign investment.

However, Kenyatta's campaign team rejected SCL's proposals and stuck with the strategy of maximising turnout by using the 'We Are Together' slogan. Essentially, they vetoed the opportunity to build a long-term brand and legacy via the word 'new', opting instead for short-term political expediency by using the word 'together'. The long-term future of Kenya was arguably less important to Kenyatta than were his immediate political fortunes, especially those of his family. As an established political dynasty, the Kenyatta family, reputedly the wealthiest in Kenya, had interests to protect. Staying in power was one way of securing their fortune. This covert intention may explain why Kenyatta's brother was so heavily involved in the campaign. At the same time, Kenyatta's running mate, William Ruto, had political designs of his own, which did not completely align with Kenyatta's. These diverging interests would eventually surface when the two men parted ways in 2020.

When the body of Christopher Msando, an electoral commission IT manager, was found shortly before polling day in a wood just outside Nairobi, many were sceptical about the idea of 'togetherness'. A post-mortem found that Msando had died of strangulation after being tortured. Bearing in mind the crucial role in administering the election results that Msando was to have played, his death certainly marred the campaign and made headlines globally. The fact that nobody has been brought to justice for his death makes some in Kenya profoundly uncomfortable to this day.

When the polls closed, Kenyatta was found to have won a total of 8.2 million votes (54.2 per cent of all votes cast) against his opponent, Odinga, who secured 6.8 million votes (44.9 per cent). These results meant that Kenyatta increased his majority by 2.4 per cent, suggesting that most members of the electorate were convinced that being 'together' with Kenyatta and Ruto for another four years was in their interest. Kenyatta's Jubilee Party also performed well in the legislative elections, winning a near-majority of 171 seats in the 348-seat National Assembly. And it won an outright majority of thirty-four seats in the 67-seat Senate. By contrast, Odinga's ODM party finished second in both chambers, with seventy-six seats in the National Assembly and twenty seats in the Senate. Kenyatta's victory showed that the 'together' slogan did what it was intended to do – it helped him to secure a second term.

This was not the end of the story, though. The result was soon declared void by the Supreme Court, which cited 'illegalities' in the transmission of results from polling stations to the national tallying centre. Even though Kenyatta emerged victorious from the second poll, held in October 2017, he only did so because more than half of the voters who had cast a vote in the August poll decided to boycott the October election. This serves as a stark indication of the disillusionment and scepticism that had existed during the original poll and points to the deep divisions within Kenyan society when it comes to the legitimacy and fairness of its electoral system. Kenyan voters knew that Kenyatta was not an original or innovative leader, a fact that was abundantly clear from his reuse of 2013's 'We Are Together' slogan. Indeed, Kenyatta was not the first Kenyan leader to use the word 'together' in a slogan, nor would he be the last. This raises wider questions about the true value of the word 'together'.

The 'We Are Together' slogan used in Kenya in 2017 provides a vivid example of how when a slogan's core message – even if framed around one of the eight hit words – doesn't resonate or fails to align with voter perceptions, it risks not just failure but amplifying the divisions it seeks to conceal. Imagine if Kenyatta used the word 'new', as he was advised to. It might have allowed him to offer the ethnically divided electorate a forward-looking vision that embraced their differences rather than demanding an unattainable consensus to further his dynastic self-interest. Though Kenyatta won in 2017, the hit word 'together' cannot be attributed to that victory – instead, its use arguably contributed to shortening his political journey. He chose a word normally used by people in the dying days of their leadership. His family ran the whole country and controlled the media and he could have used a word like 'new' to start a new journey. Instead, he was lazy and didn't pivot when the chance arose. By choosing a word like 'together', it highlighted how divided the country was and hence his inability to really bring people together.

The contradictions inherent in the word 'together' are not unique to Kenya. At the risk of stating the obvious, there will always be winners and losers in politics, and since not everybody can win, not everybody can be 'together'.

The reality of the word's inconsistencies has shown itself all over the world, from South Africa to Bosnia and Herzegovina. While some slogans may express a genuine desire for people to come 'together', many more serve as masks, hiding the true intentions of certain politicians. At the same time, the ideological malleability of the word 'together' is precisely why it is such a popular slogan word.

At the time of writing, 'Together' slogans have appeared most frequently in Europe, being used in twenty-seven countries. Africa comes second with eighteen countries, followed by Asia and the Caribbean. Left-leaning parties are slightly more represented than their right-leaning counterparts among the 'together' slogans surveyed.

'Together' slogans broadly inhabit three categories: those used to cynically advance particular interests, those that reflect a genuine desire for unity and those that end up as a desperate final plea for support from the populace. Generally, slogans that fall under the first category have a greater chance of a political journey being successful, to the detriment of rival politicians and their supporters. They superficially appeal to people's initial desire to come together so they can work in the short term, but very quickly people realise the word is a con. Authoritarian leaders make up the bulk of those who use 'together' slogans to camouflage a hidden agenda. These leaders often project themselves as amiable and reliable figures in public, an idea that the word 'together' helps to amplify. This facade belies the partisan interests or intolerance for dissent held by these leaders, which only adds to the irony of these masking exercises.

There is a long list of authoritarian or pseudo-authoritarian leaders who have used 'together' slogans in their election campaigns, including Russian President Vladimir Putin ('Together We Are Strong – We Are Voting for Russia' in 2024), Belarusian President Alexander Lukashenko ('Together We Are Belarus' in 2010 and 'Together for a Strong and Prosperous Belarus' in 2015), Egyptian President Abdel Fattah el-Sisi ('Together We'll Make a Change' in 2023), Syrian President Bashar al-Assad ('Together' in 2014) and Venezuelan President Nicolás Maduro ('Together We Can Do More' in 2018).

The list also includes the People's Action Party (PAP), the sole ruling party of Singapore since its independence in 1965. The PAP has stood on two 'together' slogans in the past – once in 2006 ('Staying Together, Moving Ahead') and again in 2011 ('Securing the Future Together'). Halimah Yacob, the PAP-endorsed independent candidate, also stood on 'Do Good, Do Together' in the 2017 presidential election. The PAP's use of the word 'together' is no surprise given it is stated as the definition of one of the party's seven 'attributes'. Like the dictators listed above, however, few Singaporeans are in reality united 'together' with the PAP, not least because of the government's heavy-handed quelling of political dissent. What the slogan actually reflects is the harmonious state of Singapore that the PAP wishes to project, rather than the reality of the ethnic tensions that simmer below the surface.

The use of 'together' slogans to cloak such tensions is one reason that the word is favoured by ethno-nationalist and ethno-religious parties. Politicians who operate in this context may not be dictators, but they tend to advance sectarian interests, which are, of course, the antithesis of togetherness. By claiming to be working 'together' with the people, these parties can conceal the divisiveness of their policies with an air of unity, while at the same time rallying their own supporters. This tactic was employed by the Serb Democratic Party (SDS) in Bosnia and Herzegovina, which used the slogan 'Together for Srpska' during the 2010 general election. Although the slogan may sound inspiring to a Serb, Bosnians and Croatians would likely find its rhetoric inflammatory, considering the party was founded by Radovan Karadžić, the Serbian general convicted of committing genocide in the Yugoslav Wars.

Indian Prime Minister Narendra Modi has also embroidered many of his slogans with the word 'together'. Examples include 'Everyone's Together, Everyone's Progress' during the 2014 general election and 'Together With All, Development for All and the Trust of All', which was deployed in 2019. Modi represents the Bharatiya Janata Party (BJP), which, like the SDS, has strong ties with a military organisation – in the BJP's case, a Hindu paramilitary organisation known as Rashtriya Swayamsevak Sangh. Such links make it difficult for supporters of the opposition and members of certain religious and ethnic minorities to accept these 'together' slogans, as they provide a progressive-sounding mask to a tacit support for nationalism.

While parties like the SDS and BJP represent more Machiavellian manipulations of the word 'together', some slogans are more sincere in their calls for unity. These are most often found in countries where there is a complete lack of unity, requiring a call for togetherness in the first place. One such country is South Africa, where 'together' slogans have been used on several occasions since its first democratic election in 1994. Four of these were rolled out by the ruling African National Congress (ANC) party in 1999, 2009, 2019 and 2021, with the Democratic Alliance and Inthaka Freedom Party having used it once each. The ANC's repeated use of the word 'together' mirrors its repetition of 'better' slogans, which emulated Nelson Mandela's desire to end the cycle of ethnic violence and disunity. However, given the ANC has been in power since 1994, some might say that the frequency with which it has used these words is indicative of its failure to make the country better or successfully bring its population together.

The lack of togetherness can also come in the form of political or ideological disunity, which has been the case in the Netherlands since support for traditional centre-right and centre-left parties evaporated during the first decade of the twenty-first century. Of the more than half a dozen 'together' slogans that have been used there this century, five appeared in elections in or after 2012, which was the last time that more than one party received over 20 per cent of the available votes. Today, at least fifteen parties are represented in the Dutch House of Representatives. Parties that have used 'together' slogans stretch across the political spectrum, including the conservative Christian Democratic Appeal (CDA), the economic-liberal People's Party for Freedom and Democracy (VVD), the social-liberal Democrats 66, the left-wing Labour Party and even the Green Party. This wide scope reflects a desire for unity in the country and the ideological flexibility of the word 'together'.

A similar phenomenon can be identified in France. Its traditional two-party system collapsed in 2017 following the presidencies of the conservative Nicolas Sarkozy and the socialist François Hollande. The fragmentation of French politics helps to explain why four of the five 'together' slogans that have been used in the country in the past century appeared in or after 2017. Voices for togetherness have been loudest on the left, where the Socialist Party vied with Jean-Luc Mélenchon's populist La France Insoumise (FI) party for the leadership of their new political alliance. The Socialists ran the slogans 'Let's Change Our Destiny Together' and 'Together Let's Change the Future' in 2022 in an effort to wrestle back control from the FI party, which had used the slogan 'The Future Together' in the previous election. Sadly for the traditional centre-left, Melanchon's party continued to dominate the left-wing vote nationally, rendering their attempt at a revival futile.

Like the French Socialists, many established governing parties around the world have attempted to extend their tenure by urging voters to stick 'together' with them as their popularity begins to run dry. The use of the word 'together' in this case can be seen as a last throw of the political dice. As with the French Socialists, the tactic has typically ended in failure. This third category of 'together' slogans relates to those who are not genuinely campaigning to bring their country together but are unable or unwilling to manipulate the word in the same way as some authoritarian leaders do. It signifies that they have burned through their political credibility. Without a compelling narrative behind them, these slogans end up being little more than a weak plea for voters' forgiveness and mercy at the ballot box.

Hillary Clinton, who ran for the presidency in 2016 on the slogan 'Stronger Together', is perhaps the standout example in this class. Despite it being her first attempt at taking the White House, she could not shake off the perception that she was merely a continuation of Barack Obama's administration, in which she had served. Many Americans had been left disappointed by Obama's inability to deliver his ambitious plans to 'change' the US and Clinton's image as a prominent member of Obama's Cabinet tarred her by association.

She was also, of course, the wife of Bill Clinton, whose record in government in the 1990s was overshadowed by scandal, turning him into a discordant political force. She made matters worse by using a campaign fundraising event to denounce 'half' of her opponent Donald Trump's supporters as a 'basket of deplorables'. This Freudian slip not only revealed the inherent contradiction of her own 'together' slogan but it also marked out the lack of original ideas in her campaign beyond presenting herself as the least 'deplorable' candidate. Many concluded that she was simply incapable of stepping out of the shadow of Obama's presidency.

In Germany, the conservative Christian Democratic Union (CDU) party faced a similar problem in 2021 after Angela Merkel announced her retirement from politics after serving as Chancellor for sixteen years. Armin Laschet, Merkel's successor as CDU leader, struggled to establish a strong brand image that went beyond Merkel's mould. When he campaigned on the slogans 'For a Germany That Sticks Together', 'Make Germany Together' and 'Crafting Germany Together', some voters interpreted these messages as Laschet begging voters not to abandon his tired party rather than giving them a new reason to place their trust in the CDU again. A further problem with Laschet's 'together' slogans was that they did not tally with the larger framework of the CDU's political journey. The word 'together' could not extend the narrative of Merkel's existing journey, nor could it start a new one for Laschet. It simply marked the end of Merkel's chancellorship.

This outcome arguably reveals one of the greatest flaws of the word 'together' when it comes to slogans. If it fails to hide a politician's political designs, it is unlikely to get past the electorate. Unlike other abstract terms such as 'new' or 'strong', the word 'together' has no descriptive quality. In contrast to a word like 'time', people do not subconsciously want to come 'together' and can easily tell when politicians do not represent their own interests.

These qualities are the reason that many strategists pair the word 'together' with a more substantive term. In both the Russian and Taiwanese cases, it was the other word in the slogan that impacted more than the word 'together'. The Taiwanese President, Tsai Ing-wen, put 'democracy' in her 2020 re-election slogan ('Today, the World Hears Democracy and Freedom, In the Future, We Walk Hand in Hand Together'), while Vladimir Putin added 'strong' to his 2024 re-election slogan ('Together We Are Strong'). Ultimately, however, 'together' slogans rarely have a long-lasting political impact. In both cases it was the other word in the slogan that was of greater significance, contributing far more to electoral victory than the word 'together'.

There is arguably no word in political sloganeering that is as cynical and contradictory as 'together'. The divisive nature of politics means that no election is likely to produce a result that pleases all – or even most – voters in any democracy, thereby undermining the sense of everybody being 'together' when the polls have closed. With voter turnouts shrinking across many democracies, even parties that win an election on a 'together' slogan must realise that the power of the word has been diminished. Can a party that wins an election with 30 per cent of the vote genuinely claim to have brought the people 'together'?

Not every politician who utters the word 'together' is without honour, but it could be described as the ultimate masking slogan word, with the power to disguise interests in the language of unity by urging voters to coalesce around a common goal. The core characteristic of 'together' slogans is harmony, which is ideal for anybody wishing to make cooperation the main theme of their campaign.

The advantages of the word 'together' are its subtlety and the sense of purpose and reassurance it provides. Its chief disadvantage is its paradoxical nature: it is impossible to bring everyone together in politics. Even those who intend to project an inclusive message may inadvertently exclude those who fundamentally oppose them. That is not to say that 'together' slogans are doomed to fail, but politicians should be wary of them.

Given the nature of 'together' slogans, those who devise their own should consider the following – especially if the slogan is intended to be part of an optimistic and progressive political journey:

1. An effective mask: 'Together' slogans can frame certain interests or intentions as part of a positive, progressive-sounding narrative.

2. A word of contradictions: The word 'together' can never truly include everyone in society, due to the nature of politics.

3. Risk of backfiring: The word 'together' can easily expose the hypocrisy of whoever uses it, thereby revealing their intentions to the public.

4. A needy word: It is hard for 'together' slogans to resonate with wider society unless supported by additional words or, in many cases, by the state apparatus.

5. Fades into the shadows: The word 'together' is relatively weak in slogans compared to more substantive words like 'strong' or 'people'.

6. The end of the road: 'Together' slogans, if misapplied, can easily become the end of a politician's political journey. If an incumbent is calling for people to come together, it merely emphasises the flaws in their own record in power, suggesting, as it does, that the people are for whatever reason divided.

'Together' slogans fit well into progressive narratives of peace, unity and societal advancement, which may explain why left-leaning parties use this word more frequently than other groups. This allows politicians to qualify their objectives through inclusive rhetoric, despite the fact that they rarely, if ever, intend to be wholly inclusive. The difference between their words and actions reveals the contradictory nature of 'together' slogans, which cannot uphold the ideals they purport to represent. Politicians can never successfully appeal to every voter during a campaign. Kenyatta's 'We Are Together' slogan is an archetypal 'together' slogan, acting as a brand image that masked his family's ambitions for political power.

It is a common misconception that a divided society can be glued back together via 'together' slogans. 'Together' slogans may be able to project a warm, fuzzy feeling of unity, especially in countries with legacies of ethnic violence and political tensions. However, they offer almost no concrete promises or tangible measure of achievement, depriving discerning voters of a convincing reason to vote for whoever uses them. Furthermore, their lack of strength almost always shows itself. When politicians have little to offer beyond bringing people together, it often signifies the end of a political journey. Voters will hear little more than a desperate plea for support and will invariably seek out greener pastures.

'Together' slogans are not the mantras chanted by those sitting in the last-chance electoral saloon, but they can sometimes appear to be so, due to the tricky nature of the word 'together' in politics. On that basis, politicians would be wise to consider what they can offer voters before settling with a 'together' slogan.

6

NEW

Politicians and political parties often use words in an election slogan that prioritise the image of themselves they want to convey over delivering any message of substance. This is certainly true of 'New Labour, New Life for Britain', which was successfully deployed by the Labour Party led by Tony Blair during the British general election of 1997. Underneath the veneer of renewal, Labour was not really 'new' at all. Fundamentally, it was quite unchanged. Other than Blair's attempt to redefine socialism by rewriting Clause IV of the party's constitution (the clause that confirmed its commitment to nationalisation), its historic links to the trade unions that had helped to form it in 1900 remained intact and many of the left-wing policies that had been adopted by Blair's immediate predecessors, John Smith and Neil Kinnock, were retained.

Party managers skilfully created the impression that the Labour movement had been radically reborn by shifting it onto the centre ground economically and embracing elements of the media with which it had previously had a poor relationship. But Blair's reputation as a youthful visionary – and the fact that the Conservatives, who had been in power for eighteen years, were a spent force – was at least as important in securing Labour's 1997 landslide victory as the idea that it was a 'new' party.

However, there is no doubt that Labour's fresh image was appropriate for the times. The arrival of the new Labour Party on the eve of the twenty-first century helped it to cast itself as modern and contributed to Blair winning two more general elections in 2001 and 2005 before stepping down in 2007 as Labour's longest continuously serving Prime Minister.

In the early 1990s, the Labour Party was facing a crisis. It had lost four consecutive general elections under three different leaders, James Callaghan, Michael Foot and Neil Kinnock, and it was considered to be disorganised, out of touch and unelectable. Margaret Thatcher had dominated British politics in the 1980s in a way that no other leader had since the days of Winston Churchill, defeating the trade unions, introducing new economic policies and reinventing the relationship between citizens and the state. Though she had many admirers, the left saw her as a deeply controversial figure and her unexpected resignation in 1990, which split the Conservative Party, was thought by many to signal that Labour would inevitably return to government. In the event, her successor, John Major, secured a surprise victory at the 1992 general election, confirming that the 'old' Labour Party led by Kinnock simply wasn't liked or trusted enough by most voters.

The sudden death in May 1994 of Labour's next leader, John Smith, presented an opportunity for Labour to put this right. This chance was seized upon. Blair's election as leader of the Labour Party in July 1994 was viewed as its best – perhaps its last – hope of returning to power. Counter-intuitively, Blair was the perfect candidate to be the public face of Labour's plans to refresh its brand image. At forty-one, he was the youngest leader the party had ever had, but his background was also atypical when compared to the working class whom Labour sought to represent. He came from a Conservative-supporting, middle-class family, he was privately educated, he had attended Oxford University and he was a qualified lawyer. He had first been elected to the House of Commons in 1983 and he rose through the ranks quickly, joining the shadow Cabinet in 1987 and being promoted to the key post of shadow Home Secretary in 1992. He was seen as charismatic and he was certainly an effective communicator.

Blair was one of the few Labour leaders since Ramsay MacDonald in the 1920s to have had no experience in government. Yet this did not suppress the Labour chiefs' appetite for change. Indeed, it merely entrenched in them the feeling that modernisation of the party must follow. This would involve a transformation both within and without. Internally, a strategy to strengthen discipline and adapt to conventional practices was put into place; at the same time, the party worked with external partners to cultivate a new public image to replace the 'old' Labour brand. The first step to electability hinged on a name for this movement, which followed a tried and tested global formula of rebranding the party as something new, and it became known as 'New Labour'. It was not exactly original, but it was an essential first step. From this grew a series of slogans, the most commonly used of which was 'New Labour, New Life for Britain'. It first appeared at a party conference in 1994 and it was used again in a draft manifesto published in 1996. It was supposed to embody not only Blair's election pledges to the British public but also the transformation of the party under his leadership and how it wished to be seen by the electorate.

Disputes as to who coined the slogan 'New Labour, New Life for Britain' continue to this day. Alastair Campbell, Blair's press secretary from 1994 until 2003, is credited by some – including Blair

– with having come up with it. He certainly recorded its use in his diary on 15 September 1994, and it is conceivable that in latching onto this phrase, he was influenced by past Labour slogans. 'A New Britain' had been used by the party during the general election of 1964 and 'The New Hope for Britain' had been used in 1983. Peter Mandelson, who played a leading role in Blair's 1994 leadership campaign and ran Labour's 1997 general election campaign, disagrees, insisting, 'I thought it was more a Tony Blair thing.'

This debate over the ownership of 'New Labour, New Life for Britain' can be seen as a microcosm of the entire movement. Perhaps the more important question relates to whether the slogan was merely a short-term publicity exercise executed for political expediency or whether it was part of a more long-term existential rebranding exercise, as Mandelson would like the public to believe. Arguably, the answer depends on how individuals want New Labour's legacy to be remembered.

'New Life for Britain' was a form of words that aimed to encapsulate the spirit of the new Labour Party, acknowledging the anguish of the past and the aspiration of the future. Mandelson says 'New Labour' was 'both a departure from [a] damaged reputation and jettisoning of unfavourable policies'. '[The phrase] wrote itself. We couldn't continue as old Labour. We were carrying a lot of historical baggage, tax and spend baggage and reputational damage from the 1980s,' Mandelson explains. He was not alone in his thinking. Everybody in the party's leadership felt that drastic action was needed if the party was to prosper.

Neil Kinnock adds that his colleagues wanted to 'make a categorical step away from the thirteen years of defeats and, by then, eighteen years of Tory government'. Philip Gould, Labour's chief pollster at the time, concluded from focus group research that Labour's reputation was so badly damaged that 'Labour's only chance was to rebuild completely from the ground up (that is, to rebuild the party's public image from the ground up, as opposed to completely changing the party)'.

The 'reputational damage' to which Mandelson refers was best exemplified by a 1978 Conservative Party poster campaign featuring the slogan 'Labour Isn't Working' against an image of people queuing outside an unemployment office. Almost fifty years later, it remains one of the most powerful and mimicked political advertising campaigns ever seen in Britain and was voted by *Campaign* magazine in 1999 as the best poster of the century. It was produced by the advertising agency Saatchi & Saatchi, which developed a reputation for negative advertisements. The poster's simple yet brilliantly effective double meaning is known to have infuriated the Labour Prime Minister of the day, James Callaghan.

However, its effects were more far-reaching than merely upsetting Callaghan. The spectre of 'Labour Isn't Working' haunted Labour to such a degree that even in the mid-1990s, the party still felt it had some work to do to convince the public that any negative perceptions they had of the Labour brand were no longer accurate. On a simple level, the word 'new' allowed the party to distinguish itself from the 'old' Labour of the 1970s and 1980s. A similar idea had first been used by the team surrounding Bill Clinton in the early 1990s, when the Democratic Party put the word 'new' in front of the party's name and slogans. Labour's refreshed brand, and the name 'New Labour', was supposed to be the opposite of old Labour: young, united and innovative. It was meant to demonstrate the transformation of the party in appearance and in substance. New Labour also served as the figurative tree trunk from which all campaign materials and publications branched off. As Mandelson explains:

New Labour is a brand, not a slogan. It captures the qualities and virtues and differences of the party. We used it as a branding for the party as a whole. Everything else emanates from it. Other things, for example 'New Life for Britain', 'Britain Deserves Better', are an extension of the brand.

Mandelson made a point of distinguishing New Labour as the brand from 'New Life for Britain' as a slogan. The distinction is an important one. 'New Labour' on its own would not have been a very descriptive slogan, not least because the public still did not know what 'new' actually meant in this context. Quite naturally, they wondered what was 'new' about the Labour Party and what, if any, journey its new leader wanted to take voters on. More concrete mission statements were needed in order to convey the ideas behind the reforms to the public. This is where slogans came in. First used just after being elected leader in July 1994, Blair introduced 'New Labour, New Britain' as the stated goal of his reforms at his first party conference, explaining how a transformed Labour Party could also transform the country. 'We have changed,' he said.

We were right to change. Parties that do not change die … We have not changed to forget our principles, but to fulfil them, not to lose our identity but to keep our relevance … The next election will offer us the chance to change our country, not just to promise change, but to achieve it – the historic goal of another Labour government.

Clearly, he hoped that the energy and dynamism of his leadership could alter Britain, just as it had begun to reshape his own party. The positivity and optimism of Blair's speech became a common thread in many slogans created by Labour for the 1997 general election. 'Britain Deserves Better', 'Britain Will Be Better', 'New Life for Britain' and 'Things Can Only Get Better' – the title of a song by the band D:Ream that the Labour Party adopted as its theme tune – were all rallying calls to Blair's cause.

The Conservative Party's response to the New Labour brand was to roll out the 'New Labour, New Danger' poster campaign in 1996. It was also produced by M&C Saatchi, a breakaway company founded by the original Saatchi brothers in 1995. It showed a photograph of a smiling Tony Blair, but his eyes had been replaced by a sinister pair of 'demon eyes'. It certainly had the desired effect in that it generated a significant amount of publicity and won an industry award. It was, however, also a piece of negative campaigning that questioned Blair's character.

In 1994, the Saatchis produced a negative slogan for F. W. de Klerk, Nelson Mandela's rival candidate, during the first free election to be held in South Africa and had clearly misjudged the public mood. The same criticism can be made of the 'New Labour, New Danger' campaign, with some suggesting at the time that in light of the many 'sleaze' allegations that had been levelled at the Conservatives as the 1990s wore on, the firm had failed to appreciate which political party was perceived by the public as the 'hero' and which was seen as the 'villain'. According to Mandelson, 'New Labour, New Life for Britain' was an antidote to 'New Labour, New Danger'. The idea of a 'New Life for Britain' countered the Conservatives' suggestion with an optimistic promise of a better life for all. 'The mood was very much for change in the mid-1990s and even more so in '97 because of social divisions and scandals in the Tory Party,' Mandelson says. 'In '97, people were crying out for change; more so than in '87. But they weren't crying out for the Labour Party in 1987.'

Labour's leadership team made sure that they did not just promise a vaguely worded 'new life' for everyone but that the public could see a plan of action that dissociated the party from its past. This is why 'New Life for Britain' became the title of Labour's draft manifesto in 1996. The document contained five pledges, in which Blair promised to improve education, tackle crime, cut NHS waiting lists, reduce unemployment and be fiscally responsible. These pledges represented the changes in policy that Mandelson refers to when commenting on New Labour. They gave structure to what this 'new life' would look like under a Labour government. It was intended to be a departure from the party's fairy-tale optimism of the past by adapting some of the more popular characteristics of Thatcherism.

By coincidence, all this coincided with renewed interest in British pop culture during an era that the press labelled 'Cool Britannia'. Bands including the Spice Girls and Oasis were gaining traction globally, as were films like *Four Weddings and a Funeral*. 'New Life for Britain' aligned itself with these cultural phenomena to project a vision of a changing Britain that was not only modernising politically but also had a greater social relevance on the world stage.

Nevertheless, there were disagreements over the delivery of the 'New Life for Britain' slogan, as well as other campaign materials. Mandelson insisted that the letter 'n' in 'new' be kept in lowercase, while other colleagues expressed a preference for a capital 'N'. The debate centred around the implications of using a capital 'N', which would have placed a lot of emphasis on the word 'new'. As Mandelson explains:

There was a lot of discussion about whether 'new' should have a capital 'N', which I didn't want. There were people in the campaign team against that. Usually, these things are finalised by July, but by the beginning of September still no decision had been made. Tony was a bit indecisive because he kept having different views put to him. His inclination was with 'new'. It had lowercase until the election when we changed it to uppercase. The reason for not being uppercase was I didn't want [people to think] that we were changing the party's name. All these things are nuanced.

The reason the leadership team eventually settled on a lowercase 'n' up until the 1997 election was to avoid overemphasising the newness of Blair's leadership. Kinnock shared this sentiment. 'Using a capital does informally retitle the party, and either because they didn't want a new title or because there were shelf-life disadvantages to using new as part of the title, [they didn't use a capital],' he says. 'Do not be mistaken: the party wanted the public to know that it had turned over a new leaf from its 1980s incarnation, which is why it kept using the word "new" in its campaign materials.'

At the same time, the party did not want to alarm its traditional supporters, many of whom were sceptical of Labour's embrace of market economics and commercial advertising. Arguably, using a lower case 'n' was symptomatic of the party's cautious approach. It wanted to get the public used to its changed status gradually before announcing some of its bolder policies, such as granting independence to the Bank of England, and the choice of lettering reflected that tactic, albeit subtly. Ultimately, the party left the job of emphasising the capital 'N' to the media – literally and metaphorically. Newspaper articles that were written about this exciting 'new' political entity used the capitalised letter in the word 'new'.

Despite this focus on the particular wording of its slogans, the Labour Party also needed an effective but secure strategy that would attract disillusioned Conservative supporters while simultaneously retaining its traditional working-class base. Merely saying 'New Labour' and 'New Life for Britain' would not have been enough to project its vision in public. A critical part of making a new slogan a success and resonating with the public lies in shaping and crafting public perception and a narrative. This was where the media came into play.

Discussion about New Labour's 1997 election strategy tends to gravitate towards 'spin' and the use of the media – especially in light of Blair accepting an invitation from Rupert Murdoch in July 1995 to speak at the News Corporation conference on Hayman Island in Australia and subsequently receiving the backing of Murdoch's London newspapers. While undoubtedly important, however, that strategy was just one facet of a larger scheme stretching back to Kinnock's leadership of the party in the 1980s. The reforms of the 1990s built on those laid down by Kinnock. It is no exaggeration to say the New Labour strategy would not have worked without Kinnock's groundwork. He changed the internal electoral system to lessen trade union influence, he cut Labour's ties with far-left factions, he expelled party members charged with corruption and he disowned controversial policies such as unilateral nuclear disarmament. With the help of Peter Mandelson, who was Kinnock's director of communications between 1985 and 1990, he also implemented some cosmetic changes, including choosing a red rose as the party's symbol. All this pointed to Kinnock seeing the value of market research, something that New Labour later embraced even more warmly.

However, this was an uphill battle for Kinnock, who encountered resistance from Labour's left wing. This faction of the party, he remembers, 'thought somehow if we became professional, we'd lose our soul … They just didn't like the idea of anything that sounded professional. I used to say, "Well I hope to God that doesn't extend to the pilot of your plane or your brain surgeon."' He adds, 'Labour never took [market research] very seriously because they were very scornful of measuring public opinion and focus groups and earnest listening to the public. The Tories took a very different view: we've got something to sell, so we'd better recruit the experts at marketing.'

Doubling down on Kinnock's strategy of employing professionals, Blair appointed Alastair Campbell – the former political editor of the *Daily Mirror* – as his campaign director alongside Mandelson. Later, he invited the American political consultant Stan Greenberg, who had worked for Bill Clinton in 1992 and Nelson Mandela in 1994, to work in the research department. The aim of Blair and his team was to focus on the sizzle rather than the steak. Visuals and language were prioritised over more fundamental reforms, which had been enacted under Kinnock's leadership, to keep the party's left wing at bay. The heart of the strategy was to use party communications, Blair's personal public image and the traditional press to present an image of what a 'New Life for Britain' would look like under Blair.

Labour Party literature was redesigned to fit the fast-emerging digital era of the late twentieth century – black-and-white printouts of party manifestos were replaced by coloured booklets filled with photographs of Blair mixing with smiling British voters. Publishing a pre-election manifesto in 1996 also gave the public plenty of time to evaluate Labour's plans in government. Targeted publications were distributed to reassure non-traditional Labour voters, particularly small business owners and pensioners. Multimedia productions and events were also held and a video titled 'Things Can Only Get Better' was released. It featured a montage of young children playing, students using computers and craftsmen using tools set against D:Ream's catchy song of the same name to symbolise the advance of the 'new' Britain envisioned by Labour. This drew parallels with Bill Clinton, who also used a theme song and relied heavily on television to inject energy and dynamism into his 1992 presidential campaign.

It is worth pondering whether any of this would have come to pass had Blair's predecessor, John Smith, lived. Smith was known to be sceptical of the type of techniques that were used routinely in American politics – indeed, he positively railed against them. Peter Mandelson recounts that when Smith discovered Blair and his close adviser Philip Gould had made a trip to Washington in 1993, he rang Mandelson and said, 'I know what their game is. We don't need any of this fucking Clinton stuff over here.' Suffice to say it is an open question as to whether such techniques would have ever been employed by the Labour Party during the twentieth century had Smith not died at the tragically young age of fifty-five.

These initiatives made the newness of Blair's leadership tangible. Between 1993 and 1997, Labour spent £23 million, including £7.3 million on media adverts, which represented a significant loosening of the purse strings compared with previous decades. The money was seen as crucial in projecting Blair's public persona, another aspect of Labour's 'spin'. Blair also allowed Campbell, Mandelson and others to advise him on public appearances, often yielding to their counsel. Mandelson, for instance, recalls Blair being 'distraught' and 'jittery' over the slow pace of campaigning. He looked to Mandelson, as campaign director, for assurance. Though there are contradictory accounts of Blair's demeanour at the time (Greenberg described him as a 'self-confident' leader), the key was in the public perception. To prevent public relations disasters, the Labour Party began to revamp its communications strategy, which was yet another aspect of Labour's 'spin'. Media messaging was tightly controlled. The goal was to dictate the narrative. As Mandelson says, 'In politics, the narrative always matters.' Campbell arranged private meetings between media players and Blair, giving them access to the Labour leader on his terms. Every aspect of New Labour's 'spin' operation served to spice up the party's public image. The production of multimedia campaign materials and the carefully crafted public personas of its leaders made the party look and sound modern.

Blair and his New Labour brand's successes showed themselves quickly. According to the polling company Ipsos, Labour's lead over the Conservatives rose up to +33 following Blair's election as party leader in July 1994, reaching +39 just one month after his 'New Labour, New Britain' conference speech. Although opinion poll numbers between Labour and the Conservatives eventually narrowed by the time of the 1997 general election, Blair won the biggest victory ever recorded by Labour in its history, securing 13.5 million votes (43.2 per cent) and 418 of the 659 seats in the House of Commons. (Interestingly, this was 575,000 fewer votes than the Conservatives polled in 1992.) By contrast, in 1997, the Conservatives suffered their worst defeat since 1906, garnering 9.6 million votes (30.7 per cent), which translated into 165 seats. The Liberal Democrats also performed well against the Conservatives, winning 5.2 million votes and forty-six seats (16.8 per cent).

According to Peter Mandelson, 'New Labour, New Britain' is 'the best slogan in history'. He likely describes it in this way for several reasons. First, it was inclusive, as all good slogans should be. 'New Labour, New Britain', along with 'New Labour, New Life for Britain', created a new set of expectations in British politics. Blair promised everybody a fair opportunity under a New Labour government, regardless of their circumstances. The message that he successfully got across was that there was a place for everyone in this 'new Britain'. The slogan opened up the field of play.

Second, the slogan rewrote the rules of subsequent British elections. The Conservatives were unable to break through the strong positivity and optimism of the 'new' slogans. Their party was portrayed as symbolising the 'old' Britain, spiritually broken by the years of division under Thatcher. In a sense, 'New Labour, New Life for Britain' weakened the Conservatives just as 'Labour Isn't Working' haunted the Labour Party for the best part of twenty years. To nail the ghost of their 1997 defeat, the Conservatives even resorted to taking a leaf out of the New Labour rulebook. David Cameron, who became Conservative leader in 2005, led the charge to create his party's own version of New Labour. Cameron swept away unpopular Thatcherite policies, embraced social liberalism and introduced so-called 'A-Lists' to prioritise women in the selection process of parliamentary candidates. George Osborne, Cameron's second in command, has even confided in Mandelson that he and Cameron studied his New Labour strategies when building their own self-described 'New Tory' project.

The similarities between 'New Life for Britain' and 'Labour Isn't Working' do not end at the unwelcome bequest made to their rival parties, however. Both slogans were deliberately light on detail. 'Labour Isn't Working' never mentioned *why* people should vote Conservative, while 'New Life for Britain' failed to paint a complete picture of what a 'new Britain' would look like and the timeframe in which it could be achieved. As Kinnock says of 'Labour Isn't Working', it was a 'resonant' and 'clever' slogan because it 'exposed everything and disclosed nothing'.

The same principle applied to a 'New Life for Britain', which may explain why it was so successful for so long. Despite the new graphic designs and the jettisoning of old policies, the Labour Party of 1997 was essentially the same party it had been in the 1970s and 1980s. Kinnock goes so far as to say that 'in '97, they hardly changed any of the policies that I'd left them'. Yet, with a few tweaks, so much about the party seemed completely 'new', which is why the word 'new' acted as the perfect long-term journey slogan for the Labour Party and its new coalition of voters. At the same time, because 'New Life for Britain' disclosed nothing, it allowed different groups to interpret 'new Britain' as they saw fit. This meant the expected destination was slightly different for everyone, even if they began at the same starting line as Blair. The – arguably – abstract slogans used by Blair, Clinton and Mandela in the 1990s had the central aim of ensuring that everybody made it to that starting line.

It could be said, however, that they devoted far less energy to monitoring how and when people finished the race. This stands in contrast to the approach taken by, say, Margaret Thatcher. She targeted aspirational voters, starting in 1979 with a campaign poster that read, 'Don't just hope for a better life, Vote for one. Vote Margaret Thatcher.' She then backed up that message by introducing policies such as the right to buy your council house and the ability to own shares in former state-owned utility firms such as British Gas. These were wealth-creating initiatives that millions of people chose to take advantage of. It is undeniable that many voters were sufficiently dazzled by the idea of 'New Labour' to vote for Blair in 1997 but were subsequently disenchanted by the New Labour government. This then left them more susceptible to voting for an organisation such as the Liberal Democrats, the Green Party or the UK Independence Party a decade later.

In this way, there was a darker side to the slogan's consequences. Contrary to the rose-tinted picture of a 'new Britain', the reality could never match the party's rhetoric. Indeed, millions were left bitterly disappointed following Britain's controversial involvement in the invasion of Iraq in 2003. There was an equal sense of rancour after the global economic crisis of 2007–8, which came barely a year after Blair decided to break with convention by standing down as Prime Minister in the middle of a parliamentary term. The British public grew increasingly disillusioned with politics following these events. Gordon Brown, who succeeded Blair as Prime Minister in 2007, failed to win the 2010 general election. For Labour, the silver lining found in 'New Labour, New Life for Britain' was that the party's positive brand image remained sufficiently strong to deny Cameron an outright majority in 2010 and force him to form a coalition government with the Liberal Democrats. This sense of disillusionment only intensified under the Conservatives, as, in common with many Western nations, they introduced austerity measures to stabilise the economy. Spending on social services was cut while tax rates were left largely unaltered, meaning most people were giving more of their income to the state but receiving less in return. Anger and resentment eventually turned to the European Union, the chief architect of austerity across the continent. The journey that for a majority of voters had begun with 'New Labour, New Life for Britain' in 1997 ended with some of them choosing to vote Leave in the Brexit referendum of 2016.

The result of the 1997 general election should undoubtedly be seen through the prism of Labour's principal slogan, 'New Labour, New Life for Britain'. It was the linchpin of their electoral triumph. For Blair and his advisers, using the word 'new' was not just another campaign accessory but a strategic necessity. That word signalled to a hungry electorate that the party that they had known as perennial losers had shed its image of the past and were ready for government.

Although New Labour is widely regarded as being a toxic brand today, its enduring legacy attests to the success of the narrative it projected through an effective use of 'spin' and the media.

The Labour Party had used the word 'new' in election slogans several times before the 1997 general election, having historically adopted a more positive rhetorical vocabulary than the Conservative Party. True to the socialist and trade unionist principles on which it was founded, the themes of its election campaigns have often been evolutionary if not revolutionary, seeking to inspire societal changes and move forward. This is why the word 'new' has been a mainstay of the party's electoral campaigns. In 1945, it used 'New Generations Deserve a New World'. In 1964, when it also won, it deployed 'The New Britain'. And in 1983, when it was not successful, it was the turn of 'The New Hope for Britain'. However, events that took place during the New Labour era of government mean that the party has never used that word again. It has for now effectively been taken out of commission.

If there is any truth to the idea that making the journey is often more exciting than reaching the destination in politics, the word 'new' is arguably the best long-term journey word of all. People tend to be far more positive about embarking on a new journey than they are about reaching a known – and usually underwhelming – destination, but only if politicians can entice them. Parties and candidates around the world have established lasting brands using 'new' in slogans, policy titles and even party names. On the surface, the word 'new' resembles the word 'change' in its appeal to those who seek something different from the status quo. Some slogans even combine the two words together, as the Democratic Party of Kosovo did in its slogan 'Time for a New Beginning, Leaders for Change' in 2017. Yet while the word 'change' is more common in developing countries, the word 'new' is used more frequently in mature democracies. In fact, the countries that have used the most 'new' slogans are almost all mature democracies. The word has been most prevalent in Britain, appearing in thirty-eight slogans since 1945. The US follows closely with twenty-nine 'new' slogans since 1912.

Election slogans using 'new' appear more often in recent years, due to voter demand for reform amid democratic backsliding, economic pressures and geopolitical tensions. 'New' slogans have also become especially common in east Asia, with the word being used in ten national election campaigns in Japan since 1987. Four presidential candidates in South Korea have also adopted 'new' slogans in four of the eight free elections held there since the late 1980s. Democratisation has been essential to this. The first time it appeared was under Kim Young-sam's 'Create a New Korea' during the 1992 presidential election, in which he successfully ran to become the first civilian President after thirty years of military rule. This was followed by Roh Moo-hyun's 'A New Republic of Korea' in 2002, Yoo Seong-min's 'New Hope for Conservatism' in 2017 and Yoon Suk Yeol's 'Newly, by the Will of the People' and 'I Will Create a New Republic of Korea' in 2022. Each of these 'new' slogans was intended to start the Korean public on fresh journeys, something which only became feasible after the removal of the military juntas that ruled South Korea for three decades.

The keys to success for a politician depend on the way they begin their political journey with the electorate, how they follow through in the long term and whether they popularise a brand through effective media messaging. No brand based on the word 'new' has been as successful in the English-speaking world as the New Deal Coalition of US President Franklin D. Roosevelt, who served from 1933 until his death in 1945. Roosevelt's 'New Deal' is still seen as a model of progressive reform for left-leaning politicians. It inspired Bill Clinton's promise of a 'New Covenant' and 'New Leadership' under his 'New Democrat' coalition in the 1990s, which, incidentally, also influenced Blair's 'New Labour' in 1997. The 'Green New Deal' popularised by progressive Democrats in 2019 similarly influenced the European Union's decision to launch its own 'Green Deal' in 2020.

There have also been conservative parties that have consistently won elections on 'new' slogans, so long as the journey was built up gradually. One example of this comes from Japan, where the Liberal Democratic Party (LDP) has governed for sixty-four of the seventy years of its post-war history. The LDP has used seven 'new' slogans in national elections since the 1990s alone, all but one of which has helped them to victory.

This journey began in 1978, when Yasuhiro Nakasone started campaigning for the LDP leadership (and the premiership) on the slogan 'Starting New Conservative Politics'. Nakasone gradually introduced the Japanese public to his mixture of ethno-nationalism and pro-market policies before he became leader in 1982. Aided by Japan's economic boom in the 1980s, in the 1986 general election he won the LDP's biggest majority since 1969 on the slogan 'Construct a Secure, Safe and Stable Japan'. Nakasone's success inspired future generations of LDP leaders to adopt various 'new' slogans, all of which have been electorally successful. These leaders include Ryutaro Hashimoto ('Open. The New LDP.' in 1996), Sadakazu Tanigaki ('New Plan, New Start' in 2010), Junichiro Koizumi ('Toward a New Japan' in 2001), Shinzo Abe ('A New Era' in 2019) and Fumio Kishida ('A New Era, With You' in 2021 and 'Through the Voice of the Regions, Toward a New Japan' in the 2023 local elections). Socialist and liberal opposition parties have attempted to adopt the word 'new' for their own slogans, which have traditionally relied more on the word 'change'.

That said, only one opposition party in Japan has ever won an election on a 'new' slogan. That came in 2009, with the Democratic Party of Japan using 'A New Japan' as one of their primary slogans, helping them to win the 2009 general election and ending the LDP's decades-long dominance. The DPJ's 2009 victory with a 'new' slogan was a rare event, driven by LDP vulnerability and a time-specific voter demand for change. Since then, the LDP's adaptability, the fragmentation of the opposition, the LPD's media influence and voter priorities have made it difficult for other opposition parties to win using a 'new' slogan.

An essential part of the framing of public perception comes from positive media coverage, as it allows politicians to portray themselves or their cause as genuinely 'new' more easily to an otherwise sceptical public. This is especially important if the party or candidate has significant baggage it needs to shake off, as was the case with the Italian Prime Minister Silvio Berlusconi. He switched from business to politics in the early 1990s and became the standard bearer of the right after the collapse of the Christian Democracy party in 1994. He won his first election the same year under his newly founded Forza Italia party, which ran on the slogan 'For a New Italian Miracle'.

To make his argument convincing, Berlusconi assumed the persona of what his former chief strategist Giuliano Ferrara described as a '"virtual reality" president'. In other words, Berlusconi relied on 'spin'. As the owner of various television channels, Berlusconi took to the airwaves to charm his audience, unafraid to show off his wealth or display his forceful personality. From flashy stunts such as signing an oversized five-point 'contract with the Italians' to explicit comments made during television interviews, he made sure that he looked and sounded nothing like the 'old' politicians from the DC party or its rival, the Italian Socialist Party (PSI). Berlusconi also promised that Italy's ailing economy would renew itself under his plan to cut taxes and loosen regulations, as outlined in documents like his 'contract'.

Ironically, his greatest strength ultimately became his undoing. The self-branded 'new miracle' leader's political career began to unravel when he admitted that 'we can't promise and can't achieve miracles' amid the 2008 global financial crisis. His overuse of spin, as well as associating his 'new miracle' with his personal brand, made his downfall much more damaging when Italians found out about his scandalous private life and alleged corruption. He resigned in 2011. A case could be made for Berlusconi and the word 'new' becoming interlinked in the minds of citizens, so that the word somehow came to represent the politician and vice versa. He used it a lot during the campaign and for several years after. Each time he introduced economic policy, he described it as part of his new miracle. The upshot was that when Berlusconi disappointed the electorate, the word 'new' not only lost its lustre more quickly but it also amplified his shortcomings. This only added to the sense of decline when the house of cards came crashing down.

Though Berlusconi could not stay in power for as long as he wished, he almost certainly remained Prime Minister for longer than he otherwise would have by leveraging the media to his advantage. Politicians who have been able to plan a long-term journey, establish a positive spin on a 'new' slogan at the beginning of that journey and exploit the media have tended to be highly successful. So successful, in fact, that many began their journey towards authoritarianism with the word 'new'.

It is noteworthy that some leaders of so-called 'illiberal' states began their political journey by winning their first election using a 'new' slogan. This includes Belarusian President Alexander Lukashenko in 1994 ('We Need New People and New Politics'); Djibouti President Ismail Omar Guelleh in 1999 ('Inject a New Breath of Life') and 2011 ('A New Impulse'), Russian President Vladimir Putin in 2000 ('New Time, New President'), Turkish President Recep Tayyip Erdoğan in 2002 ('If God Wills, a New Blank Page Will Be Opened for Turkey') and Congolese President Denis Sassou Nguesso in 2002 ('New Hope').

The ingenuity of these slogans lay in their ability to exploit the strengths of the word 'new' when circumstances allowed. Lukashenko and Putin were able to tap into voter resentment following the chaotic collapse of the Soviet Union, while Erdoğan offered a fresh start after a decade of weak coalitions and political violence. These leaders then outlined a hazy yet enticing vision of national renewal, promising to halt their country's downward spiral. This set the foundations of a decades-long journey, during which they pledged strong leadership to achieve the renewal of their country via slogans like 'National Will, National Strength' (Erdoğan, 2014) and 'Strong President, Strong Russia' (Putin, 2018). Though, of course, these leaders were also aided by a willing media, operating under the control of the ruling party.

Leaders who correctly execute a long-term journey based on a 'new' slogan can stay in power for decades, even potentially bending the state apparatus in their favour. Those who fail to seize power through charisma may find themselves relying more on brute force, as is the case in countries like Thailand and Venezuela. Nothing in politics lasts for ever, but the word 'new' can extend a leader's time in office just a bit longer, thanks to the idea that it lends strength and endurance to the enterprise.

In this way, 'new' can be a very effective word when put into a good slogan, so much so that numerous dictators have begun their political journey using it. Other leaders, like Tony Blair, have used the word 'new' as part of a rebranding exercise, which paid off handsomely. The word 'new' shares several similarities with the word 'change' and it is fair to say that many politicians who run on 'new' are subconsciously trying to deliver a message of change, as was the case with Blair's Labour Party. But 'new' is a far more productive word than 'change', and 'new' slogans tend to have a lower risk of backfiring because they are not burdened by the same sense of urgency. In fact, the human brain responds remarkably differently to 'new' and 'change'. Whereas 'change' evokes feelings of uncertainty and discomfort, 'new' can open voters to the idea of embarking on a new long-term journey in a less immediately demanding way.

'New' can project freshness and hope, but simply labelling something 'new' in an election slogan does not guarantee results. Voters must believe this originality is genuine and backed by a credible vision for improvement. For the right candidate or party, 'new' can be the ultimate rebranding slogan. The word has the power to redefine a party or politician to appeal to voters who have become disinterested in their brand. The core characteristic of 'new' slogans is transformation, and they are ideal for those wishing to make change the main theme of their campaign.

The advantages of the word 'new' are its adaptability, openness and neutrality. Its disadvantages are its short shelf life ('new' can quickly become 'old') and the fact that people can be wary of unfamiliar things. 'New' slogans can appeal to a broader audience due to the word's neutral tone, allowing politicians to impose their own interpretative meaning on the word.

But this is not to say that anyone can win an election on a 'new' slogan under any circumstances. There are five rules which should be observed by those seeing to use a 'new' slogan:

1. Seek a long-term journey over short-term political expediency: it takes a long time to realise something 'new'. Voters are willing to stay on a long journey if they think they will reach the destination at some stage.

2. The 'new' should be about the 'we' and not the 'me': people are open to making a long political journey if they believe whatever is 'new' will benefit them in the future. If 'new' is tied too tightly to an individual politician, it is very easy for voters to end their journey if the politician's career stalls or fails.

3. Have a non-specific destination: if the promise of something 'new' is too specific, then the slogan can become change-based, introducing immediacy and potentially shortening a candidate's or party's political lifespan.

4. Take control of the public narrative: the success of a 'new' slogan depends on whether the public perceives the politician or party as something genuinely 'new'. This takes time to build up.

5. Prepare ways to overcome pit stops and hurdles: nothing remains 'new' forever. Additional slogans and narrative meanders will be required to keep the journey going.

The most important of these five rules is the need for a long-term journey, something which is much harder to achieve in today's restless and unforgiving political environment – to say nothing of the disease of apathy, which continues to spread throughout

Western democracies. 'New' slogans are most effective when they point voters towards a vaguely defined utopia – one that seems real enough to achieve while simultaneously being distant enough to strive for. It is also best if the word 'new' refers to a common future or aspiration rather than simply working in the interests of the party or candidate standing for election. Fulfilling these conditions will bring a significant segment of voters to the starting line of the long-term journey, which is what Roosevelt and Blair achieved in 1932 and 1997 respectively. Voters will not be interested in any promises of a 'new' future if there is no hope of achieving it. However, politicians need to give voters an incentive to stay on that journey. The public must feel that they are benefiting from the journey and are not in danger of being left behind.

The easiest way to create this incentive is to take control of the public narrative surrounding an election campaign or a government's record. This is commonly known as 'spin' and it can be executed in several ways. It could be a clever media campaign, a backroom deal with individual journalists or it could come as the takeover or ownership of media organisations, as has taken place under Putin, Erdoğan and others. Another option is to exploit the social media landscape and speak directly to voters by catching their attention over the traditional media. Flexibility is needed to divert people's attention away from the inevitable pit stops and setbacks on the road to the 'new' destination. A narrative of strength and reliability typically works well once voters are halfway through the journey; it gives them reassurance that you have what it takes to continue taking them towards the 'new' destination. If this is carried out, leaders can be in power for at least a decade, as Blair was.

Of course, life rarely goes according to plan. If voters begin to lose interest in the journey, it could only be continued by rigging elections, by restricting access to information or by creating an environment in which voters are made to feel politically insecure. The only other way to prevent the loss of office would be to hope for an existential crisis that would keep the electorate united, thereby allowing for a 'new' future. This could naturally occur as an external war, which is what happened during Roosevelt's presidency. It could also be manufactured, just as Hungary's Viktor Orbán is doing by casting the 'liberal' establishment of the European Union as a threat to his country's national sovereignty. Either way, 'new' slogans can take a politician far, but few political journeys can be defined forever by just one slogan. What happens next will depend on a politician's judgement and ability to adapt.

7

TIME

Austria is often overlooked on the international stage in favour of its more populous neighbours, Germany and Italy. Yet this small, landlocked country in the eastern Alps has been at the centre of some significant political developments in recent decades. In the 1980s, and again between 1999 and 2002, it was the first state in Europe since the Second World War to have members of a far-right party within its coalition government. Then, in October 2017, Sebastian Kurz, leader of the conservative Austrian People's Party (ÖVP), became Chancellor at the age of thirty-one, making him the youngest democratically elected premier anywhere in the world.

Kurz took office after what had been a tumultuous time for his party. Following years of stasis under the ÖVP–SPÖ (Social Democratic Party) coalition, which between them had been in power continuously since 1945, public disillusionment was widespread and there had been a surge in support for the nationalist Austrian Freedom Party (FPÖ), which had been founded by former Nazis. This had come mostly at the expense of Kurz's ÖVP and was linked to the arrival in Austria in 2015 of more than 100,000 Middle Eastern migrants, most of whom, according to the United Nations, had fled Syria, Afghanistan and Iraq for reasons of war and persecution.

Having become party leader in May 2017 – five months before the general election – Kurz realised that he had to combat the FPÖ threat. He rebranded the ÖVP and, to emphasise the arrival of a younger generation in politics, campaigned as the 'Sebastian Kurz List – The New People's Party' under the electoral slogan 'Time for Something New'. It worked, and the ÖVP rose from third place in pre-election polls to first place in the election itself, securing 1.6 million votes (31.5 per cent) and sixty-two of the 183 seats on the National Council. The success of his campaign was underscored by the remarkable voter turnout of 80 per cent, one of the highest since 1945.

'Time for Something New' represented a major shift in Austrian politics, marking the beginning of a chapter characterised by innovation and a different approach to governance. First the far-right were invited into Kurz's coalition government for seventeen months, and subsequently the left-wing Green Party served as his coalition partners. But the choice of electoral slogan, which got Kurz into this position, was unusual. Words like 'time' and 'new' are typically used by opposition parties beginning their political journey with voters, to provide a contrast with an incumbent government – not by the party that is already at the helm of government. So how and why did Kurz use these words to convince so many members of the electorate to stick with the status quo? In an interview with me, he revealed the answers to these questions.

Sebastian Kurz was in many ways an unlikely candidate to lead the ÖVP. His ambition and dynamism were at odds with his party's traditional image and, as he was only thirty when he took on the party leadership, his youth was plain to see. The average age of an ÖVP MP was fifty-four. Moreover, many thought his radical ideas, which included calling for immigrants to be held in detention centres before reaching Europe and banning the foreign funding of mosques, were better suited to the anti-establishment NEOS party (Das Neue Österreich und Liberales Forum, or The New Austria and Liberal Forum).

By 2017, the ÖVP had been in government for fifty-five of the seventy-two years since the end of the Second World War, often as part of a grand coalition with the left-wing SPÖ. This era was known as 'Proporz', in which politicians were appointed to official positions in proportion to their party's level of electoral support. In the run-up to the 2017 general election, however, the 'Proporz' model had begun to fracture, with opinion polls from 2015 onwards suggesting a rise in support for the nationalist FPÖ as well as the smaller Green and NEOS parties. Not only did ideological differences within the incumbent ÖVP–SPÖ coalition lead to political gridlock but public discontent was worsened by a faltering economy and the complications of the 2015 immigration crisis.

The ÖVP fared worse than its senior coalition partner in opinion polls, as its right-leaning base began gravitating towards the more radical FPÖ. Established as a liberal nationalist party, the FPÖ had moved to the right after Jörg Haider became its leader in 1986. Haider's leadership attracted an influx of neo-Nazis into the FPÖ, which subsequently transformed into an ultranationalist party, espousing anti-immigrant and anti-Islam views. Like the threat posed to the Conservative Party in Britain by the UK Independence Party between 1999 and 2016 or the pressure exerted on the US Republican Party by the Tea Party movement from 2009 onwards, the FPÖ raised existential questions about the future of the ÖVP. When it overtook the ÖVP in opinion polls after 2015, it appeared to be in a strong position to win the 2017 general election.

The ÖVP realised that it must adapt or die and so turned to Kurz, the Foreign Minister. He had joined the party as a schoolboy in 2003 and then dropped out of the University of Vienna in order to dedicate himself to politics, becoming the leader of the ÖVP's youth wing and co-chair of the Viennese People's Party in 2009. He landed his first Cabinet post as Minister for Integration in 2010, when he was twenty-four. This gave him a platform on which to finesse his political skills, which he did by introducing policies to shake up the government's strategy for integrating immigrants. Among the reforms introduced on his watch were the closure of mosques linked to 'political Islam' and the demand that imams should deliver sermons in German rather than in Arabic.

Having been appointed Foreign Minister in 2013, he took a proactive role in negotiating the blockade of the 'Balkan route' amid the 2015 refugee crisis, which subsequently denied 1 million refugees access to Austria. Kurz also declined to embark on an open-border refugee policy, leading to a confrontation with the German Chancellor, Angela Merkel, who championed that policy. Despite criticisms of the perceived discriminatory nature of these positions, Kurz won admiration from many Austrians, who were fed up with government inaction towards mass immigration. The rank and file of the ÖVP saw a charisma in Kurz, which they felt had been lacking in his predecessor as party leader, 61-year-old Reinhold Mitterlehner.

Kurz understood the historical implications of assuming the reins of his party at such a young age and he wanted his colleagues and the general public to believe that his leadership would represent a break with the past. His ambitions were, accordingly, distilled into the slogan 'Time for Something New'. Rebranding is hardly unusual in politics – Tony Blair did it in the mid-1990s with the 'New Labour' moniker, while the conservative party in South Korea has changed its name four times in the past decade alone. What makes Kurz's overhaul of his party unlike these examples was how he did it and why his seemingly contradictory slogan worked.

Many politicians rely on teams of consultants when making strategic and marketing decisions, but Kurz formulated his slogan without taking any external advice. He professes a strong belief in politicians speaking their mind. 'The slogan perfectly captured the prevailing sentiment amongst the populace – it was the right slogan for that point in time,' he says. He knew that by 2015, there was a sense of disillusionment with the political establishment all over the EU, but in Austria specifically he recognised that the coalition between the SPÖ and ÖVP was no longer viable. 'Throughout the Second Republic [1955–present], Austria had been governed by a coalition dominated by the Socialists and the People's Party,' he explains.

> Despite consistently forming a coalition, the relationship between the socialists [SPÖ] and conservatives [ÖVP] was strained by the contrasting beliefs in how the country should develop. The longer this has lasted, the worse it's become and people began to show signs of frustration, especially in the last five years. So to summarise, it was a coalition of two old-fashioned parties, filled with old men who were blockading Austria's progress.

He believed the ÖVP urgently needed to reverse its stagnating electoral fortunes, having seemingly accepted its position as a second-tier party. 'Over the last thirty to forty years, the socialists were always leading and my party – the People's Party – was always in second place. I, along with many others, believed it was time for a fresh approach and a time for something new.'

That he devised the slogan personally reflects his conviction that he understood voters' concerns. Politicians often pitch themselves as the champions of everyday people, from democratic reformers like Taiwanese President Lee Teng-hui, who said he always acted 'with the people in my heart', to the murderous dictator Idi Amin, who once claimed (in seriousness), 'I am the voice of the African people, the defender of their rights.' Kurz's slogan did not merely acknowledge voters' worries, though. From a selfish perspective, it also acted as a smokescreen, allowing him to begin reforming his party internally in matters such as its candidate selection process and logo, while simultaneously giving the impression of wanting to change politics in his country – despite the fact that, ironically, he had little to offer in the way of new policies. Jörg Haider had done something similar when he had built up the FPÖ during his leadership of the party from 1986 to 2000. Haider had also been in his thirties when he first led his party, perhaps convincing Kurz that he could achieve similar success. Kurz knew that gaining such a high political position so early in life guaranteed a fascination in him, which, if harnessed correctly, could be converted into real power.

Like Haider, Kurz chose the word 'new' for his first election slogan. In 1986, Haider used the slogan 'A New Type of Politician'. Kurz, notably, inserted the word 'time' into his slogan too. Many well-known politicians have been able to run successfully on the ambiguous slogan 'It's Time', but Kurz was still trying to gain the widest possible recognition among the electorate at this point. By using the two words together, he gave his slogan an extra dimension. He calculated that in traditional conservative Austria, the public would be so taken aback by the slogan's antithetical nature – where the ÖVP had little connection to 'new' ideas – that the ensuing discussion could be used to attract media attention. Predictably enough, journalists and commentators did indeed soon begin to question what, exactly, was 'new' about the ÖVP under Kurz.

In doing so, they fulfilled his wishes. Kurz wanted to stir up a controversy around his words in order to give him a platform to explain what he was doing. One political consultant, Thomas Hofer, was typical of those who had taken the bait. 'The idea that a person whose party has been in government for thirty years could write "Time for Something New" on an election poster is bizarre,' he opined. Such scepticism was not without validity, for Kurz was felt by some to be guilty of pushing empty rhetoric. Yet from a publicity point of view, he was content. He and his party dominated the headlines without expending any great effort.

In fact, Kurz had deployed a similar tactic during a campaign in 2010, in which he lobbied for the Vienna U-Bahn to run overnight at weekends. He became the centre of attention by visiting a Viennese night club in a sleek black jeep, which he wittily called the *Geilomobil* (a double entendre, which could be translated as the 'cool' or 'horny' mobile). He also commissioned a series of advertisements featuring skimpily dressed models holding political slogans to promote this event. Not only was this visually provocative, but it was seen by some as clever. The slogan used was 'Black makes [you] cool/horny' (*Schwarz macht geil*) and was carefully thought out. The word 'black' was meant as a pun, representing his black *Geilomobil*, the darkness of the night and, separately, the ÖVP, which was known as the 'black party' for its trademark colour. The Viennese municipal government eventually adopted Kurz's idea, proving his strategy a success. 'That slogan showed that you should always stand for what you believe in and not be afraid to upset the status quo,' Kurz says.

Kurz has always claimed that during his political career, he never followed a strict strategy and, indeed, he has even said in at least one interview, 'I definitely never wanted to become a career politician.' His default setting was to project a sense of authenticity in his actions and speech, yet it is hard to accept that his success was simply some sort of fluke. With that said, his willingness to make such outlandish claims is precisely what made his approach so extraordinary. He dazzled the public with his youthful energy, flamboyant style and radical rebranding of the ÖVP. However, these characteristics were a facade that Kurz purposefully used to distract his audience. Although his slogan promised something 'new', the ÖVP relied heavily on traditional rather more than digital media for promotional purposes. His campaign stood out because he excelled at using conventional strategies to achieve his aims – other than in his choice of slogan.

Most politicians use slogans to complement their campaign. The slogan is the figurative icing on the cake. But for Kurz, the slogan was the cake itself. The campaign was built around the words 'Time for Something New' more than anything else. Kurz implemented this plan in five stages. First, he used the slogan to awaken the electorate. He admits to using this tactic as part of his overall strategy, saying that the slogan 'served as a rallying cry for those who shared our vision for a better Austria'. He wanted voters' desire for something new to be realised, a desire that was already evident from the FPÖ's lead in early pre-election polls. Once he had the electorate's attention and had begun persuading them that he could be that something new, he took them on a journey towards their desired goal. In 2017, so many parts of the world were moving in a fresh, more populist direction and there was a desire among the Austrian people to also move in that direction. This was the second stage of his election strategy and it was a crucial component, because he made it all about himself rather than the party.

Kurz was able to hark back to his time as the leader of the ÖVP's youth wing half a decade earlier, when he had embraced a risqué style that was in contrast to the ÖVP's public image as an old man's party, and to his tenure as Integration Minister, when he had embraced a hardline rhetoric on immigration from Muslim countries. These past actions allowed him to portray himself as genuine. Voters believed he would stick to his pledges to be more pro-business, more focused on the rule of law and tougher on migration because of his earlier political career.

This sense of trust allowed him to move forward with his desired reforms without upsetting the public. This, in turn, gave him more negotiating powers with ÖVP party elders, which marked the third stage of Kurz's strategy. He laid out seven conditions to the party's executive before agreeing to take over as leader in May 2017, including almost unrestricted powers to enact internal changes. The slogan formed part of Kurz's demands. These powers emboldened Kurz to speak with confidence about his transformation of the ÖVP, both internally and externally, as the slogan suggested.

Measurable action was the fourth stage of his election strategy, as he encouraged people from non-traditional backgrounds to become involved in conservative politics. 'We instantly made some statement initiatives, changing our system so that people could become candidates for the party even if they were not party members, increasing female candidates to 50 per cent and encouraging youth participation within the party,' he says. 'We also tried to get people with alternative backgrounds to politics involved, such as people from the business sector, universities, culture and science.'

These reforms proved that he was genuinely interested in pursuing a 'new' path, Kurz believes, and he remains convinced that they saved the ÖVP from its impending demise. 'Opening up the party to new voices and perspectives was instrumental,' he says. 'By allowing hundreds of thousands of people to participate in the political process, we demonstrated our commitment to inclusivity and innovation.'

The changes were certainly well reported in the media. Yet there is an argument that they said more about how Kurz wanted to be seen, rather than shedding light on what he was doing. Evidently, he cared deeply about his public image, with *Der Spiegel* typical in its description of him wearing a 'broad, boyish smile, tightly tailored suits and carefully gelled-back hair … as though he had just jumped out of the shower'. This public image was certainly part of Kurz's strategy and it formed part of the fifth stage of his campaign. His ultimate goal was to manipulate the media into becoming his public relations machine through misdirection or, as some would have it, clickbait. Kurz gave the media unprecedented access to his personal and public life during the campaign, allowing journalists to conduct interviews with him and inviting them to tag along on his foreign trips. This probably explains why his unilateral termination of the coalition with the SPÖ and call for a snap election was widely reported across the world, despite Austria's relative size and influence. Of particular interest was his alleged shift to the right, his youth and his provocative slogan. What went less reported was how little Kurz had changed the status quo he claimed to despise.

There is no doubt that he gave the ÖVP a facelift and encouraged more people of his age to join his party, but in fact most incumbent MPs stood for re-election, and by the time of the poll, the average

age of ÖVP MPs had only dropped from fifty-four to fifty-two. Similarly, despite Kurz stressing the importance of involving more women in his campaign, only 35 per cent of elected MPs were women in 2017.

Kurz knew it was essential that he didn't compromise himself by taking his own slogan too literally. Pushing the party too far in a progressive direction would have risked greater competition with the SPÖ and NEOS, the latter of which was already more age- and gender-diverse than the ÖVP. At the same time, a shift too far to the right to chase FPÖ voters could have alienated more moderate ÖVP supporters. Kurz had to try to create the biggest electoral impact with the least radical action possible by getting the media to help mask his true motives.

There is evidence to suggest that Austrians had grown increasingly mistrustful of the country's media, with research by Oxford University revealing that in 2017, pre-Kurz, only 48 per cent of the population trusted it. This meant that the more the media tried to catch the ironic and antithetical nature of Kurz's brand and slogan, the more intrigued by Kurz the public became. This allowed the word 'time' to shine, as it was the only part of the 'Time for Something New' slogan that was not clickbait. Instead, it was an appeal to the electorate to notice what Kurz was saying about renewing his party and the country more broadly, issuing an invitation to voters to join him if they agreed with his vision. The word also looped back to the first stage of his strategy, which was to awaken Austrian voters to their desire for 'something new'. Once a voter had gone through the cycle of Kurz's strategy, they became susceptible to his charm, which is more style than substance. Those whose policy inclinations were similar to the traditional outlook of the ÖVP were considered more likely to return to the fold, and those who were fundamentally opposed to the ÖVP were more likely to see Kurz as a serious challenger.

Kurz's plan certainly seemed to work. Thanks to his meticulous preparation during his time as a Cabinet minister, the ÖVP opened up a ten-point lead on the FPÖ in a poll commissioned by Austrian newspaper *Österreich* just days after he took charge of the party. The ÖVP continued to lead all major opinion polls and scored its first election victory since 2002, with 1.6 million votes (31.5 per cent) and sixty-two seats on the National Council, fifteen more than the previous election. The SPÖ slipped to second place with 1.4 million votes (26.9 per cent) and fifty-two seats, while the FPÖ captured 1.3 million votes (26 per cent) and fifty-one seats. It had led opinion polls until Kurz became ÖVP leader. The remaining eighteen seats were distributed among the liberal NEOS and left-populist PILZ, which displaced the environmentalist Greens and ousted them from Parliament. The ÖVP fell well short of the ninety-two seats needed to form a majority government, an outcome which Austria's proportional representation system ensured had only happened twice before, in the 1960s and 1970s. But, true to his word, Kurz broke away from the traditional SPÖ–ÖVP coalition and formed an alliance with the FPÖ, fulfilling Kurz's election promise of delivering 'something new'.

Public support for the new coalition government remained high in the months following the election, with the ÖVP's polling numbers consistently hovering above 35 per cent and Kurz's own approval rating reaching 60 per cent. This vindicated Kurz's use of the slogan 'Time for Something New' as his primary campaign strategy. The impact of the slogan appeared to prove the strength of his strategy, even when his government's reputation took a hammering following the Ibiza affair, a scandal in which the FPÖ leader Heinz-Christian Strache was filmed negotiating a deal with a journalist pretending to be a relative of a Russian oligarch to buy up influence in the Austrian press. Ultimately, this forced Kurz to call a snap election in 2019. In it, Kurz campaigned under a different slogan, 'Someone Who Speaks Our Language', which was, again, identical to one used in 1994 by Jörg Haider. Despite being the person who invited Strache and the FPÖ into his government, he survived the ordeal unscathed, increasing his vote share to 37.5 per cent (1.8 million votes) and winning seventy-one seats.

Substance and originality have never been the hallmarks of political slogans in Austria, which, like other Alpine democracies, is so stable that politics has tended to follow a fixed formula for decades. This sheds light on why Kurz's 'Time for Something New' attracted the attention it did in 2017. Rather than conforming to the somewhat stale political standard, he took his party in a new direction by using the word 'time' as a figurative line in the sand. As he has said, this separated him from the old ways and distinguished his slogan from the rigidity of past political messages.

The 'Time for Something New' slogan resonated especially well in the Austrian context due to its ability to capitalise on broad disappointment with the political establishment and an increasing appetite for change. The slogan enabled Kurz to present the ÖVP as a new alternative, despite its decades-long presence in government. By pairing two of the eight hit words, 'time' and 'new,' the slogan conveyed urgency and renewal, striking a chord predominately with younger voters and those disillusioned with the status quo. These words played a significant role in shifting public perception, as they cast the ÖVP not as a continuation of the old guard but as an implicit – but, crucially, not explicit – force for change. Without this slogan, the ÖVP would not have been able to distance itself from the political gridlock that had fuelled support for the far-right FPÖ. 'Time for Something New' resonated with the electorate, contributing directly to the party's rise from third place in the pre-election polls to first place on election day.

Had the ÖVP chosen a different slogan, one which failed to capture the desire for change among the electorate or appeared out of touch with the mood of the nation, the outcome of the 2017 election would likely have been radically different. A more defensive or traditionalist slogan, such as one emphasising stability or continuity, would only have reinforced the perception that the ÖVP was an old establishment party and scared off voters seeking a break from the past. 'Time for Something New' not only neutralised this threat but allowed the party to capture the dynamics of discontent, while still being positioned as a competent government party. This brings to the forefront again the greater thesis of this book: the right slogan, based on the right hit words, can be the deciding factor for the success of a campaign. For Kurz, the strategic use of 'time' was not a rhetorical trick – it was an essential part of his rebranding of the ÖVP and his electoral success.

Kurz was only the second person in Austria's post-war history to use 'time' in an election slogan, even though it is one of the most commonly used 'hit' words in political slogans around the world. Contrary to most western European democracies, continuity rather than originality has been the defining characteristic of Austrian politics for most of its post-war history. Though 'time' is not *the* most commonly used word in election slogans globally, it has had the highest rate of success, helping nearly half of those who have used it into elected office. Of course, using the word 'time' does not automatically translate into success, which hinges instead on the key questions of 'Who?', 'When?' and 'What?'

To date, the overwhelming majority of electoral victors using a 'time' slogan were in opposition (85 per cent) when they did so. The popularity of the word 'time' among opposition parties can be explained by its common use as a rallying call against existing candidates or parties, with the implication that it is now 'time' for someone else to take charge or for something new to happen. The 'time' slogan can help to boost a strong campaign for parties with a realistic prospect of forming a new government, with a success rate of 60 per cent among these parties. With that said, the word 'time' cannot create more opportunity for a candidate or party to build their brand. The word 'time' is a pre-journey slogan that merely boosts their existing chances. They must have sufficient political capital on which to build their campaign, whether via a dedicated following or thanks to abundant funding.

The Australian Labor Party (ALP) ran its 1972 general election campaign using the slogan 'It's Time' under these conditions and, ultimately, won. Key to this success was the unpopularity of the incumbent Liberal–Country coalition, which was struggling to deal with stagnant living conditions and growing discontent over the Vietnam War. The ALP won 49.6 per cent of the vote and sixty-seven seats in the House of Representatives – eight more than in the previous election in 1969. These gains were relatively modest compared with 1969, when the ALP's leader Gough Whitlam picked up eighteen new seats in the House, an achievement that was among his party's best performances in almost a decade. Whitlam ran that election on the theme of 'opportunity', promising better social policies to address inequalities in society. The 'It's Time' slogan was more of a supplement to Whitlam's 1969 campaign than a standalone success, aided by coloured film and a catchy song (also titled 'It's Time') sung by Patricia Amphlett.

The ALP was not alone in building a strong campaign against an unpopular incumbent around the slogan 'It's Time'. In 1972, the New Zealand Labour Party ran a similar campaign to its Australian counterpart and used an identical slogan, beating the National Party after fifteen years in opposition. In 1992, Bill Clinton used 'It's Time to Change America' as one of his slogans in the US presidential election, making him the first Democratic Party President to win the White House since 1976.

The same, however, cannot be said of smaller opposition parties with distant prospects of forming a government or joining a coalition. In Canada in 2011, the Green Party ran unsuccessfully on the slogan 'It's Time'. Despite the collapse of the Liberal Party, one of the two main parties in Canada, it was the larger, left-leaning New Democratic Party that saw its seat count jump from thirty-six to 103, allowing it to form the official opposition in the House of Commons for the first time. Although the Green Party did win its first seat in the Commons that year, its national vote share decreased by 2.9 per cent from the previous election. The problem for the Greens in Canada and other smaller parties around the world that have used the word 'time' in election slogans is that they never had a realistic or credible chance of winning an election, meaning that voters hardly listened to their calls for change. It might be 'time', but it isn't time for them.

This is not to say that the Greens can never win in Canada. For obvious reasons, the question of when to use a 'time' slogan is just as important as who uses one. Elections are won when voters agree that it is time for a particular candidate or party to take charge.

Parties and individuals cannot create the right moment for themselves unless they are already the recipient of the general public's affection. Those who take the political temperature accurately have won decisive victories on a 'time' slogan. For example, after a decade in opposition, the Christian Social People's Party (CSV) of Luxembourg won power in 2023 off the back of the slogan 'It's Time for a Change'. Although the CSV had to wait ten years for the right moment, it has taken far less time in other countries. Winston Churchill was returned to 10 Downing Street in 1951 under the slogan 'It's Time for a Change' after the Labour Party had been in government for only six years.

In Luxembourg, the CSV had spent a decade in opposition as the coalition led by the Democratic Party showed increasing signs of fatigue and fragmentation. Rising public concerns about housing affordability, economic inequality and political stagnation created a ripe environment for a message of renewal. The CSV's 'It's Time for a Change' slogan did more than suggest just a change of party in government – it tapped into a growing frustration with the status quo and offered a credible, centre-right alternative grounded in the party's past experience governing. Similarly, in post-war Britain, Winston Churchill's Conservatives reclaimed power in 1951 after six years of Labour government that, despite the establishment of the welfare state, had come to be associated with rationing and austerity. Churchill's return under the 'It's Time for a Change' banner worked because it signalled a shift from wartime-style management to post-war normalcy and economic revival – values that resonated with a war-weary electorate.

Similarly, Viktor Orbán led his Fidesz party to a supermajority in the Hungarian National Assembly in 2010 using the slogan 'It's Time' after eight years of Hungarian Socialist Party (MSZP) rule. Orbán might be considered a master of timing, given his understanding of the national mood at that point. The MSZP government's popularity had hit rock bottom after its former Prime Minister, Ferenc Gyurcsány, admitted during a private speech that he had lied in order to win the previous general election. Tens of thousands of Hungarians took to the streets in protest of this national insult. Orbán knew that he could capitalise on this catastrophic error. There was no need for him to add any supplementary words to his 'time' slogan because most Hungarians already knew him from his tenure as a conservative Prime Minister in the 1990s. With such a strong existing brand, voters understood what he meant by 'It's Time' and they showed their agreement at the ballot box. Orbán's success was akin to using the right equipment at the right time.

Conversely, some politicians have used the wrong tools at the wrong time. When a 'time' slogan fails, it is likely because the candidate or party using it has misjudged the electorate's readiness for change or lacked a compelling, trustworthy vision to replace what was being rejected. That was the mistake of Republican Party officials in America when their candidate, Thomas Dewey, challenged the incumbent Democratic Party President Franklin D. Roosevelt in the 1944 election using the slogan 'Time for a Change'. The US and its allies were on the brink of victory in the Second World War and Roosevelt's high approval ratings during a time of crisis gave voters little reason to seek a new leader or change direction. Roosevelt secured an unprecedented fourth term in office. Contrary to popular assumptions, the words 'time' and 'change' do not tend to complement each other well in elections, not least because the type of change being proposed can come across as vague and can have the effect of alarming voters. The human brain doesn't like change but can accept it if the change is known. When the change is abstract, it can mean anything and so the levels of uncertainty and fear are higher.

In 2019, British opposition leader Jeremy Corbyn made a similar misjudgement when he ran on the slogan 'It's Time for Real Change'. While Corbyn, a socialist, focused on socio-economic reforms, voters were far more concerned about Brexit – a subject that Corbyn largely chose to avoid. To make matters worse, he complemented his 'time' slogan with the word 'change', which, as discussed, can have the effect of alarming voters. In Corbyn's case, it served only to emphasise to Labour's opponents the extremity of the left-wing policies that he held dear and the perceived danger he posed to Britain. This combination of a weak brand image and unfavourable circumstances resulted in the Labour Party's worst defeat since 1935. The reasons the word 'time' failed Corbyn are the same reasons they have failed others who have not been elected on a 'time' slogan: he misunderstood the public mood and got his timing wrong. The supplementary word or phrase used in conjunction with the word 'time' – in Corbyn's case, 'real change' – is key. The wrong choice undermines a candidate's overall brand and is counterproductive. Incidentally, evidence from my election database strongly suggests there is a pattern to the use of the word 'time'. When it is used but isn't successful, it is because it has been deployed one election too soon, with the party that used it going on to win the subsequent election.

In this way, all is not lost after one electoral defeat. History shows there have been many comebacks. The word 'time' can assist both the emergence of a new brand in politics and the revival of an existing brand that has temporarily lost its appeal. The key to understanding this lies in the 'What?' element of the conditions dictating the efficacy of the use of 'time'. This word is a pre-journey slogan, meaning it can inspire voters to take a completely new journey or continue on an existing one in a new direction. Orbán is one example of a leader who used the slogan 'It's Time' to change course and chart a new journey in 2010. Whereas his premiership in the 1990s was based on his reputation as an anti-communist freedom fighter, by 2010 he had redefined himself as a defender of Hungary's national pride, who pledged to reverse years of socialist humiliation. 'Our revolution will be the election on 11 April,' he said during the campaign. 'A quick, striking change, the moment of truth. It will be a quick, predictable, constitutional change, but it will not take human sacrifices … It's time, Hungary; it's time, Hungarians!'

Although Orbán's victory foreshadowed the democratic backsliding he initiated after 2010, he was able to make his radical rhetoric of 'revolution' and 'change' acceptable to voters through his strong brand image as a trustworthy politician. In fact, his conservative coalition had only narrowly lost the previous election in 2006, with 42 per cent of the vote against the MSZP's 43.2 per cent. His 'It's Time' slogan in 2010 simply pushed his already-powerful campaign vehicle over the finish line.

A similar tactic was deployed by the Turkish President Recep Tayyip Erdoğan, one of Orbán's closest international allies. In 2023, Erdoğan launched his re-election campaign for President with the slogan 'Right Time, Right Man for the Century of Türkiye' after more than twenty years in power. With early opinion polls showing a statistical tie with the opposition candidate, Kemal Kılıçdaroğlu, Erdoğan faced the real prospect of losing an election for the first time in his career. He could not use 'time' as a rallying call for 'something new' in the way that Sebastian Kurz had done in Austria, but he cleverly disguised his tired brand by juxtaposing it against a new geopolitical reality. With the war in Ukraine by then jeopardising the global supply chain, Turkey's geographical position as the entry point to the Black Sea allowed Erdoğan to project its political prowess. Given his decades-long leadership and control over state media, many voters were happy to overlook his recent economic mishaps and lend him their trust again. He secured 52.18 per cent of the popular vote.

This rare success of a governing party winning re-election on a 'time' slogan shows that the potency of that word cannot be defined by either the 'Who?', 'When?' or 'What?' Opposition parties do not always win, and those running for re-election on this pre-journey word do not always lose – as long as there is purpose and a sound understanding of circumstance. This is what made Sebastian Kurz's success so unique among other examples of 'time' slogans around the world. Whereas in 2023 Erdoğan had the advantage of total control over the domestic press, in 2017 Kurz could build an entirely new brand on the slogan 'It's time for Something New' due to his mastery of the three conditions dictating the word 'time'.

Kurz recognised that voters had grown unhappy with the long-standing grand coalition between the ÖVP and SPÖ and were looking for an immediate solution in outsider parties like the FPÖ. He was able to begin his national political journey on a 'time' slogan because he embodied something 'new' – the cause he advocated. He was dynamic, charismatic and more photogenic than previous ÖVP leaders, allowing him to distinguish himself from the 'old'. This profile made his appeal to voters more compelling, as did the focus of his campaign on popular issues such as immigration. A strong body of anti-immigration opinion had already been formed and voters were prepared to abandon traditional parties in pursuit of an immediate solution. All Kurz had to do was present himself as a 'new' kind of leader and direct people's hopes to himself. Voters were willing to support him despite his party's tired brand because his slogan made sense as part of his political journey, which had begun almost a decade before in student politics. In his hands, the 'time' slogan was plausible.

If there are two words in this book that are polar opposites, they are 'time' and 'change'. Yet they are frequently thrown together and seen by those who use them as being complementary. Whereas 'change' is one of the most Machiavellian words in political campaigns because it is so rarely matched by public perception, 'time' is the most organic and least manufactured of all slogan words. Success through the use of a 'time' slogan cannot be engineered in the same way as any other word. Voters will rarely raise a point about it being 'time' in surveys or focus groups, and unlike words such as 'people' and 'better', time is neither a tangible object nor a descriptive characteristic. In other words, it is an unchanging constant. It either is or is not 'time'.

Declaring 'It's Time' can energise an electorate, but without evidence of why the moment is ripe for change, the slogan may fail. Voters want to see real urgency and a roadmap for how this call to action leads to concrete outcomes. However galvanising this word may seem, it cannot propel a candidate to victory on its own.

A 'time' slogan can be seen as the ultimate rallying call. The word has the power to inspire and unite voters around a particular cause by awaking their subconscious desires. The core characteristic of 'time' slogans is spontaneity, and they are ideal for those wishing to make immediate action the main theme of their campaign. The advantages of the word 'time' are its adaptability (it can be 'time' for many things), straightforwardness ('time' is possibly the least abstract slogan word) and authenticity ('time' sounds like a natural response). Its disadvantages are its dependence on circumstance (it either is time or it is not) and shallowness ('time' does not mean much on its own).

The word 'time' is similar to various time-related words describing the immediate term, such as 'now', 'moment' and 'today'. An action word or description typically follows the word 'time' in a slogan, with common examples being 'change', 'decision' and 'new'. The purpose of 'time' is to stress the need to implement the proposed action and rally voters to join in the effort.

Voters need to be convinced that it is the right time to take the proposed action, which can be a challenge due to the word's dependence on circumstance. With that said, given the right circumstances, almost anyone can be drawn to 'time' slogans when they are used by the right person. With these unique qualities in mind, there are four points that should be considered when it comes to the word 'time':

1. 'Time' is an organic slogan: its success cannot be engineered.
2. Get the timing right: 'time' is strongest against an unpopular incumbent or when voters are ready for a change of direction.
3. Consider supplementary words, especially if a politician or party's brand recognition is not universal: if voters need to be reminded what it's time for, the mood may well have been misjudged.
4. Use 'time' as a wake-up call: continue the journey with other slogan words.

Politicians must be able to tell instinctively whether it is the right moment to use the word 'time' as a rallying call. Given the uniqueness and volatility of national politics, there is no sure-fire way to know when it is best to deploy the word 'time', but slogans that include it are generally more effective when used by a popular opposition party against a weak incumbent. More rarely, sitting governments can also exploit the efficacy of the word 'time' when there is a strong desire among the electorate for something different, in which case 'time' can help revive an ageing brand. Sebastian Kurz, Viktor Orbán and Recep Tayyip Erdoğan are all examples of leaders who have understood timing and managed to rebrand themselves successfully with that word.

Even for a politician as well known as Erdoğan, however, 'time' is a very ambiguous word. Supplementary words like 'better' or 'new' are arguably more powerful. The importance of other words in a 'time' slogan demonstrates the importance of brand image. 'Time' itself can never be the brand. It would be best to think of 'time' slogans as the equivalent of an 'Up to 50 per cent off' sign plastered on the door of a shop. The sign can make people notice the shop, but they will only go inside if they are interested in the products that are being sold.

For this reason, 'time' slogans should only be used as a pre-journey wake-up call to rally voters to a certain cause. The word alone cannot take voters on a new journey or sustain one in the long-term, due to its lack of substance. Other words that form part of a larger brand image are capable of doing this. Examples of strong contenders for long-term slogan words include 'people' and 'new', which have been far more successfully used in this instance than 'time.' But that is not to say that the word 'time' is ineffective. It can be the most powerful slogan word when it is used at the right moment by the right people to represent the right occasion, but achieving this combination is notoriously tricky. This is the underlying lesson about 'time' slogans: politicians should only use them when they are certain that now is the time.

8

BETTER

For a few days in late April 1994, international attention fell almost exclusively upon South Africa. After decades of brutality, division and struggle, its first fully democratic general election was finally being held, ushering in a new era of multiracial government. Before this point, voting rights had been denied to its black majority population, which had been forced to exist under the racially discriminatory policy of apartheid, or 'separate development', since 1948. The introduction of universal suffrage marked a turning point in the history of this hopeful but complicated nation.

The election resulted in a clear victory for the African National Congress (ANC) led by Nelson Mandela, who had only recently been freed after twenty-seven years as the world's best-known political prisoner. Mandela's party secured 12.24 million votes, or 62.7 per cent of the total, which translated into 252 of the 400 available seats in the National Assembly. The assembly's first task was to elect its President, who is both the head of state and head of government. On 10 May 1994, Mandela, then aged seventy-five, was inaugurated as South Africa's first black leader. F. W. de Klerk of the National Party (NP), who had served as South Africa's President since 1989, became his deputy.

Mandela's triumph was remarkable for many reasons, not least that his ANC party had been officially banned until 1990. The four years of negotiations leading up to the election were fraught with tensions and violence. Mandela and de Klerk, whose personal relationship was sometimes strained, worked together to successfully dismantle apartheid, extend political freedoms and draw up a new liberal constitution in what was ultimately a peaceful process. Yet throughout this time, the country was bedevilled by disputes, demonstrations and attacks from both white extremists and black activists, so much so that there were even fears of a civil war. In 1993, they won jointly the Nobel Peace Prize for the reforms they implemented. But with such a huge weight of expectation on Mandela's shoulders, he faced enormous pressures. The bigger the margin of victory for him and the ANC, the louder the message would be internationally that South Africa had moved beyond apartheid. All of this meant that choosing the right election slogan in order to take as many members of the electorate with him on the march to a brighter future was enormously important.

To gain the trust of different groups of voters, unite the country and end the bloodshed, a simple message was required to convey a complex argument. What could be said to try to bond South Africa's people? The answer lay in the pledge Mandela made to his fellow citizens to make their lives 'better'. With this in mind, and regardless of anybody's age, race or social class, he settled on the electoral slogan 'A Better Life for All'. By ending racial oppression and mutual distrust, he hoped to cast off the shackles of the past so that all South Africans could live happier lives. This five-word campaign slogan was intended to help achieve the favourable conditions to which he aspired. It worked because it was genuine, encapsulating the benefits of political change while at the same time reflecting his personal fight as a lifelong activist. The idea was that just as Mandela's circumstances had improved, so would all of South Africa's under his presidency. At the heart of this slogan is a valuable lesson in political marketing: a slogan's proponent will, ideally, personify the meaning of the message they want to send to voters.

Rolihlahla Mandela was born in Umtata in the Eastern Cape in 1918. His father was a local chief in the Transkei region. A teacher at the first school he attended gave him the first name Nelson, though he was never told why. He qualified as a lawyer and set up the country's first black-run legal practice. He joined the ANC in 1944 and by the early 1950s had become prominent in a civil disobedience campaign against apartheid, leading to several spells in detention. After the ANC was outlawed in 1960, Mandela was instrumental in organising a three-day national strike, which led to his arrest and trial. In 1964, while in prison on other charges, he was found guilty of a catalogue of crimes including sabotage and treason and sentenced to life in prison. This gained him the status of a freedom fighter, first nationally and then internationally.

Mandela spent eighteen years incarcerated on Robben Island before being moved to the mainland. During his twenty-seven years as a prisoner, he refused to engage with the authorities, declaring that only free men can negotiate, and turned down offers of release because he would not compromise his political beliefs. From the 1970s onwards, major countries such as the US and the UK imposed sanctions on South Africa, partly as a result of the global 'Free Mandela' campaign, reducing the country to pariah status. Moves towards racial equality reform gathered pace throughout the 1980s under the presidency of P. W. Botha, who told Parliament in 1986 that the country had 'outgrown' apartheid. After Botha stepped down in 1989, his replacement, F. W. de Klerk, announced early in 1990 that he would repeal key apartheid laws, lift the ban on the ANC and begin releasing political prisoners, including Nelson Mandela. Mandela was freed on 11 February that year, setting in motion the end of three centuries of white rule in South Africa.

Mandela's call to create 'A Better Life for All' may in hindsight seem like an obvious slogan for him to have settled on in order to fulfil his political ambitions, but the journey towards choosing it was not entirely straightforward. It was not, in fact, his first choice of election slogan; nor was it much liked by his ANC colleagues, who resisted it. Initially, he was keen to use the altogether different 'Now Is the Time'.

The word 'Time' has been used so frequently by opposition parties all over the world over the past century that it has come to be seen as a somewhat hackneyed, if reliable, option. By 1990, 'Now Is the Time' had been the ANC's rallying cry for years, dating back to when it operated as an underground liberation movement calling for an end to apartheid and for the beginning of African majority rule over the country. Since February 1990, Mandela had used the phrase in several speeches, including one he gave on the day of his release in which he said, 'We have waited too long for our freedom. We can no longer wait. Now is the time to intensify the struggle on all fronts.' So why did he decide against adopting it for the 1994 general election? One of the primary reasons is that he was advised against doing so by two American political strategists, Frank Greer and Stanley Greenberg, who were drafted in to help his campaign.

On 2 February 1994, the general election was called by President F. W. de Klerk and political parties were given a specified time to register. By then, Mandela and the ANC had recruited Greer and Greenberg to work pro bono after reading an article in *Newsweek* about their involvement in President Bill Clinton's successful 1992 election campaign. Both men were affiliated with the National Democratic Institute (NDI), a non-profit, non-partisan American organisation that sends political consultants around the world to work on political campaigns, especially in emerging democracies such as Chile, where Greer had spent time in 1989 as the presidency of General Pinochet came to an end. Greenberg, meanwhile, had devoted much of his career to fighting apartheid.

The NDI had intended to send a bi-partisan delegation to South Africa, but some within the ANC were opposed to working with anybody who had links to the Republican Party. As Greer and Greenberg were Democratic Party supporters, they were welcomed. They ran a series of what were in effect 'democracy workshops', teaching South African politicians and parties about the democratic process and explaining basic practicalities to them such as how to cast a vote and what a polling station is. 'We did a several-day seminar for the leadership of twelve political parties, including the Pan-Africanist Congress,' remembers Greer. 'It was a fairly violent group. They had a slogan, "One Settler, One Bullet", and I never will forget I stood up and explained to them the philosophy of Thomas Jefferson and the founding fathers in terms of freedom of speech and respect for the rights of others to disagree.' Greer was taken aback by the force of the response he received. 'The crowd rose up and said, "What the hell! No way! We have a point of view and we're going to fight for it."'

Having completed their work, Greer and Greenberg were asked by Mandela to stay on and advise the ANC. They spent time with him over a period of months and one of the chief characteristics that struck them was his honesty. 'Mandela would say to us over and over again, "I've never been a candidate. I've been a leader of a liberation movement, I've been a leader of an anti-apartheid movement, but I've never been a candidate, and I want to learn how to be a candidate,"' remembers Greer. Yet Mandela knew that the 1994 general election was about more than mere victory. Something far greater was at stake. 'He did not want to just win,' Greer goes on. 'He really wanted to unite the country; he had the wisdom. I really give him amazing credit for not having been a political person but understanding the politics of inclusion as opposed to exclusion. He wanted to bring people together.'

Having conducted some early focus group research, Greer and Greenberg determined that the initial slogan 'Now Is the Time' ran the risk of being too divisive for many South Africans. Greer recalls that the slogan only 'resonated with the hardcore activists [of the] ANC' but did not have the same effect on anybody else because it sounded as if 'this is really going to be bad for me if I am not hardcore ANC'. Reassuring the 5 million-strong white community, which accounted for approximately 13 per cent of South Africa's population at that time, was crucial. Black Africans made up about 75 per cent of its 43 million-strong population, 'coloureds' (a legal term used to specifically denote this historically defined group of multiracial people who were neither white nor members of the black Bantu tribes) 9 per cent and those of Indian or Asian heritage about 2 per cent. Greenberg also recollects that he believed 'Now Is the Time' to be retrograde, as it had more to do with the ANC's past than its future. Moreover, by referring to apartheid even obliquely, Greenberg believed that the ANC risked walking into what he has called the National Party's 'trap'.

By the early 1990s, the National Party, which had been responsible for implementing apartheid in 1948 and had ruled South Africa ever since, had begun trying to rebrand itself as an organisation concerned with peace and prosperity. In keeping with these enlightened views, in March 1992, F. W. de Klerk held a whites-only referendum as a means of achieving a mandate for the end of apartheid. He was helped in this endeavour by the London-based advertising firm Saatchi & Saatchi, which had by then crafted many successful campaigns for the Conservative Party in Britain. In the plebiscite, de Klerk and his party secured 69 per cent of the vote. Soon afterwards, de Klerk cemented his place as a reformer by bringing to an end South Africa's nuclear weapons capacity. At the same time, the ANC stood accused of stoking racial tensions, all of which allowed the National Party to pick up support from some 'coloured' and Indian communities. Fearing that the ANC's vote share might slip below 50 per cent, Greer and Greenberg concluded that finding a fresh slogan was all the more urgent.

As somebody who describes himself as 'a believer that you need to have people be able to feel a part of the campaign,' Greer says he was instinctively drawn to slogans that promoted a sense of solidarity and kinship such as 'working together' and 'together we can'. Brevity was also paramount to him. 'One of the things we did was to talk about the fact that you needed a short and simple message to bring together diverse groups of people,' he remembers. He produced some examples of the sorts of slogan that he thought might work, most of which contained the catchword 'better'. They included 'A Better Day', 'A Better Future', 'Together, A Better Future' and 'A Better Life for All'. Of these, he thought that 'A Better Life for All' best represented Mandela's quest to unite his country and overcome its history of resentment, while also being sufficiently aspirational.

Notably, Greer considered using a slogan which included the word 'new', which was enjoying a burst of popularity both politically and commercially as the twenty-first century dawned. He decided against incorporating it in South Africa, however, because it was concluded that some South Africans, particularly white Afrikaners, might be resistant to any suggestion of a 'new' world or a 'new' order. Furthermore, Mandela's past ties to radical militant and communist elements in South Africa still spooked many of those who had governed during the apartheid regime. Promoting a 'new' way of doing things could have reawakened memories of his more ideological past. Added to this, the word 'better' was felt to have a more exact meaning than 'new', being more definitively positive and optimistic by comparison. It was hoped that this sense of precision might allow Mandela to dispel any doubts in the minds of his critics about his commitment to governing South Africa for all races.

Greenberg agreed with Greer, but to begin with, the ANC and Mandela were not convinced. In fact, Greer says they had to 'fight like hell' to make the case for the 'A Better Life for All' slogan. Mandela was, apparently, cautious about accepting any form of words that might alienate devoted ANC supporters, and he was insistent that any proposals had to acknowledge his reservations. There were, however, three factors about the 1994 general election that Mandela could not ignore, each of which would have a bearing on his final choice of campaign slogan.

The first factor was that this was the maiden election to be held in South Africa that would take place under universal suffrage. This meant, obviously, that it would be the first time that millions of South Africans would cast a vote. In contrast to the parties that had existed under the apartheid regime, therefore, Mandela had to win over many new voters, who had previously had little or no engagement with politics.

The second factor related to F. W. de Klerk. He, not Mandela, was the politician who had personally called for an end to the apartheid regime and for democratic elections to take place. By doing so, he had won the National Party some credibility, particularly internationally. It was felt that the subsequent boost to his profile had improved the National Party's standing more broadly.

Finally, Mandela had to contend with the fact that many white Afrikaners did not trust the African majority and were wary, at best, of the prospect of a black-majority government. Some of them regarded Mandela as a communist terrorist, the Communist Party having been a staunch ally of the ANC for decades. By the same token, large numbers of black South Africans were inherently distrustful of the white minority. These tensions were, seemingly, unresolvable. Yet Mandela knew that he needed to keep the leaders of the apartheid regime onside. If he lost their trust, his victory would lose legitimacy and the military might even crush this delicate democratic experiment.

Everybody in the Mandela camp understood these risks, but scepticism over the effectiveness of 'A Better Life for All' remained. As a result, Greer and Greenberg turned to research in a bid to lessen Mandela's worries and prove to the ANC that it was in its interests to switch to the new slogan. Their approach was vastly different to the ANC's. For one thing, their surveys and focus groups were more comprehensive, involving all South Africans: members of the black African community, the white community, the 'coloured' community and voters who were of Indian heritage. Greer says that the goal was to ensure that the slogan would appeal 'not just to the communities that we wanted to reach' but also to those who needed to be set at ease. 'We did a lot of research on "A Better Life for All" and Nelson Mandela sat in on some focus groups in Durban and places like that,' Greer says. 'We wanted to reassure the white community that this wasn't going to be a negative thing for them necessarily, but we also did focus groups on the hardcore ANC.' The focus groups were all-inclusive and were intended to ensure that 'A Better Life for All' would live up to those expectations.

Greer and Greenberg found that all South Africans, regardless of class or race, were receptive to the new slogan. Most encouragingly for the ANC, the African community that was sampled was not only open to the new slogan but its members seemed to like it more than other groups did. Greenberg understood that slogans matter not because of what a politician says and means, but because of what people hear and perceive. When black Africans heard 'Now Is the Time', it embodied their historical plight to such a degree that some apparently took it to mean 'Now is *Our* Time', regarding it as a motivating call to rise up against racial oppression and take back control of their land. By contrast, whites and other minorities heard something negative. White Afrikaners were especially frosty towards 'Now Is the Time', believing it to mean that it was no longer their time.

Conversely, 'A Better Life' was taken by black communities as representing the possibility of greater freedom and rights for non-whites, as well as access to quality education and employment. To white Afrikaners, the idea of a 'better life' was suggestive of a peaceful co-existence with the African community and a future free from fear of retribution or expulsion from the country. In short, all of their research suggested that the slogan's essence had the largest appeal. It did what all good slogans do: it did not exclude anybody, inviting everyone to join in creating a brighter future. Having received the reassurance that he had sought and having been convinced that 'A Better Life for All' had the ability to offer all groups who heard it a sense of optimism, Mandela accepted it as the main slogan for his 1994 election campaign.

Everybody in Mandela's camp knew that broadening the ANC's

appeal beyond its dedicated activist base and winning the election with a clear majority of votes was essential to South Africa's future prospects. Furthermore, Mandela wanted to project a positive mood internationally. Such was the goodwill of governments around the world towards South Africa at the time, they wanted to reflect that sense of hope back onto him and his countrymen. The slogan 'A Better Life for All' was an essential part of that outlook. Yet initially there was also little agreement over the campaign strategy. How would Mandela interact with voters? How should he and the ANC more generally make themselves heard in public? And, most importantly, what should be the undertone of the campaign's messaging?

Traditionally, South Africa's politicians had relied on a top-down approach. Yet, having attended some ANC rallies, Greer and Greenberg argued that in this new democratic age, the rallies were as likely to drive voters away as they were to attract them. Greer says he believed strongly in showing the 'politics of aspiration and inspiration'. He and Greenberg again recommended that the grassroots should be consulted through methodological research, which could be used to inform Mandela's campaign strategy. Greer was acutely aware of how voters perceived Mandela and he stressed the importance of including people 'so that they felt as though they were a part of the campaign'. As a pollster, Greenberg was especially skilled in modern research techniques such as empirical polling and focus groups. He thought that Mandela's campaign should target certain groups of undecided voters.

As had been the case when Greer suggested changing the campaign's slogan from 'Now Is the Time' to 'A Better Life for All', many ANC officials were sceptical of this bottom-up approach and did not see the need to pay heed to research findings. Yet like many of South Africa's political parties, the ANC was, as Greer puts it, used to being a liberation movement and well versed in being in opposition but was 'totally unprepared for what an election was'. Once again, Mandela's influence was pivotal in determining how to proceed. He took a different position from his ANC colleagues. Greer and Greenberg, plus other consultants who worked on the campaign, credited him with changing the way the party operated and presented itself to the public. Greer remembers clearly how determined Mandela was to steer the ANC away from what he calls 'the politics of resentment' towards something positive. 'Mandela knew that if he was going to be successful it was not just [about] winning the votes or the seats in Parliament; it was also trying to have something that would bring the country together,' he says. 'He felt he had a responsibility to play the role of uniter and that's where it really started.'

Mandela's moral conviction and personal philosophy became the basis of his strategic approach, which remained fiercely loyal to the interests of the ANC while being open to new ways of dealing with public relations and advertising. His willingness to embrace new techniques caused surprise, given that most people believed the ANC would pull off an easy victory and Mandela would most likely become President anyway. Yet others were less sure, partly because of the National Party's rebranding exercise. Greenberg noted later that de Klerk's National Party began to attract support from the non-African minorities, who feared the ANC's radical roots as a pan-African liberation movement. Greenberg even found that de Klerk was three times more trusted than Mandela among the 'coloured' community in Western Cape province. The conflicts between African voters muddied the waters further, as the ANC struggled to expand support in areas such as KwaZulu-Natal province, where the Inthaka Freedom Party was polling strongly. Even among the ANC's sympathisers, Greenberg's focus groups found uncertainty as to whether the ANC could deliver on the 'better life' it promised through its new slogan.

Although Mandela knew at the turn of 1994 what he had to do to win, his path to victory was far from certain. He summarised the hurdles he faced in a note that year. The seven points in it read:

1. Share developments in democratic forces.
2. Our problem is to face the very 1st democratic elections with 17 million voters who have never voted before.
3. Illiteracy rate of 67% and 63% of our voters are rural based.
4. Our problem is how to access people and introduce voters to education on how to vote.
5. We are contesting this election with the NP [National Party] which has already 150 election officers. We have none save our regional offices.
6. NP is one of the most efficient and well-organised political parties in the country.
7. Enjoy mass support – opinion polls indicate that we would emerge as a majority party. But decisive thing is to be able to carry to the voting booth.

The level of self-awareness in the note reflects Mandela's determination to transform himself and the ANC into a governing party in waiting. As such, Greer and Greenberg had the opportunity to implement their election strategy, albeit within parameters that were acceptable to the ANC. They managed to overcome these obstacles through empirical evidence from polling and focus groups, which satisfied Mandela and the ANC. While Greenberg focused on targeting the right demographic with the right message to boost support for Mandela, Greer says that what was crucial to Mandela's success was the fact that he had 'the philosophy and the heart and the instincts in terms of what was needed at a very difficult time in South Africa'.

Greenberg assigned three stages to his strategy: consolidation, contrast and reassurance. Consolidating support for Mandela meant convincing voters of the seriousness of his plan. The contrast phase would distinguish Mandela's campaign from de Klerk's via sharp attacks on the National Party. Reassurance would come about by assuaging people's doubts and fears through promoting the politics of inclusion and several public appearances by Mandela.

To consolidate support for Mandela and the ANC, Greenberg spent time with undecided voters who had already been vocal about their concerns for the future, such as rural African women and Zulu men. Comments expressed in these focus group sessions were then used in promotional material. Most advertisements focused on three themes: education, employment and race relations. The first two categories were particularly important to African voters. Non-Africans were likely to be more concerned about the latter, particularly white Afrikaners who feared retribution from the African majority. It was hoped that Mandela's slogan would address each of these points.

During the election campaign, 'A Better Life for All' featured prominently around the country on television, on the radio, in newspapers, on billboards and on hats. Once the idea it proposed had been spread via advertising, Mandela's campaign next had to find a way to convince voters why life under him would be preferable to life under de Klerk. This was the contrast phase. Greenberg and Greer made a point of advising Mandela not to launch personal attacks on de Klerk's status as an apartheid-era leader, believing it might be counterproductive and increase de Klerk's support. Any condemnation should instead concern policy, specifically education and employment.

Finally, to reassure voters, Greer guaranteed that Mandela's promotion of the politics of inclusion differed from de Klerk's divide-and-rule tactic, which involved driving non-African voters away from the ANC by suggesting that it posed a threat to their interests. Another way of reassuring voters would come through Mandela's public appearances at so-called People's Forums. This idea, designed to give him the opportunity to forge a stronger relationship with voters, was inspired by Greer's and Greenberg's involvement in Bill Clinton's town hall meetings. Mandela apparently attended at least three People's Forums per day, coming into contact with vast numbers of people in the process. This allowed him to improve his brand image and conduct politics in a new, more personal way than had previously been the case in South Africa. The lack of formality also allowed him to demonstrate his spontaneous wit and personal kindness. Through this positive and methodological campaign strategy, Mandela was able to offer his own interpretation of the word 'better' and convince voters of his authenticity, with help from his strong personal brand. It was important for him to maintain control of the narrative in this election, given how high the stakes were.

It is worth pointing out that despite the best efforts of de Klerk and the National Party's advisers, their election tactics fell short almost certainly because they failed to convince enough voters of the party's transformation into a moderate conservative organisation. De Klerk had significant resources to call on, not least Saatchi & Saatchi and the tacit support of the former British Prime Minister Margaret Thatcher, who arranged for some of her former aides, including Tim Bell, to help him. One of de Klerk's biggest shortcomings appears to have been the limited impact of his own election slogans, which were focused either on the transformation of his party or on attacking the past radicalism of the ANC. Some slogans he used were 'Vote for F. W. de Klerk and the new National Party', 'Only the NP can stop the ANC' and 'Stop Communism, Stop the ANC'. Another slogan, 'Be Sure of a Better Life', was a direct challenge to Mandela's declaration of 'A Better Life for All'.

The common theme that de Klerk's various slogans shared was that voters should stick with the government they already had. They warned voters of the potential dangers of an untested ANC government. This was representative of Saatchi & Saatchi's style of negative political advertising. It had worked well in Britain, specifically in 1978 when the agency had produced the 'Labour Isn't Working' advertising campaign, which helped propel Margaret Thatcher's Conservatives to office the following year. In 1990s South Africa, however, the sheer sense of optimism that Mandela brought to the proceedings countered most people's concerns. Some felt that Saatchi & Saatchi's negative campaigning style in South Africa looked outdated by 1994. It certainly misjudged the mood of the country, as would happen three years later in Britain when the agency unveiled its 'New Labour, New Danger' campaign (see Chapter 6). This slogan was set against a doctored photograph of the Labour Party leader Tony Blair, whose eyes had been replaced by a cartoonish pair of 'demon eyes'. The slogan failed and Labour went on to win the 1997 election by a landslide.

Less than two weeks before the polls opened, Mandela and de Klerk took part in a TV debate in Johannesburg, which de Klerk had challenged his opponent to several months previously. Mandela, who was seventeen years older than de Klerk, surprised many with the energy he displayed in the seventy-minute verbal joust. According to Bob Drogin, who covered the event for the *Los Angeles Times*, 'Mandela, in particular, dropped his usually aloof demeanour to lash out with personal attacks and bitter hostility at the white president who freed him from 27 years in prison in 1990 … De Klerk, 58, who is usually the more lively speaker, was repeatedly put on the defensive.'

Frank Greer, who was in the studio watching, remembers:

We encouraged [Mandela] to debate de Klerk. We, of course, cautioned him about being too strident … and he, of course, could not resist going after de Klerk. I was sitting in the studio thinking, 'Oh my God…' and then at the end of it he leaned across and shook de Klerk's hand and said, 'We can work together,' and he brought it all back. He was carrying the torch for what had been terrible about apartheid and how much people had suffered. But he did not practise the politics of resentment. He did practise the 'We're going to change things because it's been a terrible experience to live under apartheid, but we're going to do it in a way that is un-threatening to average people who are white or coloured'. It was a way to unify the country.

Although the ANC won the 1994 election convincingly, it did not secure the requisite two-thirds of all 22.7 million votes that would allow it to change South Africa's constitution. By the same token, de Klerk's National Party performed better than the country's demographics might have suggested it would, particularly under the circumstances, notching up just under 4 million ballots, or 20.4 per cent of the vote, enough to earn it eighty-two out of a possible 400 seats in the National Assembly.

Choosing the slogan 'A Better Life for All' was not just a marketing choice but a strategic decision that took into account the specific context of South Africa's first democratic election. Mandela's American campaign advisers understood that the original slogan was going to alienate white South Africans worried about retribution. 'A Better Life for All', however, was vague and aspirational and deliberately wide enough to appeal to a racially and class-divided electorate. The hit word 'better' was the thread that stitched the campaign together, promising improvement without attacking any group. Without it, the ANC's message could easily have been perceived to be too divisive or exclusionary and would have cast doubt on a narrative that indicated South Africa's definitive break with apartheid. The choice of 'better' was crucial – it offered hope without exclusion, a critical factor in securing 62.7 per cent of the vote.

The year 1994 was the first and last time that Nelson Mandela ran in an election. He served one term as President, stepping down in 1999, at which point the new ANC leader Thabo Mbeki was elected as his successor. The party has remained in power since then, though in June 2024 it lost its majority for the first time in thirty years. Although Mandela's presidency ended in the twentieth century, his 'Better Life for All' slogan survived in South African politics well into the twenty-first century. Indeed, the ANC and various other parties have recycled it frequently, no doubt mindful that it calls Mandela to the minds of many voters. Arguably, though, these outings have been misguided, merely serving to acknowledge that the much promised 'better life' has not so far been delivered. It is also true that every time a politician uses this phrase, they succeed in little more than confirming to the public that they are not Nelson Mandela.

The word 'better' has featured in political slogans in South Africa on more than a dozen occasions since 1994. The ANC has used it most often, featuring it in every election slogan between 1994 and 2011. Three of these slogans were verbatim copies of Mandela's original four-worded phrase. The sole exception was 'Together we can build better communities', which was used in the 2011 election. The ANC has also used the word 'together' in its slogans, mirroring the 'all' in 'A Better Life for All'. In this way, the party has continued to distance itself from its roots as a movement for black nationalists and present itself as a multiracial party. Several minor parties have also adopted the word 'better', including the Congress of the People, United Democratic Movement, African Independence Congress and the African Transformation Movement. Meanwhile, the main opposition party, the Democratic Alliance, and its predecessors have used the word 'better' twice since 1994.

Yet this strategy has been far from effective, for the ANC has largely been unable to keep its promise to make the lives of all South Africans better. The socio-economic divides in the country are still largely split along racial lines and many cities remain physically segregated. The ANC has made some strides in improving education, with the country having achieved a historically high literacy rate of 90 per cent in 2020. The average in sub-Saharan Africa is 68 per cent. But rates of those enrolled in tertiary education remain low, with only 27 per cent of all South Africans having received any form of post-secondary education in 2019. National economic indices are not any more encouraging. South Africa's GDP-per-capita growth has stalled since 2011, standing at $6,766.50 in 2023, down from the historic peak of $8,737.00 in 2011. The unemployment rate is also high, hitting 33 per cent in 2023 and rising to 61 per cent among 15–24-year-olds. As a result of its lacklustre economy, crime has soared since the ANC first took power. Nationally, the homicide rate rose to a twenty-year record high between 2022 and 2023, at forty-five murders per 100,000 people. All the while, the ANC has been beset by a series of corruption scandals, especially between 2009 and 2018 when Jacob Zuma was President. All this might help to explain why voter turnout has fallen markedly since Mandela's famous victory. In 1994 it was 86.87 per cent – a figure that had plummeted to 66.05 per cent in 2019.

Frank Greer believes that the 'Better Life for All' slogan ultimately failed for the ANC because Mandela's successors did not represent the spirit of those words, something which is a predictor of the chances of success of any election slogan. He believes that Mandela's immediate successor, Thabo Mbeki, was 'problematic', while his successor, Zuma, was the 'antithesis of "A Better Life for All"'. Greer adds, 'If the slogan doesn't fit the candidate, it's not going to keep working!'

In retrospect, it does not seem unreasonable to suggest that the 'better life' slogan worked for Mandela alone because he was a one-off. Nobody else could use the slogan and claim, in the same way as he did, that they wanted to improve the lives of others as the father figure of a nation reborn. This shows the pitfalls of simply copying a slogan. In 1994, 'A Better Life for All' was the right slogan used at the right time with the perfect brand ambassador behind it. It is hard to see that such conditions will ever exist in South Africa again.

The only leader that Greer thinks has managed to come close to symbolising the qualities of Mandela's slogan was Cyril Ramaphosa, the current ANC leader and incumbent President of South Africa, though for internal political reasons even he has not been able to reach his potential. 'Ramaphosa was very much like Mandela,' says Greer. 'He would have been the embodiment of "A Better Life for All" but the ANC went a different path.' Although Ramaphosa became President in 2018, the ANC's rhetoric has since then shifted back to the era of 'Now Is the Time', particularly in the face of the electoral threat from the hard-left, populist Economic Freedom Fighters party.

During Mandela's victory speech in May 1994, he made reference to the slogan, saying, 'This [a better life for all] means creating jobs, building houses, providing education and bringing peace and security for all.' Greer maintains that every word of the slogan he created for Mandela was necessary to its success. 'I think all of those words are equally important,' he says. 'I don't think you can have "for all" without "a better life" and you couldn't have "a better life" if you weren't talking about "for all", so every part of the slogan was essential to the core of that campaign.'

Nelson Mandela could have chosen any number of slogans or phrases in his attempt to become South Africa's first black President, but 'A Better Life for All' reflected his commitment to unity and reconciliation. This was a slogan that had to do a lot of heavy lifting by bringing together various groups, all with diametrically different interests and experiences. Very few other slogans would have worked in South Africa at that time. Most other words would have divided the population and would likely have caused irresponsible elements within their groups to be violent. Even if he had used a word like 'new', which in other countries would be considered a safe and aspirational word, in South Africa it could have caused violence by stoking fears within the white community. 'Time' and 'change' carried the same risks. 'Better' is the only non-aggressive aspirational word that could have worked in allowing both sides to envisage a future South Africa in which they could thrive. This provides a vivid illustration of why so many of the same words are used in slogans all over the word. Seemingly abstract words are used to unite disparate voting groups without exposing their differences. Slogans can reveal much about how their advocates are seen or how they want to be seen – or how they feel. In Mandela's case, he knew that no good would come of showing even a hint of bitterness for the policy that led to his incarceration for twenty-seven years, and as a result, he showed none. His willingness to proactively engage with voters and to take a new approach to politics was essential to the slogan's success. It was also key to his historic victory.

The word 'better' has been used often in the history of political slogans. It has appeared no fewer than 700 times in the past 100 years, from election campaigns in emerging democracies like Estonia to more established political systems such as those of the US, the UK and Ireland. There is no doubt that people are instinctively drawn to the positivity and optimism that this word radiates. The 'politics of aspiration', as Frank Greer calls it, usually appeals to anybody facing hardship, which is why so many parties worldwide – notably Joe Biden and the Democratic Party – employed the phrase 'Build Back Better', or something close to it, in the aftermath of the Covid-19 pandemic. This may also explain why the word 'better' is more popular in countries with a younger democratic system and a less-developed economy.

Yet socio-economic patterns alone do not determine the success of the word 'better' in any given slogan. The strength of a brand and the electorate's faith in that brand's ability to deliver their vision of things being 'better' are more important factors than any circumstantial influences on a campaign. It is also the case that politicians who misapply the word 'better' are almost always found out.

One of the earliest mainstream appearances of the word 'better' in an election slogan came in Britain during the general election of October 1931, when it was used twice by the coalition National

Government, led by Ramsay MacDonald. 'Better Punch in Than Be Knocked Out by the Foreigner. Vote for the National Government' was the first of these. The context of this slogan is rooted in the political, economic and social turmoil of the time, particularly the economic crisis following the Great Depression and concerns about Britain's position in international trade and politics. The second was 'Boom Along to Better Times. Vote for the National Government'. This slogan was deliberately optimistic and dynamic, evoking economic vitality and national pride. It suggested that voters could trust the National Government to lead Britain to prosperity.

Subsequently, both main UK parties used it regularly in the latter half of the twentieth century. The Conservatives used it to the greatest effect, winning the 1959 election under the slogan 'Life is Better With the Conservatives, Don't Let Labour Ruin it' and the 1970 election, when Ted Heath won a surprise victory, under the slogans 'Better Off With the Conservatives' and 'A Better Tomorrow'. Margaret Thatcher's first victory in 1979 was won using 'Don't Just Hope for a Better Life, Vote for One'.

The Labour Party, meanwhile, used 'A Better Tomorrow' in 1950 under Clement Attlee. The word was later revived in 1979 under the Labour leader James Callaghan, when the party opted for 'The Labour Way is the Better Way' before Tony Blair adopted 'Britain Deserves Better' as part of his New Labour rebranding exercise in 1997. The Labour Party last used 'better' during the 2015 general election, claiming that under its leader Ed Miliband, 'Britain Can Be Better'. The Labour Party have used the word 'better' more extensively than any other British party in the past 100 years, but its electoral success when it has done so have been mixed. It lost in 1950, 1979 and 2015 but won in 1997.

Labour's 1979 slogan 'The Labour Way is the Better Way' failed largely because it lacked credibility in the face of widespread public frustration following the Winter of Discontent. With strikes crippling services and economic turmoil dominating headlines, voters struggled to reconcile their lived experience with Labour's vague promise of a 'better way'. The party failed to articulate what 'better' actually meant and in a climate where trust in Labour's competence had eroded, the slogan of improvement under Labour rang hollow. In contrast, Margaret Thatcher's message of decisive action offered a clearer and more compelling alternative. Her slogan 'Don't Just Hope for a Better Life, Vote for One' placed a heavy emphasis on her credibility and her ability to deliver a better life for voters. Her use of the word 'better' was framed in emotionally resonant terms. It was direct, action-oriented and tied to a clear vision of economic stability, an end to union strikes and lower taxes.

Labour appears to have succeeded with the word 'better' only when it could clearly define what it meant by 'better', though in 1997 the slogan possibly reflected the electorate's frustrations with the Conservative government, which had been in power for the previous eighteen years and was widely perceived to be a spent force.

Slogans whose meaning cannot be explained with ease run the risk of morphing into meaningless jargon. Nowhere is this clearer than in North Macedonia, which gained its independence in 1991. Somewhat bizarrely, the word 'better' – usually in the slogan 'For a Better Life' – has been used repeatedly by both major parties in this small Balkan state since the 2006 general election. Nikola Gruevski of the VMRO-DPMNE party popularised the phrase 'For a Better Life' when he first used it successfully that year to support his campaign against the incumbent Social Democratic Union of Macedonia Party (SDSM), achieving a majority in the Macedonian Assembly. The slogan then became an integral part of Gruevski's political brand, cropping up in speeches, in advertisements and even in election manifestos. The phrase 'a better life' was repeated five times in the party's 2011 manifesto.

Ironically, another politician, Zoran Zaev of the SDSM party, then used the same slogan to bring down Gruevski's government in the 2016 general election. His interpretation of 'better' was the polar opposite of Gruevski's. For Zaev, 'a better life' meant a country that was free from corruption and that had better relations with Macedonia's neighbours. After winning the election, Zaev used 'For a Better Life' to promote his policies just as Gruevski had done, also repeating the phrase in speeches, advertisements and party manifestos. By 2020, 'For a Better Life' had become such a recognisable part of Zaev's brand that he used the slogan during that year's general election campaign. Farcically, however, the VMRO-DPMNE party did not surrender its claim to the slogan and Gruevski's successor, Hristijan Mickoski, made it an integral part of his campaign. Both parties therefore ran on an identical slogan. The election resulted in a coalition between the SDSM and the VMRO-DPMNE, and at the time of writing, both parties continue to use it.

'Better' is the ultimate utopian slogan word. It has the power to stimulate the suppressed emotions of voters who are aspiring for a brighter future by giving them a sense of hope. The core characteristic of 'better' slogans is inspiration, and they are ideal for those wishing to make advancement the main theme of their campaign. The advantages of the word 'better' are its positivity, universality (everyone wants things to improve) and status as a unifying force ('better' provides a neutral ground on which foes can come to an agreement). The disadvantages of it are its high expectations (voters expect tangible improvement soon) and impossibility (things never get continually better).

The word 'better' is similar to 'brighter', which is its identical twin and is frequently used interchangeably in reference to the state of the country or the collective future of its citizens. As such, it is commonly paired with words such as 'future', 'life', 'tomorrow' or the name of a country in a slogan. It is also used in a comparative context to show that a certain politician or party is better than another, in which case it is often paired with the word 'strong'. This pairing is ironic because the two words could not be more different. 'Better' implies a greater sense of hope and optimism than 'strong'. 'Better' slogans thrive on voters' beliefs that politicians can deliver their promise of betterment. Voters need to be convinced that 'better' slogans are not just idealistic wishes but a real programme that can be achieved, even if the details of said programme are vague.

For 'better' slogans to make an impact in an election, politicians need to understand four key points about the word 'better' in a political context:

1. 'Better' is an adjective with an antonym ('worse').
2. Better is an inherently good form of change.
3. Making something better takes a lot of time.
4. Nothing can consistently improve and get 'better' forever.

An upbeat strategy is the key to harnessing the strength of 'better' slogans. A politician's ability to influence outlook is everything when they deploy this kind of slogan. Voters cannot feel inspired if they are not thinking positively, and they will not be convinced that their situation can get better if they are not inspired by the politician.

'A Better Life for All' is a perfect example of a utopian 'better' slogan that demonstrates a good understanding of these lessons. As a long-standing anti-apartheid activist, Nelson Mandela was a celebrated hero in the eyes of many black South Africans before he entered politics. His ability to forgive those who imprisoned him made him the perfect candidate to embody a vision of a peaceful South Africa. His use of the 'better' slogan reinforced this notion in his 1994 election campaign, at a time when South African voters were desperately seeking a way out of an imminent outbreak of racial violence. His promise of a racially united South Africa, as well as his conciliatory attitude, convinced enough voters that he could turn his utopian vision into a reality.

Ironically, 'better' slogans are utopian for the very reason that makes the word so enticing. As in life, everyone wants to see their own circumstances improve, but there are always setbacks along the way. Politics is the same: the economy, standards of living and other social issues cannot consistently get 'better' as planned. These unexpected setbacks are attributed to the politician or party that made the initial promise, leading to disillusionment.

Evoking a 'better' future can be inspiring, but the word alone does not guarantee success and will not automatically transform a campaign into a winning force. Voters expect concrete proposals, credible leadership and proven ability to deliver improvement to their lives. Merely promising 'better' without a clear plan or genuine conviction rings hollow. In the end, no matter how appealing this term may be, a slogan is never a substitute for a solid, well-communicated platform.

The ANC, SDSM and others suffered from this problem when they overpromised their ability to deliver a 'better' future, leading to the long-term decline of their brand. Their lack of a clear vision and constant repetition of 'better' slogans only further reinforced the notion of failure. If politicians are able to avoid these pitfalls and learn the right lessons from Mandela's experience, then they might just succeed in standing on a 'better' slogan.

CONCLUSION

FUTURE

What does the future hold for political campaigns and slogans? Today, most voters are less politically engaged and desperate politicians are turning to new tools such as social media and artificial intelligence to try to connect with them. In future, will the eight 'hit' words featured in this book still have the power to change the world? In this concluding chapter, I will pose some questions about the prospects for political sloganeering as this century progresses and examine some possible answers.

'Future' is not one of the most-used words in the lexicon of political slogans and comes some way behind the eight words featured in this book that have shaped modern politics. But 'future' is much more than an also-ran in this contest. It could also be considered an all-encompassing summation of every slogan used in this book.

Every election campaign is essentially about trying to sell a future that a politician promises a country, even if they don't use the f-word explicitly. They might speak of 'change', or something 'new', or society being 'together', but what they are really talking about is 'tomorrow'. They want to conjure up a vision of an improved future, even if the language they use, as in Donald Trump's 'Make America

Great Again', makes it seem as if they are speaking about a return to a time past.

Indeed, the promise of a better future is always strongly implied in slogans based around the eight hit words. The underlying message is that, this time, together, something new can be done to change things for the better and to create a better society.

'Future' is itself an emerging term, used more often by politicians across the political spectrum who are seeking transformative slogans in a bid to connect with voters' aspirations. The word 'future' has been used dozens of times in election slogans over the last two years, from the incumbent right-wing Law and Justice Party in Poland seeking a third term in office in 2023 ('The Future Is Poland') to the social democrat and progressive Move Forward Party, who won the 2023 general election in Thailand with the slogan 'Good Politics, Good Living, Good Future'. So urgent is the need by politicians to stake a claim to the future that elections are now commonly being fought with several parties running against each other with a slogan featuring the word 'future'. There is no greater example of this than in the UK, where during the 2024 general election, four political parties all used a future slogan either as their main or secondary slogan. The word's prevalence at this point in the twenty-first century is striking. This is perhaps the logical conclusion of the evolution of more simplistic, abstract slogans over the past century.

Yet this type of sloganising might also be seen as part of the problem with modern politics. Politicians have always talked about a brighter future, partly to distract from the dullness of what they offer in the present. Their default setting of offering 'jam tomorrow' has long been interpreted as an admission that they have failed to deliver it today.

This problem is, arguably, more acute than ever. Electorates across the West and elsewhere feel disengaged from mainstream politics and its pre-packaged slogans, something that is reflected in falling turnouts, declining party memberships and the rise of new, 'outsider' candidates.

Political strategists are looking for new ways to connect with voters, engaging in a technological arms race using social media, AI and even neuroscience to compensate for this disillusionment. Are these new campaigning tactics a solution to the problems of modern-day democracy? Or might they make matters even worse? What does the future of political sloganising hold for us all – professional campaigners and voters alike?

• • •

This book has identified a pattern of language that has developed over the past century or so and settled on eight key words. In that time, election slogans have evolved significantly, reflecting changes in political communication, media influence and voter engagement. The brevity of modern slogans, compared with the longer, more distinctive ones used in the first half of the twentieth century, is striking. There are several reasons for this change. The most straightforward is that the expansion of electorates all over the world has had a profound impact on the nature of election campaigns and the evolution of political slogans. They have had to become more accessible and emotionally resonant as campaigns have strived to connect with increasingly large and diverse groups of voters.

When electorates were smaller and composed exclusively of elites or those with access to higher education, political discourse tended to be more nuanced. Slogans reflected a style that assumed voters would engage with and understand references to historical events, policies or complex ideas. The assumption was that these educated and often politically active voters would appreciate or even expect detailed messaging. Longer slogans provided space to articulate positions or address policy goals.

Universal suffrage changed the terms of political trade, forcing a need for slogans that resonated more widely. Shorter slogans were preferred because they were easier to remember, required less background knowledge to understand and appealed to feelings rather than intellect alone. Candidates began to rely on concise, catchy phrases and linguistic tricks such as alliteration and repetition, which would stick in the minds of voters regardless of their background.

Advances in mass media further amplified the trend towards brevity. As popular newspapers and then radio, television and digital media became dominant campaign tools, they accelerated changes in political communication. Sound bites and visually driven messages became central to reaching voters, with slogans needing to fit neatly into a short advert or even a single tweet.

The accessibility of these media mirrored the principles of universal suffrage. Just as the expansion of voting rights sought to remove barriers to participation, succinct slogans aimed to democratise political messaging. This provided a way for candidates to deliver their message to a vast, diverse audience without alienating those less inclined to engage deeply with detailed rhetoric.

Universal suffrage also emphasised the importance of making emotional connections in campaigns, as politicians sought to address a greater variety of concerns and priorities. Pithy slogans that evoked feelings such as hope, pride or fear were more effective in unifying disparate groups under a common banner. In recent years, Barack Obama's 'Yes We Can' or Donald Trump's 'Make America

Great Again' exemplify this shift. These slogans also have the advantage of avoiding details, instead fostering a wider sense of collective optimism or urgency through a general statement. Their brevity allows voters to project their personal aspirations or grievances onto a candidate's message, giving it a universal appeal.

As political slogans are the cornerstone of election campaigns, candidates will often gravitate towards words repeated from other successful campaigns such as 'Change We Can Believe In' or 'Stronger Together'. The recurring use of familiar slogans and hit words is arguably both a conscious and an unconscious strategy, designed to maximise appeal, to simplify complex ideas and to create a lasting connection based on sentiment.

Politicians rehash and recycle slogans because they think they will work. In the twenty-first century, the public is bombarded with political information. This means that conciseness and clarity is paramount. A memorable slogan can cut through the noise, distilling a candidate's message into a sound bite. By reusing themes around hope or unity, the slogan can be understood more easily by all voters.

Successful political slogans tap into the emotions of voters, creating a connection that goes beyond policy specifics. Words featured in this book such as 'strong', 'great' or 'change' can evoke feelings of power, pride and aspiration. By using such universal themes, politicians hope to appeal to diverse groups across social and cultural divides. Repetition of these ideas across campaigns ensures that the emotional resonance is familiar and comforting. Familiarity breeds trust, and slogans that echo past successful campaigns are often perceived as reliable and credible by the voters – though not necessarily by the media, which is usually quick to point out if a slogan has been used before.

Simplicity has often proved key to a successful political message. Slogans like 'A Better Life for All' (Nelson Mandela) or 'Putting People First' (Bill Clinton) are open-ended and adaptable, allowing voters to project their individual hopes and aspirations onto a campaign. Politicians or their advisers intentionally design these slogans to be inclusive, avoiding controversy while maximising potential support.

From a marketing perspective, repetition and familiarity can build brand recognition. Political campaigns, like brands, rely on establishing a strong and consistent identity. Reusing similar slogans or themes across different candidates and election cycles creates a sense of continuity. Voters may not remember the details of a candidate's platform, but they are likely to recall a catchy slogan, much as they would a strapline selling a product. It is that slogan that can have the power to act as a gateway, forming a deeper, long-term connection between politician and voter.

At the end of this long evolution of sloganising in the era of mass politics, we now find 'future' being deployed for electoral purposes by those on both the left and the right. 'Future' is a term that can potentially resonate with voters' aspirations and transcend ideological divides. It is a positive term, suggesting hope, improvement and optimism. For the left, it often conveys a sense of progress, innovation and a more just society through a push for change. The right, which tends to emphasise tradition and stability, frames its version of the future as being rooted in enduring values and security.

By invoking the concept of the future, all politicians hope that this word has the power to overcome people's dissatisfaction with the current state of politics and meet the public's desire for a better tomorrow. At the most basic level, research confirms that when voters hear the word 'future' in election slogans, they tend to look forward, recognising a sense of possibility and considering long-term outcomes rather than short-term gains – particularly if the message around the word 'future' is positive – for example, by emphasising the prospect of greater prosperity or safety.

The idea of a collective future is especially pertinent in election campaigns, when, consciously or otherwise, personal beliefs are aligned with the notion of the greater good. Politicians and parties hope that repeated exposure to slogans that emphasise a shared future together can strengthen bonds among voters who already lean towards them.

Yet despite this political emphasis on the future, voters all over the world, especially in Western democracies, appear to be increasingly losing interest in the present. Turnout is falling. Some would say that the 'sloganisation' of politics is partly responsible for this.

In the late twentieth century, a more detached form of politics and political discourse emerged. Particularly since the end of the Cold War, the old mass movements of both left and right had lost their grip on public opinion. The 1990s marked a shift in political communication, driven by rapid globalisation, the rise of round-the-clock media and changing public expectations.

A significant trend during this era was the reliance on abstract slogans by political leaders and parties, who were detached from any strong political base. While these slogans were intended to have mass appeal, their vagueness and lack of substantive commitments inadvertently contributed to declining voter trust, enthusiasm and impatience. A principal reason for this negative outcome was the growing disconnection between rhetoric and reality. Slogans like 'A Bridge to the 21st Century' (Bill Clinton) or 'New Labour, New Britain' (Tony Blair) encapsulated vague optimistic visions for societal progress but often lacked tangible policies to achieve these goals.

They may have been effective in mobilising short-term support, but ultimately, they rang hollow in the ears of many voters, particularly those facing economic inequality or job insecurity. Cynicism festered, as voters began to see political slogans as an exercise in branding rather than anything more meaningful.

Moreover, the abstract nature of these slogans often masked deeper ideological shifts. With the demise of the old left–right divide, the 1990s saw the rise of centrist 'Third Way' politics, which sought to reconcile market-driven policies with social welfare commitments. Such abstract ideas and slogans, created by academics and think-tanks with little connection to the 'real world', aimed to obscure compromises and avoid alienating specific voter blocs. But this lack of clarity left many feeling politically homeless, as they struggled to discern where parties actually stood on critical issues. This ambiguity eroded trust, as voters perceived politicians as 'all the same', more interested in managing perceptions than in addressing their needs.

The proliferation of media during this decade intensified the problem. Sound bites and slogans were tailored to fit the demands of rolling television news and emerging digital platforms, prioritising catchiness over substance. As a result, political discourse became more superficial, leaving voters short-changed. The emphasis on broad-brush messaging led to a lack of engagement, further distancing citizens from the political process.

By the end of the 1990s, the overuse of conceptual slogans had contributed to a sense of disillusionment. While slogans remained a staple of political campaigns, the lessons of the 1990s underscored the risks of favouring style over substance, a dynamic that continues to shape much political communication in the modern era.

Twenty years later, this sense of restlessness has only increased, a symptom perhaps of an expectation of instant gratification and a declining tolerance for the slow pace of political change. The rise of digital technology, particularly the internet and social media, has transformed the way people access and process information. Platforms like Twitter/X, Facebook and TikTok deliver news and updates instantaneously, conditioning users to expect immediate outcomes in all spheres. This contrasts sharply with the inherently slow processes of governance. Legislation, diplomacy and reform take time, leading to frustration among voters.

Additionally, the internet escalates public awareness of global events and solutions implemented in other countries. When voters see rapid results elsewhere, they demand similar speed from their own governments, often without accounting for the unique complexities of domestic policymaking. Donald Trump's decision to sign dozens of executive orders in front of thousands of his supporters in a basketball arena within hours of his inauguration as the forty-seventh President of the US in January 2025 offers the best recent example of this type of democratic envy. Few, if any, countries can offer this political equivalent of 'fast food'.

Misapplied use of campaign slogans exacerbates this restlessness. Politicians frequently pledge quick fixes during elections, creating unrealistic expectations. When these promises encounter bureaucratic roadblocks or political opposition, voters become disillusioned with what they regard as inefficiency or even dishonesty. Arguably, the origins of this negative feeling lie partly in the abstract slogans created in the 1990s and the cynical use of the media by the 'spin doctors' who deployed them at the time.

The recycling of political slogans serves as a reminder that the politics of the past has failed. Citizens are now likely to give a government elected on an explicit 'change' narrative less time to embark on a long-term journey, instead demanding immediate results. It seems likely that certain slogans or forms of words that have been used too often are now losing their potency, especially when used by the same old players. People have grown tired of the slow pace of change and the repetitive style of politics that is wrapped up in a slogan. A recent example is Keir Starmer's 2024 UK general election campaign, where Labour's 'Change' slogan secured victory but struggled to galvanise the public. Without a detailed long-term plan, 'change' felt hollow to many voters, reflecting the risks of relying on abstract slogans without substantive policy backing in an era of heightened scrutiny.

Given voters' impatience and disillusionment, a politician's need to find the right slogan has never been more important. Modern voters are exposed to a constant barrage of information from social media, news outlets and competing political voices. This flood of content has conditioned people to make snap judgements about candidates and their messages. As a result, a politician's slogan often serves as the first and most enduring impression of their campaign. If it fails to connect quickly, voters may lose interest or turn their attention elsewhere.

Furthermore, heightened polarisation in politics amplifies the importance of swift, clear messaging. Voters often look for cues that align with their ideological beliefs or address their most pressing worries. A strong slogan that encapsulates these priorities can create an immediate bond with the electorate and provide the first step towards a candidate building a long-term political relationship with the voters. Conversely, a vague or uninspiring slogan risks being dismissed as irrelevant or insulting, further fuelling voter discontent.

So, getting a slogan right has never been so crucial. Yet the question is: since political players are more disconnected than ever from the lives of the electorate, how are they to come up with the right words to make an impact? In response, some are resorting to alternative and even controversial methods. Politicians and their campaign teams are turning to science to help their chances of success.

I work with behavioural and data scientists at the cutting edge of campaigning. Their aim is not primarily to try to increase participation in elections. It is to appeal to the over-saturated group that is already politically engaged, using science and technology to fine-tune messages in a more personal, less universal way.

The consequences of this for political sloganising could be considerable. The eight hit words that shaped the world over the past 100 years came to the fore organically, with the aim of bringing people together. The words that politicians use to try to shape the next 100 years are likely to be far more manufactured and tailored to niche audiences – and, therefore, potentially more numerous. Whether or not they can supersede or supplement the enduring appeal of the eight words that shaped modern politics remains to be seen.

One of the benefits of working all over the world is that I come into contact with different campaigning techniques and marketing pioneers. One lesson that I have drawn from this is that winning the traditional battle of ideas is no longer considered enough. In order to be considered and heard by voters, it is now essential to win the battle of technology.

Civox is a US political AI technology company that specialises in AI-powered voice interactions for political operations. Its platform enables campaigns to engage in back-and-forth discussions with a large number of prospective voters, donors and supporters, simulating conversations that are supposed to feel like interactions with an actual person.

In December 2023, Civox, in partnership with Conversation Labs, introduced the first AI-powered, two-way voice-calling product for political campaigns and causes, taking on the role traditionally filled by people who operate phone banks and work at call centres. Each call is customised to the recipient and can be used to poll opinions, collect data, ask for donations and even to recruit volunteers.

Before the tech makes these calls, every speech that the politician has given is fed into the AI model. This allows the computer to accurately recite any policy or position a politician or party has ever held or to predict what they are likely to think and say in future circumstances. Some companies are now even able to mimic a politician's voice in order to give their response extra 'authenticity'.

Are we entering the age of the computer-generated politician? The deployment of AI in political campaigns has sparked discussions about ethics and the potential need for regulation. Doubts have also been raised about data security, the accuracy of AI-generated information and the overall impact of these developments on voters' trust.

However, the potential of AI in this context is significant. By leveraging natural language processing and data analytics, AI can analyse voter sentiment, anticipate concerns and deliver real-time targeted messaging and slogans. This level of personalisation has historically been limited by the time and resources of human campaign staff or the door-to-door campaigning experience of the politician. AI enables campaigns to provide what feels like direct communication with voters on a scale that has never before been possible. This could have huge consequences for political slogans in the future.

Whether voters will welcome such extensive interaction with AI campaign tools is another matter. In August 2024, in the run-up to the US presidential election, the *New York Times* ran a feature headlined 'The Year of the AI Election that Wasn't'. It described how thirty tech companies including Civox had approached the Republicans and Democrats offering AI campaign tools but said both parties remained 'wary', largely due to 'internal campaign polls that found voters were nervous about A.I. and distrusted the technology'. In other words, far from overcoming the problem of voter mistrust, there was a belief that the impersonal technology could make it worse. These problems might serve as a reminder that, however clever a slogan-writing system might be, politicians have never been able to succeed without talking full account of the 'human factor' and connecting with people's real interests.

Even so, others are going one step further in the quest to win, possibly taking politics even closer to the stuff of science fiction. Neuropolitics is an interdisciplinary field that examines the intersection of neuroscience and political behaviour – specifically, how brain activity influences decision-making, attitudes and actions in political contexts. By using certain technological tools, neuropolitics studies how people process political information, respond to campaign messaging and form opinions on issues or candidates. It aims to uncover what drives political preferences by focusing on emotions, cognitive biases and moral values.

The use of tools such as functional magnetic resonance imaging (fMRI) in a political context reveals much about contemporary society, particularly its focus on psychology, data-driven strategies and the increasing complexity of voter engagement. Brain activity can be measured by fMRI by detecting changes in blood flow. This allows researchers to study how people respond neurologically to political stimuli such as campaign ads, speeches and election slogans. It can even provide insights into subconscious reactions, revealing emotions and preferences that individuals may not consciously articulate. This technology is being experimented with, but the costs associated with it make it a minor activity at the time of writing. But as with all emerging technology, it's only a matter of time before this becomes more readily available and affordable.

The introduction of fMRI into politics underscores the growing reliance on data to influence decision-making. Campaigns now seek to understand not only what voters think but also how they feel at a deeper, subconscious level. This reflects a shift away from traditional polling and focus groups and towards neuroscientific methods, so that messages and slogans can be tailor-made to trigger the desired emotional response. In a highly competitive political environment, gaining even marginal advantages in voter persuasion can be decisive.

But while it might offer some valuable insights for campaigns and policymaking, neuropolitics does raise major worries about voter privacy and possible manipulation of members of the public, challenging how neuroscience should be applied in democratic processes. The potential blurring of boundaries between understanding and exploiting voter psychology is a very real risk.

The trend towards future reliance on fMRI and similar technologies confirms the growing detachment between voters and politicians. Instead of seeking direct, empathetic interactions in which a politician will try to shake thousands of hands, campaigns may prioritise optimising messages based on brain scans, reducing individuals to 'data points'. This could mean that personal connection is supplanted by scientific abstraction. Political campaigns are entering dangerous terrain when it looks as if they are trying to treat voters as data points or test dummies to be used and exploited, rather than members of a human electorate with concerns and opinions that must be recognised.

While the use of fMRI in politics highlights a technologically advanced data-driven culture that increasingly values precision in communication, those who work in this field must grapple with its implications. This type of technology could significantly influence the crafting of election slogans by offering insights into how voters respond to different messages. By measuring brain activity and identifying areas associated with emotion, memory and decision-making, fMRI could help campaigns refine slogans to maximise their psychological and emotional impact.

Although AI can enhance the efficiency and reach of voter engagement, it could lower the level of effort put in by politicians and their campaign teams to connect with voters. Whereas once people devoted many hours to addressing town halls or door-to-door canvassing, such activities can now be entirely automated. A single AI-driven system can handle millions of interactions, creating the appearance of a deeply connected and attentive campaign. Critics argue that the reduction in human effort diminishes the authenticity of voter–politician relationships. AI interactions, no matter how sophisticated, lack the genuine empathy and accountability of face-to-face dialogue. Voters may feel that their considerations are being addressed superficially, with no real commitment from the politician behind the AI.

Is the technological arms race simply trying to mask the crisis of democracy and the decline of voter participation? The reality is that this technology is trying to compensate for a lack of campaign and voter enthusiasm. But, as this book has shown, if a politician – or in this case an AI chat bot or telephone canvasser – is not able to connect with a voter on a deeper level, they will likely fail to capture their support. Given the amount of money now involved in political campaigning, especially in the US, some campaigners will not be leaving this to chance. The jury remains out on AI's long-term global impact on politics, especially when intersecting with different cultural norms around privacy and political engagement.

We might remember that while the neuroscientists and political strategists are at work trying to shape the future in their thought-factories, in the real world of politics outside the lab, elections are still being won by powerful political figures such as Donald Trump, Viktor Orbán or even Vladimir Putin, who know how to connect with the interests of millions of everyday voters. Whatever anybody might think of the politics involved, their success is evidence of the abiding importance of finding a direct message that strikes a chord in human hearts and minds.

So, what about the future of political slogans? It could be argued that AI makes it unlikely that the world will in future be shaped by the eight hit words because of the rise in universal suffrage and their ability to unite disparate groups. AI has the potential to reverse that formula – but in a negative way.

The use of AI in writing election slogans could potentially shift the trend from generic, abstract groups of words designed to appeal to diverse groups to more specific, targeted messaging. Historically, politicians have relied on broad, universal slogans such as 'better' or 'change' to unify voters across varied demographics under a big tent. AI is not seeking to unify us in the same way by bringing voters together via common language. In many ways its aim is to find our distinct differences and then appeal and exploit them on an individual level. Hyper-targeted slogans could risk deepening political polarisation by giving different groups distinct micro-messages that never converge into a shared conversation. These new technologies can be more persuasive to small groups in the short run, but you might argue that in the longer term, repeated fragmentation undermines any broader sense of collective identity. This is especially relevant in systems where stable governing majorities matter (e.g. parliamentary democracies).

AI has the potential to revolutionise political messaging. By analysing vast amounts of data regarding voters' preoccupations, it can generate multiple slogans tailored to different demographics, regions or issues. For example, one group might receive a slogan emphasising economic reform while another hears messaging about healthcare or education. This allows campaigns to engage with different voter bases more effectively without requiring the politician to expend political capital on promises they might not be able to deliver – or even to be involved in the process at all. What this ushers in is the extraordinary possibility of a politician winning an election without meeting or talking to a single voter. Neuropolitics and AI can lead to a scenario where the electorate is more 'managed' than ever, undermining the principle of free democratic choice and raising moral questions about whether democratic elections should hinge on subliminal appeals.

Yet we should also remember that those eight hit words have stood the test of time for good reason: because they have worked, for all manner of different campaigns in different countries and circumstances. Slogans are often cyclical rather than spontaneously invented, and there is likely to be plenty of life in the old 'magic words' yet. Especially given that, for all the claims of 'intelligence', AI is not really yet a creative mind of its own but more a tool for analysing and representing data and research made available by humans. If AI crunches data from election archives or this book, it may find, as I have, that 'people', 'change', 'democracy', 'strong', 'together', 'new', 'time' and 'better' remain highly effective emotional anchors.

Whereas election slogans of the 1990s left people feeling disappointed, as the 'better' future they were promised did not materialise, this new generation of slogans – aided by science – has the potential to be far more catastrophic for democracy. They will, by design, seek to hook people emotionally in a way that is much more cynical than any politician would ever dare.

In an age when trust in politicians is low, many will think carefully before immersing their campaign too deeply in the AI realm. But in the perpetual race to win, it is surely only a matter of time before even the most reluctant take the leap into the future.

• • •

The 2025 Canadian election underscores the enduring power of the eight hit words, with Liberal leader Mark Carney's 'Canada Strong' and Conservative Pierre Poilievre's 'Canada First – for a Change'. Both slogans leverage 'strong' and 'change', two of the most dominant and universal words in sloganeering. Amid US tariff threats from President Trump, Carney's 'strong' message resonated at a time when Canada's sovereignty was at risk. The slogan, evoking unity and resilience against an external threat, aligned with Carney's history as a former central banker. At that moment, Carney embodied credible and strong leadership against an aggressive Trump. But a 'strong' slogan would not have suited his predecessor Prime Minister Justin Trudeau, whose decade-long tenure carried baggage of fatigue, division and ultimately weak leadership – notably against President Trump. Under Carney, the Liberals secured a fourth term despite being as much as twenty points behind in the polls several weeks prior. Carney's use of a 'strong' slogan was undoubtedly a key part of his campaign success.

In sharp contrast to Carney's 'strong' slogan, his opponent Pierre Poilievre's 'Canada First – for a Change' slogan misfired, as it not only failed to align with the new Canadian political reality of an existential threat from the US but also used a 'change' slogan at the wrong time, with the wrong opponent in Carney. Poilievre's use of the word merely highlighted his risky platform and echoed Trump's disruptive agenda, subsequently bolstering Carney's stability narrative. Canada in 2025 is just the latest example of the universal resonance of the eight hit words. However, though they undeniably appeal to our collective emotions, to succeed they will always require alignment with context and candidate credibility.

Whatever the future holds for political slogans, among the thousands of words that have been written or spoken in the dual pursuit of our hearts and our minds, only eight words have consistently impacted our life: 'people', 'change', 'democracy', 'strong', 'together', 'new', 'time' and 'better'. What makes these words remarkable is not just their frequency or popularity but also their timeless resonance and capacity to reflect fundamental human desires – to be included, to improve our lives, to project strength and to believe in a better future.

This book, I hope, has demonstrated how these eight deceptively simple words wield extraordinary influence across ideologies, cultures and continents. We've seen the impact of these words in mobilising voters, toppling entrenched regimes, birthing new political movements and fundamentally transforming the direction of nations. The power of these eight words lies precisely in their universality, allowing them to resonate across ideological divides and to capture the mood of any era. Democratic politics, at its core, hinges on language as the means to articulate visions of the future.

For the first time, we can clearly see that the history of democracy is not only in big events and in larger-than-life personalities but written in words – words that have consistently shaped and re-shaped our world. These eight words, above all others, have proven themselves indispensable tools in the hands of those political story-tellers who seek to inspire meaningful change. Indeed, these are more than words; they are catalysts, capable of changing the world again and again.